THE
FLORIDA
KEYS

Also by Joy Williams

NOVELS

State of Grace
The Changeling
Breaking and Entering

SHORT STORIES

Taking Care
Escapes

THE FLORIDA KEYS

A History & Guide

1995 Edition

Joy Williams

Illustrations by Robert Carawan

Random House • New York

Library of Congress Cataloging-in-Publication Data

Williams, Joy.
The Florida Keys: a history & guide/by Joy Williams:
illustrations by Robert Carawan.—1995 ed.
p.   cm.
Includes index
ISBN 0-679-75773-2 (pbk.)
1. Florida Keys (Fla.)—Description and travel—Guidebooks.
2. Florida Keys (Fla.)—History.   I. Title.
F317.M7W54   1991
917.59´410463—dc20   91-52658

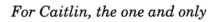

For Caitlin, the one and only

CONTENTS

INTRODUCTION

The Florida Keys do not run due south. They drift southwest, Route 1 running more east–west than north–south. The Gulf side is actually Florida Bay, the upper reaches of which belong to the Everglades. The bay side is called the "back country" or "outback." The Atlantic side is actually the Straits of Florida, where wide Hawk Channel runs out from shore to the reef, which stretches the length of the Keys. Beyond the reef is the Gulf Stream—"out front"—that great oceanic river whose demarcation is clearly seen, the water being a profound and fabulous blue. Beyond the Gulf Stream lies, then, the ocean.

The Keys run from Biscayne Bay to the Dry Tortugas, a distance of some 180 miles. No road runs to the keys north of Key Largo—Sands, Elliott, and Old Rhodes—and the Tortugas are 70 watery, wild miles from Key West. The distance accessible by car is some 106 miles—from Key Largo to Key West. That road, originally built in the 1930's, replaced Henry Flagler's Florida East Coast Extension railroad line, an amazing piece of engineering which had linked the Keys since 1912 and which was destroyed by a hurricane in 1935. The Mile Markers which are referred to in this guide—green signs with white numerals, posted on the right-hand shoulder—were first placed along the Keys by the railroad.

On a map, the Keys look fairly improbable—and Route 1, the line that drops down their sprinkled length, improbable too. The possibilities are vast, but the road itself is simple, which explains why some travelers begin at Key Largo, hang onto the steering wheel, and don't stop until Key West, heeding the billboards' urging, Go All the Way, with all its attendant, randy implications of reckless fulfillment. Other travelers arrive in the Keys, love them, stick close to Islamorada, and wouldn't dream of going all the way, considering Key West weird, if not bizarre, as though that singular and raffish place was at the bottom of an ever-darkening well.

But of course the Keys don't really go from light to dark. The Keys sparkle downward, warm and bright, full of light and air and a bit of intrigue. The Keys are relaxed, a little reckless. The

Keys are water and sky, horizon, daybreak, spectacular sunsets, the cup of night. The least interesting thing about them is
the road, but the road, as is its nature, allows entrance. The
road is the beginning.

There are some automobile guides, such as the old Sanborn
Guides to Mexico, that are wonderfully jittery backseat companions, not pointing out cathedrals and markets (because the
route in question is manifestly lacking in cathedrals and markets), but taking great pains to point out everything else. A
child selling an iguana is *here;* half a kilometer down the road
you will pass a most peculiarly shaped boulder; a bit beyond
that there was once a Pemex station, though unfortunately, a
Pemex station is no longer there, only a tire dump; two kilome-
ters away the road curves. . . . And so on.

The Keys once lent themselves to this sort of innocent treatment, and in a way they still do. There is the road, and there
are the dutiful descending markers accompanying your every
mile, suggesting that a trip is little more than coloring your
own experience between provided lines. At MM #—— there is
an egret; at MM #—— there's a pretty view between two violet
jacaranda trees; at MM #——, if you can wait that long, is a bar
where the bartender wears live snakes wrapped around her
neck and wrists—her "pretties," she calls them. . . . And so on.

Time passes, of course. The snake lady is run over one night
as she is crossing the road. Someone builds his dream house in
front of the pretty view, cutting down the jacaranda trees in the
process. But the Keys, though no longer the empty, silent
stretches they once were, still markedly lack (you might as well
be told) historical and cultural monuments. And the osprey still
builds his nest larger each year at MM #——. And the tarpon
still roll and flash each spring under the bridge at MM #——.
And certainly at MM #—— the disreputable bar remains. The
best way to enjoy the Keys is still to seek out their simplicity
and their eccentricity.

The Keys have been largely ignored until recently, the lack of
fresh water being the real inhibitor to development. The Navy
had built an 18-inch pipeline in 1942 that ran the 130 miles
from the Everglades wells in Florida City to Key West. The
water took a week to travel the route. In 1982 the old pipe was

replaced with a 36-inch pipe, increasing the quantity fourfold, providing indeed an oversupply of water and accelerating building and population growth. Oddly, the pipeline, as well as the construction of new bridges and wider roads, took place seven years after the state had designated Monroe County, which is the Keys, an "area of critical state concern" in an attempt to slow development (a perfectly nice word that unfortunately has been stolen away—undoubtedly while we were not looking—by the developers). A peculiar event occurred recently. Realtors dressed up in wood rat costumes and organized motorcades and rallies to protest new state guidelines that would restrict development in the Keys. It is true. People who felt themselves endangered by environmental laws dressed up like the cotton mouse and the wood rat—present inhabitants of mangrove swamp and hammock—and, aroused by lawyers and politicians, made a long, noisy trip down the highway to Key West, where the governor was speaking, picking up additional incensed rat- and mouse-garbed people along the way. This is typical oddball Keys, but in this case, peculiarity has a threateningly modern and consumptive edge, which is familiarly Floridian.

W. C. Barron, the founder of Wall Street's *Barron's* magazine, said early in this century that the only values in the state of Florida are the values created by man. This was how the state was perceived by the wealthy who came from elsewhere to exploit it. Florida, that splendid, subtle, once fabulous state, has been exploited, miscomprehended and misused, drained and diked, filled in and paved over. The values of man have been imposed with a vengeance.

Half of the historic Everglades is now farms, groves, and cities, and this marvelous ecosystem isn't working anymore. Over the last 50 years, 90 percent of the 'glades' wading-bird population has been lost. To read the roll of its endangered species is heartbreaking. The reef is becoming increasingly stressed by sewage that flows quickly through the porous rock of the Keys and into the ocean, as well as by agricultural runoff from the mainland that gets dumped into Florida Bay from the Everglades.

The bill is coming. It's not like the bill from a wonderful

restaurant, *Louie's,* for example. It's not the bill for the lovely fresh snapper, the lovely wines, the lovely brownie with bourbon ice cream and caramel sauce at the lovely table beside the lovely sea. It's the bill for all our environmental mistakes of the past. The big bill.

"Keys" comes from the Spanish word *cayos,* for "little islands." The Keys are little, and they are fragile. They cannot sustain any more "dream houses" or "dream resorts." The sustaining dream is in the natural world—the world that each of us should respect, enjoy, and protect so that it may be enjoyed again—the world to which one can return and be refreshed.

Time passes. There are more of the many, and they want too much. What the traveler wants, of course, is not development but adventure, and this is still possible in the Keys. The Keys have always been different. May they remain that way. Here's to them.

THE
UPPER KEYS
Key Largo
to Long Key

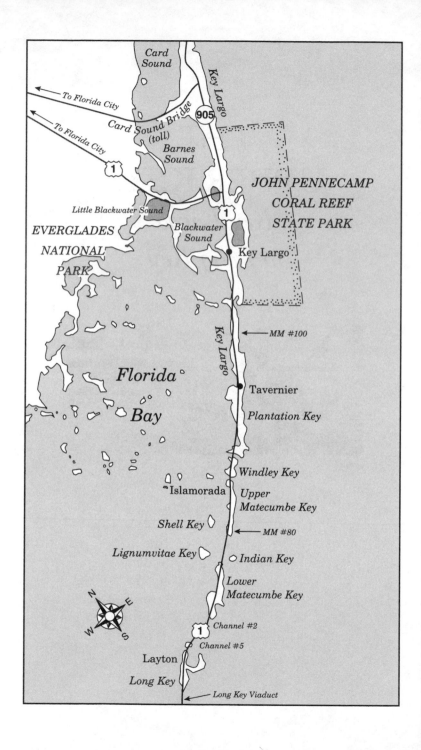

T HE Spanish first found the Keys in Ponce de León's 1513 expedition and promptly called them, with inquisitional flair, *Los Martires*—the martyrs—because they seemed twisted and tortured. They logged out the mahogany that grew here early on, and probably enslaved the native Caloosa Indians, but they were indifferent to exploring or settling these stony islands. There was no gold, no fresh water, and many, many bugs. They mapped and named the Keys principally as an aid to their ships, which, laden with gold and silver, used the Florida Straits as their route from the New World back to the Old.

The first settlement in the Keys was at *Cayo Hueso,* or Key West, in 1822, more than two decades before Florida became a state. The other keys remained pretty much deserted until 1874, when the government surveyed them and plotted land for homesteading. The early homes were primitive, built from the local "coastal store"—the beach—with wood and materials washed up from shipwrecks. The biggest plague of the settlers was mosquitoes. The mosquito was king of the Keys. Mosquitoes blackened the sides of houses and obscured the shapes of animals. Mosquitoes blackened the cheesecloth which people swathed their heads in as they slept. If you swung a pint cup, the saying went, you'd come up with a quart full of mosquitoes. Smudgepots burned constantly inside and outside the drift-wood houses. Burlap bags filled with wood chips soaked in old engine oil were hung to drip over stagnant water holes in an attempt to kill mosquito larvae. With mosquitoes gnawing on them day and night, a few pioneering families nevertheless managed to claw a living from what one writer of the time referred to as "worthless, chaotic fragments of coral reef, lime-stone and mangrove swamp."

The people who first made their homes in the Upper Keys were hardworking Methodist fishermen and farmers. They spoke with a Cockney accent, were closely interrelated, and bore the names Albury, Pinder, Johnson, Russell, and Lowe.

Their more flamboyant wrecking neighbors were in Key West, but life in the "outside keys" was earnestly drab, farming rock being somewhat Sisyphian in nature. But farm the rock they did, burning and clearing the land and planting coconuts, citrus, pineapple, and melons in the ashy interstices between the coral. They homesteaded on the Atlantic, and transportation between the scattered houses was by shallow-draft boat. These boats also took the produce out to deeper waters, where it was off-loaded onto schooners which sailed to Key West as well as to northern ports.

In 1905, Henry Flagler, a former partner of John D. Rockefeller in Standard Oil and president of the Florida East Coast Railroad, began extending the train track from Homestead, through the Everglades to Key Largo. Flagler was always pushing southward, legend has it, because his wives were forever wanting to be warmer. That is why he pushed down from St. Augustine to Palm Beach. (Flagler also altered Florida history by having the state's strict divorce laws changed when an early wife of his went mad.) But the reason he desired the terminus of his Florida railroad to be in Key West was because it was a fine deep-water port. Shipping out of Miami was limited by the 12-foot depth of Biscayne Bay. Flagler was seventy-five years old when construction started and died only a few months after the project was completed in 1912.

For seven years, the track and train, freighted with peril and mishap, inched their way down the Keys to Key West. Settlers in the Upper Keys longed for the railroad to be completed, believing that it would put them in closer touch with their markets and make them wealthy. But eventually the railroad meant the end of their little coastal communities and their large fruit farms. Key West became a receiving center for produce from all over the Caribbean and South America, and cheaper fruit was introduced to the mainland. Too, the few inches of Keys' topsoil that had supported such exotics as Porto Rico, Abbakka Queen, and Sugar Loaf pineapples was soon robbed of all nutrients, and the plantations failed. Towns like Planter, which once shipped out a million crates of limes, pineapples, tomatoes, and melons a year by schooner, simply disappeared, a victim of sporadic hurricanes and the railroad.

Other communities that sprang up along the track vanished too, when the 1935 hurricane blew the train away.

It was this hurricane—*the* hurricane, the nameless one—that made the history of the Upper Keys. It swept across the Matecumbe Keys on September 2, 1935, with an 18-foot tidal wave and 200-mph winds. Matecumbe is a name of obscure origins, but it may be a corruption of the Spanish *mata hombre*—"kill man"—which was also the meaning of Cuchiyaga, the Indian name for the island. In any case, it was a fated place. More than eight hundred people died in the hurricane, many of them members of the second "Bonus Army" of World War I veterans who, seeking early military benefits, had been hired instead by the Federal Emergency Relief Administration for work projects across the country. In this instance, they were building a road from Lower Matecumbe to Grassy Key so that the ferry route could be eliminated. Most of them died when the train sent down to rescue them was blown off the tracks in Islamorada. Of the eleven cars, only the 106-ton locomotive, "Old 447," remained upright, saving the lives of the engineer and the fireman. Many of the dead were burned in funeral pyres overseen by the National Guard in the sunny days after the storm, while others were buried in a common crypt marked by a monument in Islamorada.

Besides winds, the history here is in the waters—in the wrecks and reefs. The waters off the Upper Keys conceal a remarkable number of wrecks, from Spanish galleons to British frigates to World War II freighters. Cannon from the HMS *Winchester,* a 60-gun British frigate which went down in a hurricane in 1695, are displayed on dry ground at Pennecamp Park, and the adventurous diver can frequently see less restored and considerably wetter and blurrier artifacts. A wreck that is not present but that has left its contemporary and eternal mark is that of the *Wellwood,* a 400-foot Turkish freighter which ran aground within the park's boundaries in the fall of 1984. The *Wellwood,* filled with chicken feed, and captained, it would certainly seem, with some incompetence by a C. H. Vickers, ignored the 45-foot flashing light that marks Molasses Reef on the southernmost boundary of the park and ploughed into the reef, annihilating four acres of living coral. It made a portion of

CONCHS

Englishmen, descendants of the "Eleuthera Adventurers" who settled Eleuthera and the Great Abaco Islands in the Bahamas, explored the good fishing and turtling grounds off the Keys in the late 1700's but did not settle on the land, preferring instead to wait offshore for ships to founder on the reef. Particularly popular were the waters of the Upper Keys, where ships foundered regularly. "Wrecking," which occasionally bordered on piracy, was much practiced by the Bahamians, who would salvage the cargo from sinking ships and sell the goods in the port of Nassau. Shortly after Spain ceded Florida to the United States in 1821, however, the Bahamians were forced to become residents of this country if they wanted to continue to engage in wrecking. They began to move their families to the new town of Key West, where an admiralty court had been established to legalize and regulate what had become a major industry. These Bahamians were called "Conchs," after the large sea snails they ate in considerable amounts and perhaps because they used the conch shell as a trumpet. With a hole correctly placed at the tip, the shell could produce a plaintive wail heard for up to half a mile, a way of announcing, "Wreck ashore." The strange collective nickname may have been used disparagingly at first, but today a Conch, a lifelong resident of the Keys, descendant of Conchs, is proud of the shrewd and stubborn individuality the name represents. Key West will maintain that the only true Conch is a person born on the "Rock" of Key West, where the birth of a baby was once announced by putting a conch shell on a stick in the front yard. It should be remembered, on the other hand, that until well into the 1900's *all* Keys' babies "went to Key West to be born," there being no doctors or midwives elsewhere. The creature that began all this associative lore—the conch—has been mindlessly overharvested and, almost gone, is at last protected in the Keys' waters. Restaurant conch is not local. Even though conchs mate and lay eggs at the same time, they just can't keep up with our "demands" on them.

that fabulous tract, all the peaks and valleys and colorful caves bright with life, as flat and as gray as a parking lot.

The reef that runs along the Atlantic coast of the Keys, close to the great Gulf Stream, is fantastically fragile. All reefs are complex and highly particular life-forms, requiring lots of sunlight and clear, warm water. The Florida Keys tract (the only reef in the continental United States) exists at the northernmost limit of tropical reef development. It is threatened by this potentially chilly location. It is threatened by its own wonderful accessibility. It is threatened by development on land, by boat bilge, by silt dredged up from marinas, by the effluent and rainwater runoff from condo complexes and parking lots. It is threatened by overuse and misuse. With all this close at hand, it seems cruel and unnecessary for fate to bring tons of chicken feed blundering out of the darkness for the singular purpose of extinguishing part of beautiful Molasses Reef, but blunder out of the darkness the chicken feed did. (More recently, a 147-foot freighter carrying candy and cigarettes deliberately grounded on Western Sambo Reef in the Lower Keys during a winter storm, demolishing that.) The Park Service has marked off the damaged tract with yellow cone-shaped buoys and are monitoring it for signs of regeneration, which they do not expect to occur. The part of the reef visited by the wayward *Wellwood* has ceased to exist. It has become part of Keys history, as gone as the Caloosa Indians, the railroad, and the green turtle.

KEY LARGO

By car there are two approaches to the Keys. The most commonly traveled is Route 1, which skirts the savannah of the Everglades, crosses Jewfish Creek (which is part of the Intracoastal Waterway) and broad Lake Surprise, so named by the first railroad survey party in 1902, who apparently had not anticipated its existence. The other, slightly longer way of entering the Keys is over the Card Sound Bridge—a toll that will deposit you farther up in the mangrove and hardwood hammock land of North Key Largo.

Sometimes it's nice to contemplate things that *aren't* there. The 11-mile strip between the wealthy and very private Ocean

Reef Club (once considered by the FBI to be one of the most secure resorts in the country before it was battered by Hurricane Andrew in 1992) and Card Sound Road's convergence with Route 1 is empty, but grandiose projects have long been planned for this area. In 1955, speculators bought up 1,500 acres of virgin land here and incorporated it as the city of North Key Largo Beach. It was a phantom city with a phantom government but with very large intentions. It would be a city of 100,000 people to begin with, which would have increased the population of the Keys by 150 percent. It would be a super-city, of course, with much modern gadgetry, like monorails. The land was rescued from this ghastly inspiration when the Nature Conservancy and the Fish and Wildlife Service purchased it for their Crocodile Lake National Wildlife Refuge. Construction of the notorious "Port Bougainvillea"—described by its developers as "an imitation Mediterranean coastal village" of almost 3,000 units, pocked with "baylets" and man-made lakes—was halted because the very enormity of the project bankrupted its backers. Many other condos and hotels have been planned for the Card Sound Road, but so far three homely beasts have prevented them from being built—the alligator, the wood rat, and the cotton mouse. Modest and much-maligned but all federally protected endangered species, these three have kept bulldozers from overrunning the Keys.

Card Sound Road and Route 1 converge just after MM #109 at Lake Surprise, and one enters the Florida Keys. A sign with a leaping sailfish says so on your right. Following quickly on your left is another sign. This one says, Hell Is Truth Seen Too Late.

Key Largo Key was once a series of barely connected keys with a few high ridges. Railroad construction filled in the channels between the islets, leaving us with what we now experience as a single long key which stretches all the way down to Tavernier. A four-lane road runs the length of the key, divided from MM #100 down to MM #92 by a wooded median.

The town of **Key Largo** was originally known as Rock Harbor. Real estate promoters sought to cash in on the publicity given the 1948 Bogart-Bacall movie and circulated a petition to have the name changed. The request was granted by postal authorities in 1952, and Rock Harbor became Key Largo.

The movie *Key Largo,* with the exception of a few interior set scenes shot inside the bar The Caribbean Club, was filmed entirely on a soundstage in Hollywood. The film itself may be drenched with Bogart charisma, but it certainly is counterfeit Keys, with director John Huston ornamenting the script with California touches such as fog and kelp. However, the fact that the actors never came to Key Largo, and that the film was not shot here, did not faze the town's boosters. Key West had Hemingway, why shouldn't Largo have Bogie? To compound matters, the owner of the Holiday Inn, maintaining that "Key Largo is laden with memories of the great actor," bought the riverboat used in the Bogart movie *The African Queen* (which was filmed mostly in England) and now offers "excursions" in it from his dock. As a random touch, he has the original Chris-Craft boat that was used in the movie *On Golden Pond* there as well.

What Key Largo is far more justifiably known for is the reef, for here is the beautiful and unique **John Pennecamp Coral Reef State Park**. The coral reef is one of the world's most ancient and involved life-forms, and the easy availability of this spectacular other world is what makes a trip to the Florida Keys so special. The reef, lying between four and seven miles offshore, runs parallel to the Keys from Largo to the Dry Tortugas. It protects the Keys from storms and is also the reason why there are no sandy beaches on these islands—the reef absorbs the roll of waves which, if they came ashore, would gradually wear away rock to sand. The depths at which the most variety

The queen conch

of life and geological relief occur is between fifteen and thirty-five feet of water. At greater depths there is not as much diversity, but the corals, sponges, and fish are larger. The living animals that form and build the reef are coral polyps that feed on plankton—the tiny organisms that float past on ocean currents—which is also the food of great whales. There are both hard and soft corals. The hard ones have a flexible skeletal structure which undulates in the moving waters. These are the *gorgonians,* named for the snake-haired sisters of Greek myth, and they come in shapes of tubes, plumes, whips, and fans and in a multitude of colors. One of the most beautiful and easily recognizable is the common sea fan, the color of which is the most spectacular peacock blue. The hard corals are the castle builders. They are the brain, the staghorn and elkhorn, the pillar, the star and flower corals. Other hard corals have descriptive names like sheet, leaf, saucer, scroll, ribbon, tree, tube, and bush. Some colonies of polyps create massive spiraling structures that can rise as high as thirty-five feet from the ocean floor or spread out as boulders with deep, swirling convolutions. These coral polyps, building on the dead skeletons of former colonies, have a life span of centuries, but the reef grows with exceptional slowness. Staghorn and elkhorn corals grow only scant inches a year, and a good-sized brain coral may be hundreds of years old. The reef is perhaps the most complicated of all ecosystems, for nowhere else in the animal kingdom do so many organisms live together and participate in such interdependent relationships. More than five hundred species of fish live, feed, and are protected in its coraline caves. Some fish, like the dramatically streaked neon gobie, and crustaceans, like the banded coral shrimp, enjoy freedom from predation by grooming other fish of parasites. The gobie inhabits the deep grooves of brain corals, which other fish seem to regard as cleaning stations, while the coral shrimp actually lives within the jaws of the toothy moray eel.

Before marine sanctuaries were established and federal and state laws passed, commercial collectors were dynamiting the reef for coral, as well as removing it with crowbars and even cranes. It's remarkable that there's anything left of the living reef at all. But there is some left and it's enchanting. It's also irreplaceable and unrenewable.

Peculiarly enough, one of the first establishments that greets you as you enter Key Largo is **Shell Man** at MM #106, a "decor" emporium filled with corals yanked out of the peaceful and astounding depths and lined up on dusted shelves beneath fluorescent lights. Mystery has been transformed into mere novelty. (Does someone back home desire a toilet seat with seashells laminated deep within? This is the place to get it, perhaps the only place to get it.) The corals have been imported from the Philippines, since the taking of coral is prohibited in the Keys, but there are no signs posted to tell you of this fact. Instead, the place is almost an invitation to the unaware to go diving, discover a pretty piece of coral, break it off, and take it home. *All* corals, including the "soft" sea fans and whips, are protected all along the Keys' 150-mile reef tract. If you see anyone taking coral or harming or molesting other protected marine species turtles, rays, and manatees—contact the Marine Patrol (743-6542) or, in Pennecamp, the park ranger. The area code for all the Keys, including Key West, is 305.

DIVING

The first of the many dive shops you will see on the Key is **Capt. Slate's Atlantis Dive Center** at MM #106.5 (Phone: 451-3020). Those who dive with Capt. Slate, at least according to the pictures in his brochure, like to put largish dead fish in their mouths and feed them to even larger fish. If this is not to your fancy, however, Capt. Slate offers the usual—snorkel and scuba charters, instruction, and night dives.

As well, there are **American Diving Headquarters**, MM #106 (451-0037); **Quiescence**, MM #103.2 (451-2440); **Sea Dwellers**, MM #100 (451-3640); **Ocean Divers**, MM #100 (451-1113); and **Divers' World**, MM #99.5 (451-3200).

Dive shops all along Key Largo Key down to Tavernier dive Pennecamp Park. There is an extensive dive concession within the park itself, but in general you have the potential of visiting a wider variety of reef sites with shops located on Route 1. Make sure you know how many will be aboard so you won't have the disappointment of ending up on a "cattleboat." There are heavily dived reefs and there are areas that aren't even named, yet are beautiful and exciting. Many shops offer multi-day dive packages, and some will even arrange for motel or camping accommodations. (Conversely, most of the larger motels in the area offer dive packages.) Rates usually run around $20 for a snorkeling trip, with about one and a half hours of diving time. Scuba trips are usually $25, with rental equipment running around $20. Wet suits can be rented for $15, not a bad idea in the winter, when even first-felt-warm waters can turn chilly after an hour. Other equipment, such as underwater cameras, can also be rented. Boats leave early in the morning and early in the afternoon. Call for reservations. Inquire as to advanced instruction classes and certification.

For experienced scuba divers, a dive at night is an especially remarkable experience. The coral polyps open like flowers to feed on the plankton floating by, and the water is lit by luminescent organisms corkscrewing through the blackness. Some fish, like the triggerfish and the big blue-and-green parrotfish, snuggle into crevices and seem to sleep at night. Others, like the bizarrely beaked filefish, come out to eat their favorite foods, stinging fire-coral and black long-spined sea urchins. Many fish change or lose their colors at night, while sea fans seem veined in fire. Big-eyed squid appear—and octopuses, those boneless, enigmatic forms which, because of their highly developed nervous systems, are believed to be more intelligent than anything in the sea, except for mammals.

The new fad in Key Largo is **Jules' Undersea Lodge**, a two-room "hotel" at the bottom of the lagoon. "Through this wonderful experience of sub-surface habitation, we open to the public one of the planet's last frontiers," one of the owners says. This particular frontier is only one hundred feet from shore and thirty feet below the surface, and has air-conditioning, television, a VCR, telephones, and "bathroom facilities." Perhaps you'll feel that this is not much of a creative step. It's $300 per person per night and you're provided with hookah-type diving gear for when you venture outside. If you're not a certified diver you can learn how to use this equipment in a "Resort Course" that costs another $50–$75. You can have lobster, steak, or chicken for dinner (just like on an airplane) and Belgian waffles for breakfast, but no alcohol is permitted unless you're on your

The Coral Reef

honeymoon. Then you're allowed some champagne. There are plans to create a six-acre "undersea leisure park" here—sort of a Snorkel World. Jules' is located at the Koblick Marine Center at MM #103.2 (phone: 451-2353).

Contact **Reef Relief Environmental Education Center** in Key West for their brochure on the proper ways to see and protect the reef when snorkeling and diving. Call (305) 294-3100. The Center, located at 210 William Street in Key West, has great videos and attitude.

JOHN PENNECAMP CORAL REEF STATE PARK

America's first underwater state park was established in 1960 and named for one of its most dedicated and determined advocates, John Pennecamp, a Miami newspaper editor who was also instrumental in creating Everglades National Park. Park waters stretch more than 21 miles from Carysfort Reef to

Molasses Reef and inshore to the coastline. With the additional protected waters of the Key Largo National Marine Sanctuary, the preserve extends more than eight miles into the ocean and encompasses 178 square miles. There are two small beaches on park grounds (in the shallow waters off one of them, the state has reconstructed a galleon wreck) and two nature trails, one winding by boardwalk through the mangroves. But the real meaning of the place is all beneath the water's surface.

If this is your first time out to see the reef (remember, the reef lies several miles offshore—you can't just wade out, dip your face down, and see it), your first glimpse of the fanciful, lacy, undulating terrain and the beautiful bright fishes in the clear water will be startling. You will first be amazed. Then may follow, fleetingly, suspicion. Has the place been stocked? Have the fish been placed here by the concessionaire? Have these fish somehow, even, been *hired*? But your suspicions are unfounded. They fade away and wonder returns.

The park's concession stand does stock a good number of informational booklets about the reef. For an even more extensive selection of bird, coral, and fish identification guides, go to **The Book Nook** at MM #100 in the Waldorf Plaza Shopping Center, which has an excellent offering of Florida books in general as well as NOAA (National Oceanic and Atmospheric Administration) charts. These charts are absolutely necessary to the boater.

The entrance to Pennecamp is at MM #102.5. For camping reservations and information, call the park at 451-1202. For information on snorkeling and scuba tours and boat and equipment rental, call 872-1127. Entry fees at Pennecamp and all state recreation areas are $3.25 a car and 50¢ per person. Camping is $25 per night.

The park offers several types of diving trips and programs (for example, a one-day course in scuba diving costs $150 and a four-day certification course costs $325). A snorkeling tour leaves at 9 A.M., noon, and 3 P.M. and costs $25 per person. A snorkeling and sailing tour on a 38-foot catamaran costs $32 per person for a half day. Scuba trips cost $32.50 per person and leave at 9:30 A.M. and 1:30 P.M. The dive shop rents all equipment as well as a variety of boats. An 18-foot motorboat costs $95 for a half day, $160 for a full day. Other reef boats can be rented for about $25 an hour. High deposits are required on boat rentals. If you do decide to go out on your own, it's important that you be able to read charts well. The park service has white mooring buoys scattered around the most frequently dived sites. Tie up to these. If you must anchor, do so on a sandy spot. *Never* anchor on the coral itself. Careless anchoring is highly destructive to the reef, for when coral is broken, the wound invites invasion by algae and other organisms which spread rapidly and can destroy an entire colony. When diving, always display the red-and-white "diver down" flag and stay within one hundred feet of your boat. A lot of boats are cruising around these waters, and the flag speaks of your presence.

There are nine diving sites in the park, each distinguished by some fascinating peculiarity. Park-based dive boats usually go to White Bank Dry Rocks, French Reef, and Molasses Reef. The **Benwood** wreck, a mile and a half north of French Reef, is a popular scuba destination. The luckless freighter was first torpedoed by a German submarine during World War II and, while limping home, was then accidentally rammed by another boat. Her hull was used for bombing practice for a while, and then she was dynamited and sunk. Her battered and scattered remains are now host to large schools of fish, and home, too, to the secretive and commandingly repellent moray eel.

White Bank Dry Rocks is the largest of the snorkeling reefs. It is a shallow garden wealthy with staghorn and elkhorn beds and star and brain coral heads, and full of the brilliant flitting movement of small tropical fish of dots and stripes and bands and bars, tiny wrasses—fish so darkly purple their bones are blue—curious and fearless angelfish, rock beauties, triggerfish, and damselfish (these last being the most aggressive fish on the reef and the ones most likely to bite you—this dismaying prospect tempered, however, by the fact that they are no more than two inches long). This is a perfect reef for the novice diver to explore. **French Reef** is primarily a scuba site, noted for its caves, winding canyons, and large fish. **Molasses** is the biggest reef in the park and has what many divers consider the greatest variety of both terrain and fish. There are shipwrecks, and sandy channels winding through towering coral wells. It's very likely you'll see beautiful manta rays here.

Dive shops on Route 1 visit the middle and more northern

areas of the park. If you have a particular site or wreck that you are interested in exploring, inquire, remembering that trips are dependent on visibility and weather and that visibility in winter can sometimes be disappointing. **Carysfort Reef** (named, with an inexplicable alteration of the last letter, for the HMS *Carysford,* a frigate which had run aground there in 1770) is located at the extreme northern end of the park and is marked by a 100-foot lighthouse. This is a nice diving area and not a particularly busy one. The **Elbow**, marked by a navigational light, is the closest of the reefs to the cleansing and swift Gulf Stream, making visibility there almost always excellent. There are more shipwrecks located around here than almost anywhere else, and the fish have been fed so frequently by divers that they seem actually expectant of handouts. **Key Largo Dry Rocks** is the site of the nine-foot **Christ of the Deep Statue**, a duplicate of the Christ of the Abysses Statue in the Mediterranean off Genoa. The bronze Christ with upraised arms placed here in twenty feet of water was donated to the park by an Italian industrialist and sports spearfisherman, and much flowery rhetoric swirls about it. A park bulletin, reprinting the original dedication of the Abysses statue, says, "The dead shall no longer be lonely. . . . Ships and phantoms of ships will crowd around Him; living men and dead men. The shadows of all those who lost their lives in the sea will be present, without discrimination of nationality, blood or color. With His liberal gesture of invitation, He will welcome everybody. . . ." And so on. The statue's liberal and equitable invitation is blurred frequently by algae. "It's real pretty when it's all scrubbed up," a park ranger says. "We've got to get out there more and scrub her up." What can't be scrubbed up is algae-smothered coral, and this is becoming an increasing problem throughout the park and sanctuary. A large area near the Dry Rocks is covered with green-brown coats of algae that look like fur and stringy yellow strands of algae that look like hair. *Wherever does this gross stuff come from?* you might ask. (See Florida Bay, page 26.)

   Not far from the Christ of the Deep is **Grecian Rocks**, a good reef for snorkelers because it has shallow waters and very little current. Close by is the intriguing **Cannon Patch**, where a number of cannon from unknown ships lie scattered about. Far-

THE GLASS-BOTTOM BOAT

The **Discovery** leaves three times a day from the park, at 9:30 A.M., 12:30 P.M., and at 3. The $2\frac{1}{2}$-hour trip costs $14 for adults and $9 for children. It is rather like going from Hyannis to Nantucket on the Hi-Line, except that at the end of $2\frac{1}{2}$ hours you are not in Nantucket. *Discovery* trips are very popular, and reservations should be made in advance by calling 451-1621. The vessel winds through South Sound Creek and out six miles to Molasses Reef, which is the only reef it visits. Many people are disappointed that they do not see the Christ of the Deep Statue, but that is miles to the northeast. There is about a half hour of viewing time through the glass panels in the ship's hull while the *Discovery* wiggles and churns about. The trip is most enjoyable if undertaken with a large group of children, who will be highly vocal in their enthusiasm for what they do and do not see. They will invariably spot the seasickness bags in the shelf above the panels and yell *Look at the barf bags* while the guide is pointing out a parrotfish. They will always insist that they have seen a shark, and they will have a very good time. Actually, it is not likely that you will see a shark, a turtle, or any of the larger or shyer inhabitants of the reef with all the bustling about the *Discovery* does, idling, then scooting sideways with a grand flourish of bubbles, leaving sea fans waving frantically in the propeller wash like shipwrecked maidens. What you will see are big basket sponges, a good variety of corals, and schools of porkfish and grunts. And you will frequently see barracuda wearing their customary peevish expressions.

The 'cuda is enjoying a period of revisionist thinking at present. He is no longer considered the aggressive man-mauler he was once believed to be. The new attitude is that if he does blunder into you with his razory teeth it will be because of poor visibility or because you were wearing something shiny. In any case, it will be a mistake. Another mistake—this time one that people make—is eating barracuda. The fish shows his considerable resentment at being eaten by infecting the eater with ciguatera, a violent fish poisoning, although folk wisdom claims that if you cook a dime with a 'cuda and the dime stays shiny, it's safe to eat him. If the dime turns black, though, you'd better not.

A *Discovery* trip is undeniably the driest way to see the reef, but it is probably the least satisfying. If you're able to swim at all, it's far more enjoyable to take one of the dive boats out and snorkel the reef. The reef is another world which you can enter, and to be able to do so with the rudiments of a glass mask and a plastic tube is almost miraculous. Besides having that silly name, snorkelers *look* silly to the non-snorkeler, floating flatly around, making occasional rude noises through their tubes. But a snorkeler is not what he appears to others. He is what he sees. He has a magic glass wrapped around his eyes and he is in a world of beauty and color. Graceful movement. Silence.

ther south, beyond the park's boundaries, is pretty **Conch Reef** and the site of three Spanish galleons, the *Capitana,* the *El Infante,* and the *San Jose y las Animas,* all shipwrecked here in a 1733 hurricane. Even the ballast stones—mere stones, after all—are fascinating here. **Conch Reef** drops off to a depth of 115 feet, but close to the surface is a large stand of elkhorn coral, and there are stumpy remnants of formerly large colonies of pillar coral. (It was the devastation of Conch Reef by collectors that prompted state legislators to prohibit the taking of coral.)

WHERE TO STAY

Exploring the reef and taking advantage of the different packages the dive shops offer take days at the very least. Many places to stay are completely booked in the winter season and on weekends. Reservations are always a good idea. The motels are clustered in two areas—just south of the entrance to Pennecamp, and below MM #100, just beyond where the four-lane road divides. Most of them are on the bay side.

There's a **Howard Johnson's** at MM #102 beside the splendid monolith of Southern Bell, and the aforementioned **Holiday Inn** at MM #100, recently renovated with a jungle theme—lots of zebra-patterned area rugs. Best of the chains is the **Sheraton** at MM #97 (bay side), not far from the Wynken,

Blynken and Nod Trailer Park, where ancient immobile homes
reside on streets such as Tweety Pie Terrace, Thumper Thor-
oughfare, and Little Miss Muffet Lane. The Sheraton is trying
to give a new resort feeling to Key Largo, and a standard room
here runs around $200 in season. It's a well-laid-out, luxurious
place, concealed from the road by a buttonwood grove. Suites
overlooking the bay are $400 in season; over the trees
$160–$200. Good discounts are available. And there's tennis
too (852-5553).

Although there are many more chains and deluxe resorts in the
Keys than there used to be, small cottages and more eccentri-
cally personalized lodgings can still be found. Many people stay
in these places for weeks, bringing their own coffeepots, broil-
ing up the fish they catch, eating from the mismatched plates
stacked in the cupboard (ant motel tin discreetly tucked in the
corner), shaking the scatter rugs out each day, and sitting outside on the dock at twilight with their compeers, sipping martinis they have mixed exactly to their taste. There's always a
little boat tied up that the kids can use, and the swimming pool
is usually part of the bay itself, set off by flaking cement walls,
its depth dictated by the tides.

Basket sponges and a barracuda

Largo Lodge, less than a mile south of the park at MM #102, is a cool, jungly enclave—very refreshing after a day on and under the bright water. The grounds, though not extensive, are unique for their lushness. The palms are towering, the orchids profuse, and every healthy leaf shines. The cottages are large, with screened porches and separate kitchens, and can sleep four. There is a boat ramp and a little dock on the bay, on what is here called Tarpon Basin. The place is very pleasant, the landlady jolly, but the rule in this Eden is that no one under the age of sixteen is allowed. Prices are $85 a night for two, $5 for each additional person. Telephone: 451-0424.

Rock Reef (852-2401) and **The Seafarer** (852-5349) at MM #98.5 both have cottages on tree-dotted grounds and little man-made beaches. Rooms and efficiencies range from $61 to $113 in winter; a cabin on the water is $100. **Popp's** (852-5201) and **Stoneledge** (852-8114), farther down at MM #96 and MM #95, are similar in style and rates.

In a class by itself is the **Blue Lagoon Resort** (451-2908) at MM #99.5. This is an intense little jumble of trailers and cottages, the office manned by clerks of many nations. There was a time when you could rent a room in a trailer here and share it with an enormous TV for a mere $25. You could fantasize that you were in a fifties movie. On the lam. Escaping from something terrible. You would sit on a green plaid bedspread and listen to your breathing. No one would ever find you here. They still won't, but prices have risen frightfully. It's $55–$75 to feel there's something wrong with you now.

WHERE TO EAT

Key Largo has many eating establishments that there's no need to write home about (perhaps more places than most) but there's no need to resign yourself to yet another awesome blizzard from the Dairy Queen.

Tiny **Harriet's**, close to Popp's around MM #95, is good for breakfast, as is **The Hideout** at MM #103.5 on the water at the end of a street peculiarly named Transylvania Avenue. In a humble house, very much unrestored (close to Jules', "one of the planet's last frontiers"), you can have fish and grits and biscuits for breakfast. It is common knowledge that nothing beats fish and grits and biscuits for breakfast. You can have it for lunch too. Open 7–2 seven days a week. Telephone: 451-0128. **Mrs. Mac's Kitchen** (451-3722) has basic burgers and good chilli as well as cold Key lime pie that will make your teeth sing. Authentic-license-plate decor. Open Monday–Saturday 7 A.M.– 9:30 P.M.

The Italian Fisherman at MM #104 is large and open with big white statues gleaming nakedly in the parking lot and lots of outside dining on extended terraces. The place has a sprawl- ing, free-form quality—it's been expanding now for twenty years. The bar is the place to watch Key Largo sunsets. The ambience here is better than the food, which is, however, rea- sonably priced. The portions are large. They seem to worry about the conch dishes somewhat. ("Have you ever had conch before?" the waitress asks. "Maybe you should have it parmi- giana.") It is the beginning of the Keys up here, but if you're try- ing conch, try it the simplest way possible. The more elaborate the preparation sounds, the tougher it's going to be. Open from 11:30 A.M. until 11 P.M. (451-4471).

Coconuts (follow the loud signs) is a big, casual place on a stuffed marina. Their specialty is a fish covered with a sauce of bananas, oranges, pineapple, and rum. Other dishes are gath- ered under peculiar headings. Meat and fish are under For Real Estate Lovers, while salads can be found under For Those Who Care (451-4107).

Snapper's Waterfront Saloon at MM #94.5, the place with the mermaid sitting on the turtle is far nicer and appreciated by many. Overlooking the waters of another marina, it has decks, three bars, a big and easy menu, and is open from 11 A.M. to 10 P.M. (852-5956).

TAVERNIER

At the end of Key Largo Key at MM #92.5, just north of the com- munity of **Tavernier**, is the turn to the Keys' original settle- ment of Planter, which was homesteaded in 1866. **Harry**

Harris County Park occupies the ocean site today. At the
turn of the century, Planter had the only post office between
Miami and Key West, but the town was abandoned when the
railroad came through and people moved inland to be around
the station, founding the new town of Tavernier, named for a
small key offshore which the Spaniards had previously named
Cayo Tabona, or Horsefly Key. If you want to go to the park,
take a left on Burton Drive, wind your way past many streets
filled with houses and trailers all festooned with Styrofoam lobster pot markers, and you will eventually reach it. There is a
sandy beach and many concrete picnic tables that look like
small temples dedicated to hibachi gods. Before you advance to

A BAR

Right beside The Italian Fisherman is **The Caribbean
Club Bar**, the bar of movie myth. A sign inside says
Absolutely No Dogs Allowed. Outside, there's a bit of littered
waterfront and some benches and beer bottles scattered
about. Inside, in the morning, there are men drinking shots
and playing pool and women sliding off their stools. It certainly doesn't look like the kind of place where a dog wouldn't
be welcome.

But there is an explanation for the sign. Once dogs wan-
dered in and out of here freely. They slept, snarled,
scratched, and drank beer here. It was a democratic place.
One man who frequented The Caribbean Club would often
bring his pit bull bitch in. She was a champion pit bull, and
she had a litter of puppies. So the man brought her in one
day with a few of her puppies. While the man drank, the dogs
went for a dip. One of the puppies, frightened of the water,
climbed on the bitch's back and would not let go, and managed to drown its very own mother. The bitch was a champion who had been worth a great deal of money, and the
owner, as well as being upset, was disbelieving. He gave the
drowned dog mouth-to-mouth resuscitation and pounded on
her heart, but the dog remained drowned. He was so mad at
the puppy he kicked it to death. The management decided
that dogs hanging out in the bar were a potential problem.
Now dogs are not allowed. Absolutely.

THE UPPER KEYS 23

the beach, picnic temples, and playgrounds, however, a great many signs will place grave demands on your sense of freedom and delight. Stop, they say. No Dogs, they say. No Parking. Stop. Slow. No Sports or Games, they say. Perhaps you will find it more congenial to turn back to Route 1 and drive down to **Harry's Place** at MM #91. Harry's Place (it's the same Harry Harris actually, an early restaurateur and county commissioner called Hi-Rise Harry for his lucrative friendships with developers) is inexpensive, with weekend buffets and breakfast served as early as 6 A.M. The bar stays open until 4 A.M.

The development of Tavernier was inhibited by the depression of 1929 and the almost constant arrival of hurricanes, the most severe of all being the storm of September 1935, which devastated most of Tavernier's structures and erased all signs of habitation eight miles south on Matecumbe Key. A peculiar result of the hurricane for Tavernier was the subsequent construction of "Red Cross houses," built with the help of the Federal Emergency Relief Administration and the Red Cross. These were four-room houses built of reinforced concrete containing 80,000 pounds of steel, with steel rods anchoring the house to bedrock. The floors and roof were also made of concrete, and the walls were a foot thick. The window sashes were made of steel and contained double-strength glass. The houses were ugly as sin, of course, but built to withstand anything short of the Apocalypse. Unfortunately, seawater was used in the mixing of the cement, which rusted the steel reinforcing rods so that all the structures cracked.

But Tavernier is proud of these oddities, proud indeed of anything that dates at all, for the Keys, with the exception of Key West, are scant on old buildings. The town plans to establish a historical district that will include these hurricane houses as well as the simple wooden structures that remain from the days of the railroad, when Tavernier was the first station stop in the Keys. Tavernier was once considered an outpost—subdued, but an outpost nonetheless. No longer an outpost, the town remains subdued, hugging the road in a mannerly fashion. It has a new shopping center, **Tavernier Towne** (complete with dignified *e*), at MM #91.5, and the only movie theater in the Upper Keys. It's a modest, rather dusty community and seems far removed from the water, although the water is there, of course, and

---

CUCO BOBO

In the Depression, a round-trip ticket from Miami to Key West on the railroad cost a dollar. When the train stopped for water just south of Tavernier, passengers would dash into the lime groves and gather Key limes to liven up their rum drinks. In Key West, a Cuban called Cuco Bobo made a living in bars by imitating the railroad as it chugged down the Keys. Cuco was attired somewhat militarily, with a dazzling array of medals and ribbons. He would stand on the bar, move his arms like an engine gathering steam, shuffle his feet, and make toot-tooting noises. Several drinks were purchased for him during this process. He'd blow a whistle, eliciting further drinks. Then he'd start to call out the stops—*Tavernier! Islamorada! Matecumbe!* Oh, it was a long, dry trip. *Grassy Key!* Very seldom was Key West reached before Cuco Bobo fell off the bar.

---

along the ocean where the early settlers built their lonely little homes, situated to catch the breezes and keep the mosquitoes away, are the large weekend retreats of Miamians, each equipped with a slick car and a motorboat. Hurricane bunkers these houses are not.

PLANTATION KEY

Across Tavernier Creek at MM #90 and running down to Snake Creek at MM #87 is **Plantation Key**. Centuries ago it was inhabited by the Caloosa Indians. Remnants of a considerably large midden can be found on the bay on the northernmost end of the key. As you are probably aware, however, Indian mounds and middens are very boring, consisting of dirt, small grimy shells, and once-useful stones—dumps of non-acquisition. These middens are of most interest to enterprising gardeners, who can be seen carting away buckets of the old, rich soil for their own flowery purposes.

At the turn of the century, the first large schooner in the

Upper Keys was built on Plantation Key by "Brush" Pinder. It was built "by the idea," without plans, the same way it was done in the Bahamas. Pinder named the 60-foot, 40-ton schooner, which was made of Everglades mahogany, *Island Home,* and she sailed Keys' waters for fifteen years, carrying ice, pineapples, passengers, and mail before the coming of the railroad.

A small group of mangrove islands off Plantation are called The Cowpens. Manatees were once so numerous that they were herded into these watery corrals to await their future as meat. The odd, gentle manatee is now almost extinct.

Plantation Key boasts the restaurant **Marker 88** (located helpfully at MM #88), often described as "a destination of gourmets." Open for dinner only, it is attractive, expensive, requires reservations, and is quietly placed among trees on the bay. Inside, however, it is anything but quiet. The tables are set very close together and the noise is beyond discordance, beyond clamor, beyond din or hubbub. It is not that the waitresses scream at one another or drop trays—it is the shrieking, babbling, crowing uproar of the patrons themselves. The kitchen may create inspired bisques and sauces and stuffings, but it is difficult not to be more impressed by the surrounding cacophony. Marker 88 is open from 5 P.M. For reservations, call 852-9315. (**The Naughty and Nice Gag Shop** has appeared just across the highway, hoping to get some of the gourmet trade too.)

A mile away, at MM #87, is the **Plantation Yacht Harbor Resort**, with its big marina and its candlelit Commodore Room for those who regret ever having left Ft. Lauderdale. Reservations: 852-2381. Open 6–11 P.M. Adjacent is the more casual El Capitain Room, open 8 A.M. to 3 P.M., and 5 to 10 P.M., when the children are screaming for nachos or potato skins. Rooms are available at the Resort, most of them overlooking extensive areas of denuded land, faintly green, which appears to be waiting for a golf course to happen to it. Telephone: 852-2381. Rooms $95 in season, $75 May 1–November 30.

A bit of old Keys funk is a half mile away on your left, in the shape of a small and startling perma-stone castle—the former home of McKee's Museum of Sunken Treasure. When you toured the Keys in the 1950's, you'd do some fishing, eat some fish, and visit Art McKee's museum. McKee was a well-known local treasure diver of the 1940's and '50's who built his minia- turized version of a Spanish fort in 1949 and filled it with the things he'd found in nearby waters—cannons, muskets, swords, and gold coins. The museum closed in 1976, and the "castle," for sale for years, recently became **Treasure Village**, with lots of candles and crafts and dried flowers. The best thing about it now is the gigantic spiny lobster sculpture out front. Very invit- ing, but No Toque Esta Langosta. Across the road at MM #86.5

FLORIDA BAY

Florida Bay, the great nursery, is in the throes of environ- mental collapse, falling apart, as one researcher put it, "like a rotting piece of cloth." The Dead Zone, clearly visible from airplane and boat, sprawls farther each year—a spreading area of massive turtle grass die-off that has fueled an algae bloom in which marine life perishes or from which it flees. Many people will tell you how clear the Bay's waters used to be, that you could see 30 feet straight to the bottom in sub- marine canyons that wound through the shallow flats, that you felt as if you were flying, that looking into the water was like looking through the air. Now visibility is measured in inches. Once crystal waters have turned murky and opaque, a milky green, a pea green, even a phosphorescent green. Loss of sea grasses has turned underwater acres into mud meadows. Where the algae passes, the die-off of sponges is 100 percent, and it is those sponges that have provided food and protection for young fish, shrimp, and spiny lobsters.

The nursery is shutting down: Florida Bay is becoming a hypersaline, superheated lagoon, a hot death soup for marine life. This is a direct result of the dying of the Ever- glades itself: years of flood control and government water- management practices there have promoted cities and farms, and just about accomplished their original mandate of suck- ing the Everglades dry. Books could be written about this, of course. Millions of words *have* been written, most of them assuring those who care that steps are being considered (if not yet taken) to bring the Everglades back from the brink of death. And the health of the Florida Keys is utterly depen- dent on the health of the Everglades.

> There is a man named Wayne Huizenga and he has a
> vision. He is the Blockbuster sorcerer and his vision is the
> biggest tourist attraction in America. It will be a gargantuan
> sports and entertainment complex covering 2,500 acres,
> located just three miles from the parched lip of the Ever-
> glades. He wants to call it Wayne's World and he has all
> money and permits he needs to build it. In addition to all the
> arenas and stadiums, there are plans to build a big virtual
> reality amusement center as well. Perhaps you can pay the
> fee and enter the Keys that so recently are: see the bright
> and extraordinary worlds of water and sky where remark-
> able creatures, not of our kind, existed. Of course, it will real-
> ly be make-believe.

is **The Rain Barrel**, with more crafts shops. This is not the
place to buy the armadillo pocketbook you've always wanted, or
coconuts with spangled, painted faces. There are artful things
back here, where printmakers, potters, jewelsmiths, sculptors,
and wood and leather workers all exercise their talents. It's as
though the entire graduating class of the Putney School in Vermont had come down to Plantation Key.

If you want to explore the reef off Plantation, local dive shops
will take you to a variety of areas, usually visiting the reefs of
Inner and Outer Conch and the ledges and drop-offs of
Davis Reef and **Crocker Wall**. Outer Conch has a zigzag
maze of ridges separated by long, winding valleys of sand,
where huge rays can often be seen gracefully swimming. Sometimes captains bring bags of bread crumbs and chopped sea
urchins to feed the fish. Other trips concentrate on spearfishing, or lobstering. Dive boats make morning and afternoon
trips, and the costs usually run about $30 for a two-tank scuba
trip, $35 for night dives, $20 for snorkelers. Make reservations,
and inquire as to location and group intention; you don't want
to be happily feeding a fish and have your dive companion nail
it right before your eyes:

Lady Cyana, MM #86 (664-8717)
World Down Under, MM #81.5 (664-9312)
Holiday Isle, MM #84.5 (664-4145)

A popular wreck dive here is the *Duane,* a 327-foot scuttled Coast Guard cutter. The county is looking into the possibility of getting, and sinking, surplus army tanks as well. It isn't yet known what kind of fish will favor a tank environment.

An in-shore patch reef, easily accessible if you're just poking about in a rental boat, is **Hens and Chickens Reef**. This reef, originally named by the Spanish, lies three miles offshore and is marked by a navigational light. Large star-coral heads once grew here, but the reef was killed in 1970, when a particularly cold winter brought cold water laden with sediment out of the bay through Snake Creek into the Gulf. The living coral is gone but the structures remain and are being repopulated by soft corals. Fish and lobsters still live among the rocky remains, and many moray eels also lurk about here. As is often the case with reefs close to shore, visibility at Hens and Chickens is frequently nonexistent.

THE BACK COUNTRY

To the west of Plantation Key are the waters of Florida Bay, the "back country" that, once you pass the Intracoastal Waterway, which roughly and rather closely parallels the Upper Keys, is the Everglades National Park. These uninhabited islands of the upper and central bay have names like Caloosa, Buttonwood, Triplet, Tern, Eagle, Black Betsy, and Manatee. All are mangrove, red and black, the red the pioneer, its roots graceful as hooped skirts, clumping forward, building land. There are primitive campsites on some of the keys in the bay, including Nest in the eastern portion and Rabbit and Man of War keys in the Dildo Key Bank (there is a modest explanation for this name, one is certain; there *is* a native cactus called the dildo, which has loping, three-angled thorny stems, but that doesn't clear up much epistemologically). For the interest of etymologists, the grim name of Arsenic Bank nearby is a distortion of *Arsenicker,* in turn a mispronunciation of these keys' *real* name, Marsh Sneaker.

The back country is unique and mysterious, both subtle and

grand. It's a silent wilderness of extravagant rushing clouds, shallow waters brightened by sun and darkened by the shapes of fishes, green islands appearing as if by magic on the horizon, and 360-degree sunsets. The northwestern part of the bay is home to the secretive, slender-snouted crocodile, rarer than the freshwater alligator. Crocs are said to have five distinct calls, all to do with love and warning. Poachers say that their red eyes look just like dollar bills. In the warmer months, the beleaguered manatee grazes on the succulent grasses of these flats. A docile, dallying creature, its biggest enemy is, of course, man, this time piloting the motorboat that churns thoughtlessly across its great, browsing bulk.

The grass beds of the back country support large numbers of redfish, trout, snook, mangrove snapper, tarpon, and the small, fast, hard fighting gamefish jack crevalles, and provide a nursery for lobsters and crabs. And this is where the bird rookeries are, the nesting islands and feeding grounds, the resting areas for those who make long migrations. Brown pelicans nest in great numbers, favoring a new key each season. The American Bald Eagle, too, nests here, usually raising his young on one key and fishing and hunting on another, perhaps not liking to dispose of his most immediate neighbors. There are a multitude of herons who work these waters—Louisiana, Little, Green, White, and Blue. And egrets, terns, turnstones, plovers, skimmers. Some stalk or spear. Some glide and scoop. Others sprint

A Keys' gator

through shallow water, striking right and left. Others dabble and probe or are masters of the surprise attack. One of the most beautiful birds that live and breed here, though not in great numbers, is the roseate spoonbill. No one who sees the brilliant colors of this bird against the dark green mangroves and blue back-country sky will ever forget it.

These are fabulous waters to explore in a small boat, although the back country takes years to know, and voyaging into its quiet wonders should not be undertaken lightly by the casual boater. Channels are complex, usually little more than a tortured winding through mangroves and hammocks which suddenly open out to basins and flats. Always stay in channels and do not stray into the shallows, where prop damage can wreak havoc on fragile seagrass meadows. The time of high and low tides can differ several hours between locations only a few miles apart. Basically, you can tell water depth by color. If it's brown, you're going to run aground. If it's white, you might. In the winter, the bay can be whipped by winds into choppy foam. In the summer, the waters can be flat as glass, with faraway boats seemingly floating in the air and the sticks that mark channels turning into long-legged herons that fly away. At any

---

THE ROSEATE SPOONBILL

"It is as though an orchid had spread its lovely wings and flown," an enthusiast once described the spoonbill.

The spoonbill had almost been exterminated by plume hunters at the turn of the century. The feathers were not as popular as those of the egret for ladies' hats, but the wings were torn off and made into fans, though the buyer was often disappointed when the brilliant colors quickly faded. Knowledge of the horrors of avian carnage gives reading Edith Wharton a new dimension.

Julian Huxley once noted that the "bird mind is not yet complicated by reason." The roseate spoonbill is a simple and shy creature of many troubles, yet garbed in glory. The young are an immaculate white and only gradually become suffused with pink. Three years must pass and three moltings occur before the bird achieves its full brilliance of nup-

Roseate spoonbills

tial plumage—in rose and carmine and orange—and will
mate. The drawing of the spoonbill in John Audubon's *Birds
of America,* considered not to be by Audubon, does not reflect
the true radiance of the bird's colors. It is not likely that
Audubon saw many of them. In his remarks, he noted that
their flesh was oily and poor eating, and that they were difficult to kill. (Some years later, in 1874, a man named Freder-
ick Tingley Jencks, realizing that the species was growing
scarce, visited two nesting colonies in the Lake Okeechobee
region of Florida. He found eradicating the birds time-
consuming but not impossible. He returned day after day,
shooting all the birds in both colonies until no spoonbill
remained. He "collected" a total of twenty-six skins.)

By 1939, the only nesting site for the birds in the state of
Florida was on Bottlepoint (now called Bottle) Key, off Tavernier in Florida Bay. Robert Porter Allen, an ornithologist
working for the National Audubon Society, made an intensive study of the colony in 1939 and 1940, camping on the far
end of the key away from the birds and on a skiff offshore,
observing their courtship, breeding, and feeding habits, and
writing a charming book, *The Flame Birds.* The spoonbill
favors the little killifishes of the marly flats of shallow man-

grove pools, grazing the opaque water, swinging their sensitive bills to and fro, feeling through the water as "one might with the fingers of the hand." Mating between the birds is decorous, the female showing her willingness by isolating herself upon a pleasant bush and shaking convenient twigs or branches with her bill. After a seemly amount of bill-clashing and twig-rattling—which usually goes on for two weeks—the male perches behind the female, reaching across her back and grasping the twig she is fiddling with in his bill. Together they grip the twig. Then the twig is dropped, and the male grasps firmly the slender middle portion of the female's bill with his own. Progression progresses . . . and so are baby spoonbills begun!

Roseate spoonbills now nest in April and May on several of the islands in Florida Bay, including the keys named for Allen himself and the Audubon sanctuary, Cowpens, through which the Inland Waterway cuts a swath. They remain far from common, so to see them is indeed an event—their bright existence making the beautiful back country of the Keys even more beautiful.

time of the year you should be prepared for very rapid weather changes—waterspouts in the summer, brisk squalls, and sudden wind shifts. Your boat should be equipped with binoculars, good charts, a compass, and a push pole (a 10-foot pole with a spatulate end, which you use to push yourself off mud banks, pole across the flats, and anchor in the marl). The marly bottom of the bay is alarming to the uninitiated who, hopping over the side of the boat, will promptly proceed to sink. Visions of Amazonian quicksand movies flash through one's head, but it is not quicksand, and it will not devour you, although it is sucky, sticky stuff. Always wear sneakers when tramping around either Bay or Gulf waters, for protection against coral, spiny sea urchins, and other skittering, perhaps stinging, perhaps slimy things.

Duly informed, but not unduly alarmed about squalls and slither, make an effort to get "out back." The experience of birding, fishing, and exploring in the bay is something you should not miss in the Keys.

WINDLEY KEY

Eric's Floating Restaurant could once be found just across the Snake Creek Bridge at MM #86.5. It was a houseboat ambiguously decorated with animal skins and heads, and lace tablecloths. There was also a vague Viking ship motif. Some occasional nymph statuary as well. It was all . . . uncanny. But it sank. No diners were reported having gone down with it. Close by this ambiguous site is the casual **Hook's**, which has an easygoing menu ranging from crabcake sandwiches to steaks. Beer and wine. Telephone: 664-2600.

The bridge at Snake Creek got stuck during Spring Break in March of 1988. A gust of wind misaligned the spans when they were in their highest open position—a gust that bartenders for ten miles in each direction considered "an act of God." People were stranded for seventeen hours. Beer was delivered in iced-up wheelbarrows. It was the wheelbarrows that made the moment "Conch."

Holiday Isle is one of the best-known pleasure and partying meccas in the Keys, but if you want a smaller, quieter place to lay your head, there is a cluster of little motels here on the ocean. The **Drop Anchor** is pretty and relaxing, with a palm-studded beach and a resident great white heron. In season (December 15 to mid-April), rooms are $50, two-room suites $115, kitchenettes $65. Summer and fall, prices drop $10 to $20. Telephone: 664-4863.

Windley Key was once two separate islands named the Umbrella Keys, but they were joined with fill by railroad construction. The key was quarried extensively for bridge and causeway fill, and after the railroad was completed, various companies continued to quarry the beautifully patterned fossilized coral rock for use as decorative veneer on buildings. The rock was known as keystone. The living reef runs along the Keys. The dead reef is the foundation of the Upper Keys. The exposed rock of the quarry walls shows the patterns and borings of polyps, gorgonians, and other inhabitants of the ancient reef. Three of the old quarries can be found on the bay side of the highway shortly after the Snake Creek Bridge, and there are hopes of

HURRICANES

Reading about hurricanes and having hurricane parties are, naturally, much more enjoyable than evacuating for a hurricane, preparing for a hurricane, or assessing the damage from a hurricane. The Keys haven't had a hurricane in a very long while. Awful Andrew barely grazed the islands. Most people have never experienced one, and many think that those who voice their fears about hurricanes are just trying to put their bad mouth around the Keys. A hurricane is a monster whirlwind. It has a name and massive amounts of rain. It has winds of between 74 and 200 mph and stirs up giant waves and strong tides. It is born of blazing sun, still water, and warm, wet air in either the Atlantic Ocean, the Gulf of Mexico, or the Caribbean Sea any time between June and November, although it's most likely to occur in the autumn equinox between mid-August and mid-October. It begins life as a vacuum, a *beckoning* vacuum, attracting faraway breezes which approach it in a clockwise-twisting curve, only to reverse and swirl excitedly in ever-tightening counterclockwise gyres. Cool air arrives, is sucked up and made warm, everything climbs higher and faster, creating wind and rain, and then this thing starts to *move,* gorged with water power, fatally attracted to land (which will weaken and eventually extinguish it)—a real 3-D monster. Conchs know that a hurricane is coming when the poinciana loses its leaves or doesn't blossom, or when land crabs move to higher ground or ants climb straight up the walls or dogs and birds start acting peculiar. Scientists know that a hurricane is coming by reading their satellites, radar, and computers. But no one can forecast with true accuracy where a hurricane's point of landfall will be. A computer's reliability for predicting where a hurricane will hit ranges from 10 percent at 72 hours to almost 75 percent within 12 hours. Even with a half day's notice, the margin of error on a hurricane with a breadth of 150 miles remains at 65 miles in either direction. If the Hurricane Center in Miami forecasts 12 hours in advance that a storm will hit Marathon, it could strike anywhere from Key West to Key Largo, requiring total evacuation of the Keys. But the feasibility of complete over-the-road evacuation is nil, and if it were possible, it would take at least 35 hours. Besides, behavioral studies have shown that 25 percent of the population in a hurricane's path wouldn't leave their homes even if ordered to.

So, what to do! According to a NOAA (National Oceanic and Atmospheric Administration) Coastal Hazards Program booklet, if you're at home you should stock up on candles, masking tape, and radio batteries, fill your bathtub and washing machine with water, and throw your aluminum furniture in the swimming pool. You should secure your boat in a safe harbor or tie it up in the mangroves. You should keep your ear pasted to NOAA weather radio. If you go to a Red Cross Shelter, you should bring food and bedding. You should not bring intoxicating beverages, pets, or firearms. You should probably not bring John D. MacDonald's *Condominium* for reading material, either.

Some people feel that the Florida coastline is a disaster waiting to happen, and project 20-foot tidal waves sweeping over the Keys. Others trust in the offshore reefs to break up any mass of water before it reaches land, or don't even trouble themselves to think of hurricanes at all, believing them to be obsolete, rather like kerosene lamps. Whatever, almost everyone would agree that trying to determine which direction the wind is going to blow is like trying to chart the course of a leaf on a giant river.

acquiring this area, which spans more than thirty acres, as a state geological site and park. As well as the fascinating quarries, there is a dense hardwood hammock running along the high land above the walls with large mahogany, torchwood, joewood, and white ironwood, all rare native trees of the Florida Keys.

Theater of the Sea at MM #84.5 was created from one of the old quarries the railroad crews dug in 1907. It was flooded with seawater and stocked with fish as a tourist attraction in the 1940's, which makes it one of the oldest marine parks in the world. There are some very amorous sea lions here, and a number of more locally grown cheerful and acrobatic dolphins. They put on a very nice show for children. Shows are continuous from 9:30 A.M. to 4 P.M. Admission is $12.25 for adults, $6.75 for children 5–12; under 5, free. There are also some gloomy sharks and a blind crocodile. They do not put on shows.

Holiday Isle (MM #84.5) is big and brassy, with the mood of a speeded-up film. From the road it looks as though something tumultuous—even disastrous—involving a great many people has just occurred, and it usually has. On winter weekends five to six thousand people ready to fish and rock out crowd this complex, which is said to include ten bars—even taking double-vision into account a considerable number. (You will see a lot of pliers in these bars, and in fact in all the bars scattered along the intensive fishing grounds of Islamorada and Marathon—machismo being measured by the size of the pliers sticking in belts or jeans pockets, as pliers are used for wrenching the hooks from the mouths of huge fish.) The resort sponsors off-shore power boat races and windsurfing and fishing tournaments throughout the year. For these special events and all holidays, minimum stay requirements apply. Languid it's not. December 15 to May 1, economy rooms $105, ocean view $150, suites $220–$360. Rates drop $20 to $25 between May 2 and Labor Day and drop slightly again between September and mid-December. All rates, however, go up between $10 and $25 each year. Telephone: 664-2321.

Within dueling distance, at MM #83.5, is the **Whale Harbor Restaurant and Marina** with the adjacent **Chesapeake Motel**, marked by a shell-plastered toy lighthouse. Hurricane Donna struck here vigorously in 1960—the area seems a popular landfall for storms. There's a good upstairs tiki bar here over the charter boat docks, and an extensive seafood buffet served daily from 4:30 P.M. for $12.95. Sunday the buffet begins at noon and costs $9.95. The Chesapeake is quieter and less wildly sociable than Holiday Isle, yet close enough to make one's indulgences and then retreat to roomy villas and nicely landscaped grounds. Again, there's a three-day minimum stay during holidays and special events. Motel rooms are $125 a night; a nice room on the water is $170–$195. Villas range from $130 to $350 in season, $10 or so less at other times. Telephone: 664-4662 or 664-4663. Reservations are important during the season.

UPPER MATECUMBE KEY

On the morning of September 2, 1935, large red-and-black hurricane warning flags were flying along the Keys. The foremen

Hurricane!

for the hundreds of workmen who were building a road here telephoned the Overseas Railroad headquarters in Miami and begged for an evacuation train to be sent down for them. A rescue train left Miami late in the afternoon, stopping at Homestead, the last mainland stop, to shift the locomotive from the front to the rear of the train, the engineer planning on pulling out of the storm rather than backing out of it. When the train stopped at Snake Creek at 7 P.M. to take on evacuees, a cable, torn loose by winds that were blowing over 150 mph, snagged on the engine cab, and more than an hour's effort was required to free it. By the time the train had backed down to Islamorada, winds had reached 200 mph. Hundreds of people were on board when a tidal wave engulfed the train and tore it from the tracks.

After the hurricane, one could stand in the middle of the key and see from ocean to bay and from one end of the island to the other. Nothing remained standing except the angel that marked a grave in a tiny cemetery on the beach in Islamorada. The angel can be seen today on the grounds of the Cheeca Lodge (of all places) between the Cheeca's Ocean Front Villas south and the golf driving range and heliport pad—a bit of *memento mori* in the midst of the good and fancy life.

> *This lovely bud so young so fair*
> *Called home to early doom*

Just called to show how sweet a flower
In Paradise would bloom

The angel is missing a hand and part of one wing, but she is still there, watching over the grave of Etta Dolores Pinder, who was born in 1899 and died in 1914, the only child of one of the early homesteading families of the Upper Keys.

Just beyond Cheeca, around MM #81.5, is a hurricane monument that marks the mass grave of many of those killed in the storm. The monument is constructed of locally quarried limestone and bears a striking art nouveau impression of palm trees bending in the wind.

ISLAMORADA

Most of the restaurants, resorts, and shops on Plantation, Windley, and Matecumbe keys running from MM #88 down to MM #73 and Channel #2 use **Islamorada** as their address, for that is the community and post office which serves these keys.

For many people, this area is easily comprehended by its attractions (**Theater of the Sea**), the concentration of restaurants (unnerving buffet excess is available at the **Whale Harbor Inn** at MM #83.5 and **The Coral Grille**), and its accommodations (which range from the calm and dignified **Cheeca Lodge** to the playful, disorderly **Holiday Isle**) and is their ultimate destination in the Keys. Here, within a few miles, are the big marinas at **Holiday Isle**, **Whale Harbor**, and **Bud 'n' Mary's**, these three providing the largest concentration of charter fishing boats in the entire island chain, a fact which allows Islamorada to claim for itself the title "Sport Fishing Capital of the World."

People come here to fish, eat, drink, fish, drink, and fish. From December to May there is the annual South Florida Fishing Tournament. In February there's the Ladies Sailfish Tournament. There's the Bonefish Fly Tournament in April, and the Ladies Invitational Tarpon Tournament. In the summer there are Shark Tournaments which allowed, until recently, the use of shotguns and baseball bats. There are Great Grunt Rodeos and Dolphin Scrambles. In the fall there are more bonefish tournaments and billfish tournaments and sailfish tournaments. Tournaments are usually sponsored by breweries and resorts, and there are cash prizes and trophies and patches and plaques and citations. Prizes are given for the biggest fish, the smallest fish, the weirdest fish, and the most fish.

For tournament and charter information, contact:

Whale Harbor Marina, MM #84 (664-4511)
Holiday Isle, MM # 84.5 (664-2321)
Bud 'n' Mary's, MM #80 (664-2461)
Abel's Tackle Box, MM #84 (664-2521)

For a great day of fly-fishing on the flats, contact Mike Collins, an exceptionally able and articulate guide. It's $325 for a full day. Flats boats are too cool to have names. Call 852-5837.

For a brochure containing the names, addresses, telephone numbers, and specialties of fishing guides, write to **Marathon Guides Association**, P.O. Box 65, Marathon, FL 33050. Key West captains have finally admitted that there are "really too many" charterboats operating in the Keys, but you won't hear such heresy up here.

WHERE TO STAY

The Cheeca Lodge (MM #82). Cheeca sounds like something meaningfully Indian, but in fact it's just a preppy nickname for Cynthia Twitchell, who with her husband ran the lodge as a private club in the fifties. Known for years as one of the Keys' few resorts, it had an understated, clubby atmosphere, a forgiving nine-hole golf course, a preppy white-sand beach, and a seemingly endless 525-foot fishing pier, down which all guests were obliged to trek. Everything went on in a low-key way until new owners decided they wanted to spend $40 million. Everyone thought that was a lot, so an expensive study was commissioned to see if it was possible to spend that much. The study determined that it was possible. Cheeca now has 203 rooms, more than double the original number, two more tennis courts, another pool, a date palm–lined courtyard, parrots burbling in cages, and a series of meandering lagoons. Cheeca's elegance isn't so low-key any more, but it is still a romantic and friendly resort. Rooms run $225–$500 in season, suites $275 all the way up to $800. If you have $1,000, you're welcome to stay in the Presidential Suite as well. There are extensive activity programs for children, and special room rates if you go out fishing. They've adopted an odd "availability" policy, "just like the airlines." If you arrange for your room far enough ahead of time, you get a better rate. But if you're the more carefree, spur-of-the-moment type, well, you suffer. Telephone: 664-4651.

The Islander (MM #83) occupies almost the same amount of land as the Cheeca Lodge—25 acres—and has a nice beach and two pools (one saltwater, one fresh), but lacks Cheeca's cachet. It is sparsely landscaped, with a large number of units arranged so that they look out upon the backs or beginnings of other large numbers of units, and rooms are decorated in garish colors. Ample spaces, however, and modest rates. In season (December 15 to mid-April), rooms $65–$71; with kitchenettes, $77. A lanai of one's own is another $10. From mid-April to mid-December, rates drop $10 to $15. Telephone: 664-2031.

The Moorings (Beach Road off the old highway). Hard to find. Everyone knows where it is but it's still hard to find. Stay on the old road that parallels Route 1 after Manny and Isa's heading south and turn down Beach Road toward the ocean. This is a wonderful spot, 17 palmy acres on a lovely beach. Old, comfy, carefully restored housekeeping cottages on the right, and newer, tasteful, but less interesting houses with suites on the left. The original fishing camp here was built after the '35 hurricane with Arm and Hammer money. It has become a very popular place to conduct fashion shoots, so you will see some unnervingly perfect people here in bathing suits. Quiet, classy, simple. Children and their parents are encouraged to stay over at Cheeca, where there would be "more for them to do." The old cottages have a two-night minimum stay and run between $115 and $145 a night. A two-bedroom cottage on the beach is $1,500 a night. Telephone: 664-4708.

Breezy Palms (MM #80). Much smaller and very pleasant. Nicely furnished rooms and efficiencies on the ocean by the towering Ocean 80 resort. No beach really, but small, busy piers, assorted sunning spots, and a pool. Winter rates $75. An apartment by the pool $105. Telephone: 664-2361.

Oceanside Motel (MM #82.5).   Most famous for the abduction of Bert, a peacock who blew in after Hurricane Andrew in 1992. Two carpenters from Miami snatched the bird but were arrested by alert sheriff deputies who saw Bert's tail feathers sticking out the van's sliding doors. "No matter what their intentions, I think it was a real bad thing to do. The bird was happy here and all of a sudden he was kidnapped," the manager said. You can see Bert (one hopes) and even enjoy a great suite on the ocean with a wraparound balcony for $170 a night. Telephone: 664-3681.

WHERE TO EAT

Ziggie's Conch at MM #83 is small, crowded, and plain, with an extensive fish menu and a popular bar. A longtime eccentric favorite, it's tamed down a bit and now may be . . . just another restaurant. Open 5 P.M. Closed Thursdays. Telephone: 664-3391.

Lorelei (MM #82 at the Islamorada Yacht Basin). The tiki bar outside is friendly, the gathering place at the end of the day for back-country guides. The restaurant has lots of glass and lovely bay views, although you may be seated by a large mermaid with a tail of glued-on tarpon scales which occupies one wall. Lorelei has many steak, lobster, and rich seafood casserole offerings. Their snapper stuffed with crabmeat is good, but expensive even by Key West standards. Open 11 A.M. to 3 P.M. for lunch, 5:30 to 9:30 P.M. for dinner; Saturdays 11 A.M. to 9:30 P.M. Telephone: 664-4656. Nearby is **Woody's** (664-4335), a popular place for pizza and pasta but most renowned for its lounge life after ten, when a band called Big Dick and the Extenders play.

Green Turtle Inn (MM #81).   Popular, crowded, cluttered, the Green Turtle has been around since 1947, when patrons really tucked in the turtle steaks. In 1970, just before the government passed laws prohibiting the killing and selling of green turtle, the owner of Sid and Roxie's Cannery across the street was processing over a thousand pounds of turtle meat weekly. The turtle steaks and chowders you now get at the inn are from freshwater turtles raised in farms around Lake Okeechobee. Several old cottages have been joined to make up the restaurant, which is cozy and hearty, the walls covered with photographs of jolly, beaming patrons and framed newspaper headlines of puzzling relevance—*Another Jap Warlord Kills Self.* At night there's a piano player who'll play anything you request. "I'm Back in Baby's Arms" seems to be popular with the diners. Maybe you'll be on hand for the "turtle wave," which everyone seems to know how to do. Open from noon until 10 P.M. Closed Mondays. Telephone: 664-4918.

Papa Joe's (MM #80).   A nice old place at the end of Upper Matecumbe, overlooking Tea Table Channel. Italian dishes, fresh and inexpensive fish dinners. A tiki bar is cantilevered over a bait shop in back. Open from 11 A.M. until 10 P.M. Closed Tuesdays. Telephone: 664-8109. You can arrange for rental boats and back-country charters here too. The marina's number is 664-5005.

Manny and Isa's (MM #81.6). Manny has an orchard behind his tiny restaurant, and each summer he squeezes 9,000 Key limes for you. The pies are classic: $1.75 a slice, $10 for the whole statement. Open 11 A.M. to 9 P.M. Closed Tuesdays. Telephone: 664-5019. Don't expect ambience here, just good . . . pie.

LIGNUMVITAE AND INDIAN KEYS

Between Upper and Lower Matecumbe keys lie two unconnected, uninhabited keys of considerable historic and natural interest—Lignumvitae and Indian.

Lignumvitae, a 345-acre island, along with Shell Key and Indian Key, was purchased by the Nature Conservancy and the state in 1970. Arrangements can be made at **Long Key Recreation Area** for a two-hour interpretive tour, where small groups are escorted through the island by a ranger.

Of all the Keys, Lignumvitae is the highest—sixteen feet above sea level—and is a true island. Although the giant mahoganies were removed in the nineteenth century, and although some building and introduction of exotic plants and animals took place in the 1920's, Lignumvitae is considered to be virgin hammock, the last untouched bit of tropical forest in Florida. Botanists say that to enter Lignumvitae is to enter the primeval past. Certainly, it is to see a portion of the wonder that Florida once was.

The history of the Keys is a harsh one of dynamiting, burning, collecting, and developing. Lignumvitae has miraculously escaped all that. Its last owner, a Miami dentist, wanted to build a bridge from Lower Matecumbe Key and develop a resort there. He liked golf, so there would have been a golf course. Restaurants. The works. Amazingly, this didn't happen. Lignumvitae was saved. Perhaps it's blessed. It has never been burned like the other keys; fire has never destroyed the organic humus that takes centuries to form over the coral rock. Farmers never cleared and seared the land to get a year or two of good fruit production. Snail collectors never discovered it and burned the hammock when they left, as was their habit. (All of Florida's tropical hammocks were home to varieties of tree snails, which with their varied markings were astonishingly popular with collectors throughout the world. The snails of each area had evolved distinct color patterns on their shells. It was common for a collector to go to a hammock, collect a few snails, then set the land on fire to increase the rarity and value of the variety he had collected. The snail peculiar to Lignumvitae has a shell neatly circled with fine bands of red and green on a base of cream.)

Lignum vitae is a tree noted for the extreme density of its wood. Because of the rich resins which keep it from drying out, it has been used in boat outfitting, outlasting even steel and bronze. Lignum vitae was first described in *Ortus Sanitatis,* one of the major botanical works of the fifteenth century, as a tree in the Garden of Eden. Whoever consumed it was said to be strengthened with perpetual health, clothed in immortality, and protected from anxiety, weakness, and infirmity. It was described as being not only nonflammable, but purified by fire, and it was the wood from which the Holy Grail was created. In the Bahamas today, lignum vitae is called holywood or broke-iron tree and is used as a cure for impotence.

The Matheson family, which owned Lignumvitae from 1919 to 1953, built the large limestone house visible from the dock, as well as the windmill and cistern. They decorated the lawn with six cannons from the wrecked HMS *Winchester,* which ran aground on Carysfort Reef in 1695 and was discovered in 1939. They built an airstrip, brought in a bulldozer to maintain a trail, and imported burros, Galapagos tortoises, Angora goats, round-eared brown rabbits, Indian geese, ducks, and peafowl. They also made extensive plantings of exotics with the assistance of their friend, the famous botanist David Fairchild.

The strange species are gone, along with the other disturbances. The house remains, the only interruption in the mangrove shoreline, facing east away from the sea, untouched by the 1935 hurricane that cut such a narrow and ferocious swath between Tavernier and Marathon. Around the house are huge mastics and banyans and sapodilla trees, and beyond is the forest of the hammock. There are 133 varieties of trees here, including the thorny plants of the low, hot woods on the western shore—prickly ash, cockspur, hog plum, and cat's claw. There is also an enigmatic 3,000-foot coral rock wall built no one knows when, or why, as well as a Caloosa burial ground.

For years before the state purchased the key, the caretakers of the property were the remarkable Russel and Charlotte Niedhauk. *Charlotte's Story,* a 1930's diary of the Niedhauks' caretaking of Elliott Key, north of Key Largo, is available in local bookstores and is a charming and guileless account of risk, ingenuity, and adventure in a primitive Florida.

Tours of Lignumvitae are conducted daily except Tuesday and Wednesday at 10:30 A.M., 1 P.M., and 2:30. The Park Service used to run a boat from Indian Key Fill at MM #79, but the boat broke in '93 and the state hasn't given them money to fix it yet. You can rent a boat at **Robbie's** (MM #77.5) or **Bud 'n' Mary's Marina** (MM #80) and motor over yourself. This will cost you $75 for a half day, $100 for a full day.

A nice time to visit Lignumvitae is during the first two weeks in April, when the trees are in bloom.

The Spanish named **Indian Key** *Matanzas,* which means slaughter, purportedly because four hundred shipwrecked Frenchmen were killed by the Caloosa Indians here. The slaughter seems more legend than fact and may just be another example of the Spaniard's gloomy penchant for bloody place names. Once again, however, the name proved historically fateful.

In the 1830's, the tiny 11-acre island was a flourishing town, the personal kingdom of a wrecker named Jacob Housman, who established a salvaging station here so that he would not have to obey the rules and pay the fees set by Key West courts. Indian Key had a post office, three streets, twenty houses, wharves, warehouses, and a resort hotel called The Tropical. There was even a bowling alley in this best of all possible worlds, the bowling balls probably made of lignum vitae wood.

Audubon anchored offshore on the revenue cutter *Marion* for a week in the spring of 1832 and discovered birds there which were entirely new to him, including the roseate tern, the double-breasted cormorant, and the reddish egret. He extensively used the services of one of Housman's pilots, a man named Egan. Egan took him along the channels and through the maze of mangrove unerringly to the objects of his desire. "Not a Cormorant or Pelican, a Flamingo, an Ibis, or Heron, had ever in his days formed its nest without his having marked the spot," Audubon wrote. While George Lehman, his background artist, drew the key itself, Audubon sketched the birds.

Audubon was not a precociously gifted draftsman. Even after he had perfected his method, in which freshly killed specimens were run through with wires and arranged in lifelike positions, he still had to keep shooting the same species over and over, so that he could sketch them in different positions. In *The Birds of America,* he wrote of the brown pelican, "This superb male whose portrait is before you . . . was selected from a great number. . . ." In his writings he also shares with us a disappointment he suffered:

Lo, I came in sight of several pelicans, perched on the branches of the mangrove trees, seated in comfortable harmony, as near

each other as the strength of the boughs would allow. I ordered
to back water gently. I waded to the shore under cover of the
rushes along it, saw the pelicans fast asleep, examined their
countenances and deportment well and leisurely, and after all,
levelled, fired my piece and dropped two of the finest specimens I
ever saw. I really believe I would have shot one hundred of these
reverend sirs, had not a mistake taken place in the reloading of
my gun. A mistake, however, did take place, and to my utmost
disappointment, I saw each pelican, young and old, leave his
perch and take to wing.

Audubon loved the singular plants, the gorgeous flowers, and
the "salubrious" air of Indian Key. He gives an account of a raucous party the islanders threw, complete with fiddles and di-
luted claret for the ladies.

Jacob Housman was a wealthy man and a law unto himself,
but he still had to worry about the Indians. He arranged to have
the Navy's Florida Squadron, a fleet of seven ships based on
nearby Tea Table Key, to protect his holdings, but the
squadron, known for spending more money on "medicines," primarily rum, than all the other units of the Navy combined,
were to be of little use to the townspeople of Indian Key.

By 1840, Housman's town had fifty-five inhabitants, including a physician-botanist, Dr. Henry Perrine, and his family.
Perrine established a nursery on the northeast end of Lower
Matecumbe and did plant research on Indian Key. All in all, he
introduced more than two hundred plants to tropical Florida.
He had many interests, including silkworms and stingless bees,
but his true obsession was *agave*—a plant cultivated for its
sturdy sisal, a durable fiber, and also, less prosaically, as a
source of hashish. Dr. Perrine also treated the sick, including
Seminole Indians. Housman, on the other hand, ever enterprising, was trying to negotiate a contract with the government
which would permit him to hunt and kill the Indians at two
hundred dollars a head.

On August 7, 1840, with the Naval squadron away, the Seminoles, no doubt having heard of Housman's income-producing
scheme, attacked the island, burning every building except the
home of the postman, Charles Howe. Howe was a Mason, and
his Masonic apron with its all-seeing eye and other mystic sym-

bols was found spread upon the table. The eye may have given the Indians pause, but they went on anyway to kill sixteen people, one of whom was Dr. Perrine. Those who escaped the massacre hid in turtle kraals near the houses or in the cisterns beneath them, although gruesome popular history claims that some who sought safety there were boiled alive. Housman and his family survived, but he never reestablished his empire. He returned to Key West and worked on a former rival's salvage vessel, dying in a ship accident six months later. His body was buried on Indian Key, and there is a historical plaque identifying the site. Someone has stolen the skeleton, to say nothing of the tombstone, although fragments of the stone were recovered and taken to Lignumvitae for safekeeping. Other markers identify the house site, the hotel cistern, and so on.

A new community was formed on the island in the 1870's, when the key became a site for building schooners and sloops. It was also on this tiny key that the construction workers for the Alligator Reef lighthouse, built in 1873, lived, and where the iron pile structure, built and dismantled in a northern foundry, then shipped to Florida, was stored before being transported to the reef.

Indian Key is certainly not the unblemished paradise that Lignumvitae is. It seems ironic that it ended up as a historic site rather than a botanical one, when one considers Dr. Perrine's extensive introduction of exotic plants here. Damage was done in the 1930's and 1940's, when treasure hunters dynamited it to search for valuables they thought had been buried there. Tourists were even brought over at $5 a day and furnished with shovels so that they could dig. Today the landscape seems almost Mexican, with its sisal plants and prickly pear, descendants of the doctor's plants, but there is also a restful wild tamarind grove, the delicate, feathery foliage softening the glare of the sun.

As with Lignumvitae, you must acquire or hire a boat to get over to Indian Key, but then you're on your own. You may explore from 8 A.M. to sunset.

A mile south of Indian Key is the wreck of the *San Pedro*, a ship that went down in 1733. It lies in eighteen feet of water and consists mostly of ballast stones, although it has recently been enhanced by replicas of timbers, anchors, and cannons.

LOWER MATECUMBE KEY

Judging from the amount of tangled monofilament around the power lines, some of the worst fishermen in the Keys frequent the catwalks over Indian Key and Lignumvitae Channels. Fishing here and along the bridges that span Channel #2 and Channel #5 between Lower Matecumbe and Long Key is very good, offering catches of snapper, grouper, and, in the spring and early summer, snook. In the winter, after a cold snap and the ensuing nor'wester, shrimp leave the cooler waters of the bay and can be netted from the bridges at night.

Alligator Lighthouse, the most beautiful on the reef, white and stately, is visible off the Matecumbe keys. Over five hundred species of fish have been found on the reef the light marks. **Buddy's Dive Shop** at MM #79.5 makes trips to Alligator. Buddy's also takes experienced divers to an artificial deep-water reef, created when a 65-foot trawler loaded with marijuana was deliberately scuttled. The "Cannabis Cruiser" sits upright on the bottom, still loaded with its ruined bales, and makes an interesting wreck dive.

Lower Matecumbe has a number of troubled time-shares, most of which would be thrilled if you rented a room for the night. Developers went into a greed frenzy in the early 1980's, when they came up with the idea of selling both space *and* time. The new structures are circular, erected on pedestals, with an ambience of early space station. The old ones are old motels. **Caloosa Cove** at MM #73.8 covers all bases—it's a time-share condominium resort with a full marina, charters, room and boat rentals, tennis courts, and a bar which is inexplicably called The Safari and filled with African "artifacts." The establishment leaps into the void of hyperbole with its billboard slogan, Paradise at Your Command. Telephone: 664-8811.

A far lovelier sight is the watery stretch between Lower Matecumbe and tiny Craig Key at MM #72. This area has some very pretty picnicking spots and some of the most beautiful views to be had from the highway in the Keys. You will see many birds feeding here—little blue herons, which when young are pure white; white ibis, with their bright orange curved bills;

PELICANS: COLORS AND A LEGEND

Brown pelicans can be seen everywhere, all year long, in the Keys. The white pelican breeds in the summer near the mountain lakes of Montana and Utah and is only a winter visitor to the islands in Florida Bay. (Unlike brown pelicans, white pelicans don't dive for fish. Instead, their fishing is a communal effort, with ten to fifteen birds forming a semicircle and herding the fish to shore, where they can then scoop them up with their bills.) Many of the brown pelicans you see begging for fish off docks and bridges are young birds. A pelican in his first year has a brown neck and wings and a very white belly. In the second year, his body is more gray than brown. By the third year, his belly is quite dark. In the summertime, the adult pelican's head is white with a dark brown stripe on the back of the neck. In early fall, the brown stripe molts to white, and yellow courting plumage appears.

The pelican is a bird of myth as well as droll actuality. His image is common on ecclesiastical heraldry and was often engraved on chalices. Many medieval bestiaries include a story in which the mother pelican caresses her offspring with such devotion that she kills them. When the father returns to the nest, he so despairs over the death of his young that he tears at his breast with his bill, and the blood from his wounds revives the dead birds. Dante, in the *Paradiso* (Canto XXV, line 113), calls Jesus Christ *nostro Pellicano*—mankind's pelican.

Pelicans feeding

white egrets, with their black legs and beautiful long breeding feathers, which are called "aigrettes"; and great white herons, the largest of the herons—over four feet in height, with a wingspan of seven feet—readily distinguished from the egrets by their much greater size and their light-colored legs. The great white is rare except in the Keys, where it is frequently seen. This very limited range, however, indicates few total numbers, and their small population is devastated by storms and hurricanes.

Craig Key once had several fishing shacks built out over the water and even a post office, established in the late 1920's because President Herbert Hoover had once anchored his yacht close by and it was thought that he might want to mail something. Storms blew everything away, but in the 1960's, a concrete-block mansion was built on the bay side by the Twitchell family, the original owners of the Cheeca Lodge. Concealed behind a stone wall and a grove of pine, the manse has five bedrooms, two full kitchens, eight baths, and a mirrored bar modeled after Cheeca's. Mrs. Twitchell was an A&P heiress who was known for her sense of humor. Mrs. Twitchell's sense of humor is responsible, it is said, for the air jets in the front door jamb that would blast air up ladies' dresses.

The road curves sharply after Craig, crossing Channel #5 and the Intracoastal Waterway, which links the ocean and the bay at MM #70. The next key, **Fiesta**, is a fill, as is Craig. Fiesta was originally called Jewfish Key, then Greyhound when the Greyhound Corporation built a post house there for its bus passengers, shortly after the highway was pushed down to Grassy Key in 1937. Now it's the site of a KOA (Kampgrounds of America) campground.

Layton is a city, incorporated in 1963, but certainly a modest one. Once, two locked black-and-white police cars (actually, one of them was only painted to *look* like a police car) were parked on either side of the highway near MM #68 and people thought they were somewhere and slowed down, but these were recently hauled away, one of Layton's biggest events in years. Nevertheless, the city has what every city should have—an Italian restaurant, sailboats, and sharks. Rather, it used to have sharks at the Sea World Shark Institute, once open to the public but recently closed to the public so that the facility, now known as Sea World Marine Science and Conservation Center, could get research grants while it continued to collect and provide Sea World's Orlando ocean aquarium with Keys' fish, turtles, and dolphins. Who knows what takes place back here in the specimen holding tanks and on the wet tables? More blood chemistry and blood gas level tests, one would imagine. More sea urchin studies. Passing through these gates is more difficult than a rich man's getting into heaven. The secretary who guards the place will tell you she believes there's a cute manatee back there, a manatee you are most certainly not allowed to see.

Dive shops in this area visit **Tennessee Reef**, one of the least-dived reefs in the Keys because of its rather remote location. Much of the collecting undertaken by the Sea World facility takes place here. There's a lot of variety on Tennessee. Tall walls and drop-offs support large corals and fish. There are lots of shells and conchs hopping across the sandy patches. And around the 1930's wreck of the USS *Tennessee* herself, which lies in twenty feet of water, many brilliant tropicals dart singly or in schools.

Reddish egret

Lime Tree Bay Resort at MM #68.5 (664-4740) has the eccentric quality of old-time Keys accommodations: a zoo, a paperback library, a shuffleboard court, and a postage-stamp beach on a grassy bay. Rooms and efficiencies run $80 to $100 in winter. A two-bedroom "tree-house" apartment is $145. Each room is decorated in a different motif. You might be given the bullfight room, for example—toreadors everywhere!—or the mounted-fish room. There's a simple restaurant that serves breakfast and burgers, and someone may be banging away on a musical instrument in the beer and wine bar at night. Close by is **Lewis Rents Boats** (664-8060), where you can rent well-maintained daysailers, Hobie Cats, Windsurfers, or canoes.

LONG KEY

Long Key State Recreation Area at MM #67.5 is one of the three state parks on the Keys. The swimming here is poor—you see people far, far from shore and they're still only up to their knees—and the beach is narrow, squeezed close to the park road and the speeding parade of humanity on Route 1. There is a nature walk through the mangroves on a recently constructed boardwalk complete with interpretive signs that urge you to reflect, ponder, and mull. One invites you to imagine a Caloosa Indian poking about the mangroves doing his inscrutable Caloosa Indian thing. "Life must have been so different then . . . ," it trails off wistfully.

The walkway is called the Golden Orb trail after the spectacular spiders that weave their webs here. The webs are heavy and huge, the female spider a royal red and gold. The males are tiny little things crouched in the corner, or not around at all. They spend so much time searching for females, courting them, and mating with them that they neglect eating, and often drop dead from exhaustion.

You can rent a canoe for $2 an hour and explore a winding tidal lagoon. Very pretty. Watch out for the "skinny water," where the coral cap rock lies close to the surface.

Off the beach the snorkeling is a great deal of fun—you'll see lobsters and octopuses—and the beachcombing can be interesting if you're able to block out the astonishing amount of dis-

---

BUGS

Mosquitoes are big here. They have been called the most reliable defenders of wilderness in the state. Sandflies are big. They're called "flying teeth." Palmetto bugs, the southern cockroach, are very big, and shiny, too. You'll see them in the best of places as well as in the wilds. At a pool party at an elegant home, a guest was heard to exclaim, "Oh, look at the little turtles!" as a family of these creepies lumbered across the patio. If you crush them, there is a terrible smell of almonds.

---

carded plastic. Always there seem to be dolls' heads on remote beaches, and Long Key is no exception. Here, too, scattered amidst the plastic, can be found the rubbery, flattened egg cases of turtles.

There's quite a bit of bird activity on the flats. The best show is put on by the reddish egret as he attempts to acquire lunch. This is a gangly, charming bird—a two-toned heron, the head and neck reddish brown, the body slate gray. He also goes through a white phase, when you could easily confuse him with a variety of herons and egrets, including even the immature little blue. But what distinguishes the reddish egret is his peculiar eating habits. Other wading birds have dignity. They stalk. They stand motionless. They are patient and aloof. The red selects the minnow he wants and chases it until he gets it, in a frenzy of running, lurching, splashing, and zigzagging, flapping his wings and clacking his bill until the minnow, exhausted, surrenders in a blur of foam.

Campgrounds in the Keys are very popular places, in both the winter and summer months. The state parks have an ingenious system of reserving 50 percent of the campsites, leaving the other half available on a first-come, first-served basis. You have to make reservations early, though not *too* early—not more than sixty days in advance, and by telephone, not mail. Checkout time is 2 P.M., and there's a two-week maximum stay, with a fee of $23.50 a night; $25.75 with electric hook-up.

The seaweed that coats the beach here is a kitchen cupboard for the birds, jumping and crawling with tasty amphipods. But

for you, the adventurous camper, the seaweed after the sun
goes down becomes a jumping, crawling hell. You cannot imagine how many bugs creep, crawl, and fly on a Keys beach after
dark. So don't undertake your overnighters lightly, with a
beach towel and a can of Coke. Bring lots of insect repellent and
cover-ups, so that you can enjoy the enormous sky and the glittering ocean phosphorescent with life.

By 1906, construction of the railroad had come as far as Long
Key. Henry Flagler built screened cottages for his workers
while they labored on the Long Key Viaduct. Other workers
were housed on large covered barges called quarterboats. When
a hurricane struck Long Key in the fall of 1906, one of these
quarterboats broke its moorings and was swept out to sea,
drowning more than a hundred men.

After the viaduct was completed, Flagler turned the construction camp into a fishing camp, The Long Key Fishing Club,
for the wealthy who arrived by yacht and rail. He supplemented
the bungalows with a luxury lodge on a white-sand beach
on the ocean side, and even built a narrow-gauge railroad that
ran through a tunnel beneath the tracks for the convenience of
his guests.

Zane Grey (Was he really christened Pearl Grey?) was one of
the camp's most famous guests. The well-known writer of west-
erns first visited here in 1913 and organized the club's fishing
contests, established "to develop the best and finest traits of
sport, to restrict the killing of fish, to educate the inexperienced
angler by helping him and to promote good fellowship." Grey
brought sailfishing into vogue. At that time, sailfish were considered pests and were called spikefish or "boohoo" because of
the disappointment they often caused by slicing through lines
intended for more popular quarry, such as kingfish. Grey introduced light tackle methods, and taking sailfish became an art.
He found the fish the gamest and most beautiful fish to catch on
light tackle, with its pirouetting leaps and its great sail spread.
Grey visited the fishing camp frequently over the years, in January and February, adhering to a schedule of rising early, writing for one hour, fishing for ten, then writing for another hour
or two in the evenings. He worked on books such as *Code of the
West* and *The Light of Western Stars* here as well as doing a
great deal of exploring and photography. "So much beauty and

wildlife," he wrote, "so wild it was tame." Grey was also known for releasing trophy-sized catches and not mourning the ones that got away. He wrote of a lost tarpon, "Into my memory had been burned indelibly a picture of a sunlit, cloud-mirroring, green and gold bordered cove, above the center of which shone a glorious fish-creature in the air."

The Long Key Fishing Club was completely destroyed in the 1935 hurricane. Just south of the boat rentals in Layton there is an historical tablet commemorating the site if not accurately marking it.

THE
MIDDLE KEYS
*Long Key Viaduct
to Bahia Honda*

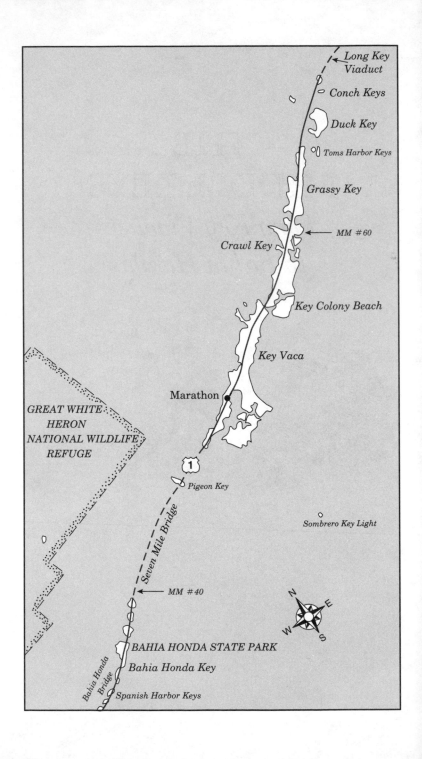

Forty-two bridges link the Keys, but it is in the Middle Keys where the three longest and most impressive ones stand. Beside them are their shadows, the bridges recently built. The road now traverses these shadows—the strong old bridges run emptily alongside. Everywhere there is water, water that becomes sky, the shadows of rays like clouds moving across the blue. Water loves light. The light changes. Dawn and sunset break. Thunderclouds mass. The water is black, emerald, azure, sheer, and the vault of sky becomes the vault of water. Flocks of egrets fly bone-white across that impossible interstice. The Keys are lovely litanies of colors and creatures, fishes and birds.

If one were to know the Keys only by car, this passage over the bridges of the Middle Keys is the most impressive. The trip by train must have been astonishing. John Dos Passos in a letter to Hemingway called it a "dreamlike journey." The trains crept across the bridges no faster than fifteen miles an hour and seldom exceeded forty miles an hour over the mostly deserted Keys. The dreamlike journey made possible by the railroad was created with swarms of vessels, workboats, dredges, seagoing cranes, pile drivers, quarterboats, and floating cement mixers. At one point, Flagler's general manager, Joseph Parrott, had every freight steamer on the Atlantic coast that flew the American flag under charter to bring in materials.

Before the railroad, there were few people on any of these keys. There were salt-works on Duck Key in the early 1800's, but they had been abandoned by 1837. A few Bahamian families lived along Key Vaca, but they had deserted it by 1860. In 1926, the population of Marathon was only seventeen. It was not until the 1940's that sportfishing created a reason for the town's existence. Other, now highly populated areas are of even more recent invention. In the 1950's, causeways were built to islands such as Duck Key, and even islands that weren't, such as Key Colony Beach. One best perceives the beauty of this area—its remaining wilderness—from the great bridges, even though, as in the case of the newly installed utility poles which run the distance of the Seven-Mile Bridge, modernization has reduced the awesome effect.

People remember traveling on the old bridges with fondness, even though delays were common. Accidents and breakdowns would jam up the narrow lanes. The drawspan on the Seven-Mile Bridge would stick. Small airplanes would sometimes make emergency landings. These were usually occasions for a party. People would abandon their cars, throw out a fishing line, set up the cooler and the radio, become tight friends with complete strangers, and socialize in the sunshine, beneath the merging seas and the sky.

The beautiful **Long Key Viaduct** at MM #65.5 was Flagler's favorite bridge, and the one he used in photographs advertising the railroad. One hundred eighty arches span two and one half miles of water, making it the second largest span in the Keys. Be sure to pull off the road to the left just before crossing the new Long Key Bridge built close alongside. Walk down the embankment, where in spring there will be a profusion of flowering vines and stacked crayfish traps, and look at the graceful old arches, darkly Roman against the green tropical waters and far nobler than the sensible modern piers.

Stacked crayfish traps are once again in evidence on the other side of the bridge during the closed season, April 1 to July 25. Here at MM #63 is **Conch Key**. Conch Key consists of sixteen acres, every inch of which is covered with houses and crayfish traps. The crayfish, or "bug," or Florida spiny lobster has long antennae, many legs, and no claws. All the meat is in the muscles of the tail, which is used for backward propulsion. Fishermen, lobstermen, and retirees inhabit Conch Key, along with hundreds of crayfish traps.

Crossing the bridge over Tom's Harbor Cut at MM #61, you will see on your left **Duck Key**, dominated by the striking green and pink **Hawk's Cay Resort**. The colors, according to the designer, are actually seafoam green, salmon, cabbage green, and paper-bag brown. This is no place to bag your lunch, however. For luxury, this is *the* place in the Middle Keys—awash in Jacuzzis, chefs in white hats, chaise lounges, linen tablecloths, and fresh cans of tennis balls. Hawk's Cay used to be the Indies Inn before the Indies became ramshackle and slipped into receivership. Fifteen million dollars' worth of renovations later, it is now ready to receive you. It's very tasteful, very comfortable, very elegant, with lots of French doors, wicker furniture, and gleaming tiles, but there is the flavor of the Board Room in some of its larger pavilions and terraces. The clay tennis courts are called gardens here, for they are set amidst some sea grape and palm, and there is a marina a short distance away that offers fishing charters, and a nightclub with a dance floor. Many are the planned activities at Hawk's Cay, and adult guests are treated rather like shy campers who must gently be introduced to fishing rods and tiny sailboats and even, behind and beyond the mannered affluence of the place, Nature. A bizarrely named "Scratch 'n' Sniff" tour will take you by rubber raft past the canals and expensive stuccoed homes of Duck Key and encourage you to observe starfish bumbling across the flats or herons clinging to a bit of undisturbed mangrove. And it will bring you back to the resort in time for lunch.

In season (mid-December to mid-April), large suites are $465 a night, smaller suites are around $370. Rooms run $195. Through the summer and fall, suites cost between $240 and $300 a night, rooms $125. A three-nights' deposit is required at Christmas, New Year's, and Easter. A lavish breakfast buffet is complimentary daily. Telephone: 743-7000.

Below elaborate Duck Key lies **Grassy Key**, where Flipper's Sea School used to be the big attraction: Flipper, the film star, whose real name was Mitzi, is buried here, and a 30-foot-tall monument to a dolphin mother and baby still stands on the bay side of the highway at MM #59. Flipper's moved to a new and more elaborate site in Key West, invested a fortune in advertising, and promptly went out of business. The facility on Grassy Key became the **Dolphin Research Center** and is open to the public on a limited walking-tour basis. The inquisitive dolphins rise to greet you as you stand on the rickety causeways between the pools. They chatter and click and turn to be patted and stroked and fix you with their marvelous eyes. There is modest research and training done here, but it's so relaxing on Grassy Key that dolphins from more high-pressured attractions and institutions come here for R&R. (A well-known instance involved two dolphins who were flown down for a vacation from the National Aquarium in Baltimore. Because of poor lighting and bad tank design, the dolphins had been constantly seeing their own reflections and with no privacy from each other or themselves, they had become anxious and eventually developed ulcers.)

Dolphins are curious, playful, social, and very sexy. They're bisexual. They have complex brains which are larger than man's. They have several stomachs and no sense of smell. They have an incredibly refined capacity to form auditory images and "hear" the texture of objects around them, suggesting that they can look into each other in eerie ways and read emotional states. They once lived on land, and gradually, for unknown reasons, took to the seas. One story, and why not believe it, is that they approached man around the time of Plato and Aristotle but that philosophers and religious men rebuffed them, so they retreated into the depths of the sea to await a better time for communication and understanding. They have remarkable memories and can comprehend simple sonic sentences. They become bored easily. When they give birth, there is frequently another female close by acting as midwife, assisting the new mother in bringing the baby to the surface for his first breath of air. Dolphins breathe through their blowholes, emitting occasional whiffs of sweet-smelling air, almost like chlorophyll. (Some Japanese fishermen, complaining that dolphins compete with them in catching cuttlefish and yellowtail, herd them ashore and club them to death.) Dolphins have their own legend. It is said they believe that one day a few humans will break through to a new, transhuman level of consciousness and make contact with them. There are several versions of this legend. One is that these humans, true philosophers who comprehend the whole in all its parts, will join the dolphins and never return. Another is that they will return to the world of men and be locked up as lunatics. A third has them join forces with the dolphins, stage a bloodless coup d'état, and establish a peaceful and paradisiacal rule over all man- and animalkind. And, of course, the last version is that the dolphins, totally fed up with even the philosophers, will lead an insurrection of all the beasts and eliminate the human race because of its grave threat to the planet.

There was once a sanctuary for injured birds here—hawks, herons, and pelicans harmed intentionally or unintentionally by man. Most of the injuries to pelicans are the result of fish hooks and monofilament. Never discard old fishing line for a bird to become entangled in. Don't toss away those eternal six-pack grippers either. A pelican looks like a large bird, but it weighs only six pounds. Its bones are hollow and usually can't be set. (The sanctuary, **The Florida Keys Wild Bird Rehabilitation Center,** has moved up to Tavernier and is located at MM #93.5. This is not a fun experience but it is a moving one. If you find an injured bird, call the Center at 852-4486.) The Dolphin Research Center offers something now more geared to the tourist—you can partake of the latest craze and swim with the dolphins here—though you don't just swim with them, you "encounter and interact" with them, but by appointment only. It costs $90. For the more serious devotee of the divine dolphin, there is Dolphinlab, a seven-day course of lectures, films, and field trips to the reef and back country. Write to P.O. Box 522875, Marathon Shores, FL 33052, or call 289-0002. Reservations must be made the first day of the month prior to the month of your encounter. This "ultimate experience" is very popular. Tours of the facility cost $7.50 and leave at 10 A.M., 12:30 P.M., 2, and 3:30. Call 289-1121 for confirmation of this. The Center is closed Mondays and Tuesdays.

The difference between dolphins and dolphins

THE DIFFERENCE BETWEEN DOLPHINS AND DOLPHINS

Dolphins are spiny-finned gamefish of flamboyant colors, the brilliance of which fades instantly with death. They are of the genus *Coryphaena,* family *Coryphaenidae.* People catch them and eat them because they taste very good. Dolphins are also the smart and friendly mammals who nurse their young, speak in "clicks," and like to play around boats. They have little teeth and big smiles. Hemingway once remarked that he would shoot his own mother "if she flew in coveys and had a good strong flight," but most people would feel that dining on these individuals was rude, if not cannibalistic. These dolphins are small-toothed whales, genus *Delphinus,* family *Delphinidae,* and have a distinct and easily recognizable snout. The name *porpoise* can be applied only to a few species of *Phocoenidae* that lack this pronounced beak and have spade-shaped rather than conical teeth. However, most fishermen, restaurant owners, and even some scientists call mammalian dolphins porpoises to distinguish them from the gamefish dolphins. The best-known of the mammals is the bottle-nose dolphin—the one seen in "shows"—which you can refer to as a porpoise if it will make you feel more comfortable while you're chowing down the dolphin fish, which perhaps should be called what it is in other parts of the world—dorado or mahi-mahi. Dolphin sounds so pretty, though. Most fish have such goofy epithets—jewfish, mullet, turbo, snapper. Bonefish. Permit. Grunt.

For eating out, the **Grassy Key Dairy Bar** at MM #58.5 is *the* place to go. The name is strange, but the food is the best for miles. There are two squat cement ice-cream cones in front. Seafood and beef dinners, with wine and beer, are served from 5 to 10 P.M. Closed Sundays and Mondays. Telephone: 743-3816.

Rainbow Bend Fishing Resort at MM #58 is a relaxing alternative to the hustle and sprawl of Marathon, eight miles farther down the road. A tiny place, hardly a resort but with a tidy beach, pier, and pool. Most of the units are suites and efficiencies and run around $200 a night. The management at times can be a bit cool, and draconian deposit/cancellation reservation rules are in effect, but as their guest you get the free use of a Boston Whaler or sailboat, great for exploring the reef at Coffins Patch or fishing the flats off Duck Key. Coffins Patch was once called "Atlantis" because of the tall pillar coral that made exotic fishy cities there, before collectors and shell shops hauled off the larger specimens. (Pillar coral grows approximately one inch every forty years, so it's unlikely you will ever see what the "collectors" did.) The airy, second-story restaurant here is called the **Hideaway**, and the food is so fancy that they say people come all the way down from Miami to eat it. (That is, they don't do anything else here. They eat it and go back.) Prime rib, filet medallions, seafood delmonico. Cognacs and creams, special sauces and bouquetieres. Amaretto frequently figures. There's a good wine list. Call the Rainbow Bend at 289-1505.

Just beyond, on Crawl Key at MM #56.5, is a road to the left that leads to **Valhalla Beach Motel**. On the road maps, a town named Ecstasy is mentioned, but Ecstasy is hard to find. You might, in fact, spend a very long time hunting around for Ecstasy. Valhalla Beach Motel, however, can be attained, and it's a nice little place with a sand beach on a tidal creek and bird-busy mangroves all around. You should make reservations (289-0616), for there are only a dozen rooms. Most of these are efficiencies that run about $65 a night. No credit cards. It's a return to a simpler, sweeter Keys back here, a sleepy exception to the wired development of so much of the area. The beautiful views seem almost illusory, a scrim before the pumped-up, pumped-out communities of Coco Plum Beach and Key Colony Beach beyond.

The next several miles are empty of all but mangroves. The water pipe that runs the length of the Keys is clearly visible here on the right. Activity begins just beyond the old Pull-and-Be-Damned Creek—the scourge of railroad workers who had to row supplies across its strong currents—a part of Vaca Cut now filled in. Here is **Adventure Island**, a feverish dream for the highly active, where there are sailboat, catamaran, sunfish, and jet-ski rentals. You can also have the thrilling, rackety fun of a helicopter ride. There was ambition here once—there are twenty-seven picnic tables behind the tiki bar—but excited intentions have given way to exhausted somnolence. A bored

Rottweiler is tied beneath a broken barbecue stand by the helicopter pad, and parrotfish with toothy smiles graze in the waters off the dock.

Beyond Adventure Island and to your left at the traffic light and over the causeway is the city of **Key Colony Beach**, created in 1959 by dredging up bay-bottom and adding it to low-lying offshore Shelter Key. It has houses, condos, time-shares, boatels, tennis courts, a golf course, a marina, three miles of canals, and earnestly cared-for lawns. And there it is. Key Colony Beach is notorious for sponsoring, in 1969, a sailfish tournament in which 553 sailfish were caught in four days of fish horror. The tournament continues to be held each November.

A bit farther south on Route 1 is **The Diving Site**, a dive shop behind which is **Coral Lagoon**, a motel with bright, spacious efficiencies on a canal. It's a bit Florida-suburban but it's quiet and sunny (289-0121). The rooms are $65 a night in the fall, $85 in the summer, $100 in the season. There are tennis courts and a pool, the good pool close to the bad pool, a deep, dark, unappetizing thing which seems to be connected to the dive shop. *Whatever was this for?* you might ask. . . . *Ahhh, I think they kept turtles in it or something* . . . someone will say, . . . *but there's nothing in there now.* . . . You peer at the slick, sad water and can't imagine . . . turtles.

Diving in the Marathon area is generally based more on the grimmer activities of spearfishing than on reef exploration. Spearfishing is not allowed in the Upper Keys down to Long up to three miles from shore. Below Long, it is permitted at distances of more than one mile from Route 1. Because of the configuration of the Keys, speargunning often takes place close to shore, particularly under the bridges. The fish in Pennecamp are practically tame, plump with cracker crumbs and popcorn and used to having divers swim among them. There are giant grouper in the reefs off Largo that are routinely petted and hand-fed by divers. The reefs off Marathon, however, are combat zones, and the dumb fish that expects to be pampered here will end up skewered.

Divers hunt fish around **Delta Shoal** and **East and West Turtle Shoals** and search the coral heads of the **Content**

Keys for lobsters and stone crabs. The shallow Content Keys are on the Gulf side, southwest of Marathon, a good snorkeling area for windy days. The areas most dived are **East Washerwoman Shoal** and the lighthouse at **Sombrero Reef**. Sombrero has nice coral formations and impressively gaudy colonies of tiny fish safe from everything but aquarium collectors, for all tiny tropicals are poisonous if eaten.

The only wreck dive in the Marathon area is the *Thunderbolt*, an old Army cable-laying vessel, intentionally sunk for divers, five miles south of Key Colony Beach.

The bridge over Vaca Cut brings you into the Marathon area. **Captain Hook's Marina**, on your left at MM #53, is worth a stop. There are live-fish pools and a complete and helpful tackle shop. Both a party boat, *Marathon Lady,* and a charter boat operate from here. The charter is a 25-foot open boat with bimini top which offers a variety of fishing trips, including night expeditions and Everglades trips.

KEY VACA

The Spaniards might have originally called this key *Cayos de Bacas,* which means "berries," or *Cayos de Vaccas,* which means "cows." If it was cows, they were referring to the manatees that once thickly browsed on the vegetation offshore. Or they may have named it for one of their own conquistadors named de Vaca. The name's obscure, to be sure. Key Vaca runs from Vaca Cut at MM #53 to Knight's Key at MM #47, the terminus of Henry Flagler's railroad from 1908 to 1911, while workers constructed the Seven-Mile Bridge.

Marathon and its remoralike subdivision, Marathon Shores, have consumed Key Vaca. There is simply nothing of Key Vaca which is not Marathon.

Optimistic travelers have for years harbored the hope that there is more to Marathon than what they see, but unremarkably this is not the case. Marathon is exactly what they see and what you will see as well—a careless, unrespectable town who presents her homely face to you without a bit of a blush—

although under more demanding perusal she will turn a bit defensive, for she lacks panache, although she can show you a good time. Old football stars love her.

Sunset and a Beach

Marathon offers a very nice sunset, you'll be relieved to know. In the winter, go to the tiki bar at **Shucker's**, which gives good food as well as view. It's down 11th Street just before the Seven-Mile Bridge. Sitting or strolling on the old bridge is the thing to do at dusk too. The bridge, of course, generously delivers sunset. There's a parking area at MM #46.8. The walk to Pigeon Key is just over two miles. **The Sunset Cafe** at **Buccaneer** (page 72) also does rampant sunset. They even shoot off a cannon.

All down the Keys, at the uncanny hour, drivers will be swerving their cars off the road to pause and pay their respects to the sun as it squashes down on the horizon.

The beach is **Sombrero Beach**, down Sombrero Road at MM #50. The swimming is good, for the water is deep, the beach is immaculate, and the carefully mowed grass of the adjacent park offers not one single sandspur. The park, which is on Hawk Channel and the Atlantic, also has a little playground and a softball diamond with a burrowing owl who stubbornly makes his home behind second base. The island off the southwest boundary of the park is Boot Key, joined by a costly bridge to the highway in 1959. The bridge, complete with drawspan and bridge tender, is maintained by the county, and in the finest tradition of mystery bridges leads absolutely nowhere, a developer's scam having failed to produce anything on the key except access to it. There is a radio tower, and a road that wanders nervously about until it vanishes.

Crane Point Hammock

In the middle of Marathon, opposite the Gulfside Shopping Center, the typical paved wasteland that Kmart and McDonald's like to dis-create from nature and call home, lies the lovely

Crane Point Hammock, recently acquired by the Florida Keys Land and Sea Trust. This is a true tropical forest, a magnificent 64-acre hardwood and thatch palm hammock on the Gulf. It's a different world back here—a glimpse of the real Florida. But, too, there's a rather retro and overdesigned museum, **The Museum of the Florida Keys**. There are dioramas with stuffed birds, and one room depicts the reef as it might appear inside a very peculiar person's head—stuffed fish suspended from the ceiling and a clicking, whispering, gurgling soundtrack. The trail through the hammock, as it is now designed, is only a quarter of a mile loop. There is a brochure that informs you about the trees. Try to avoid the woman behind you reading from it. " '. . . Stop Five. If you are lucky and quiet you might encounter a raccoon or rosy rat snake. . . .' Ichhhh, let's make noise." The museum is open 9–5, noon to 5 on Sundays, and costs $3.50.

MARATHON

Marathon is a strip, heavily developed. Residents do live here very happily, it is assumed, off the highway, in subdivisions and along long canals that accommodate their boats, but to the traveler, inching along the congested road, this community (for Marathon is not a town and has no form of local government, being more or less run by the Chamber of Commerce) appears a soiled servicing station for those enjoying the abstraction of "The Heart of the Keys." It's prettiest at night, when the neon lights, appearing after the blackness of Crawl Key, suggest a jackpot possibility.

Marathon's history is that of the railroad that virtually created it. It began as a base camp for thousands of railroad workers, the most reliable of them being men from the Caymans and from Spain. The rest were derelicts from Philadelphia and New York, shanghaied by railroad recruiters. After the 1906 hurricane, Flagler housed the men in wooden barracks on land rather than on quarterboats. The camp on Key Vaca consisted of not only tents and barracks but cottages, a hospital, a power plant, and repair shops for the locomotives. Railroad workers named their new settlement Marathon—legend has it—after their own endurance, and built gyms and basketball courts for themselves.

Eighty-six miles of the Overseas Railroad had been completed by 1906, and miles of open water remained. A long trestle and dock were built on the southernmost end of Key Vaca at **Knight's Key** so that steamships could meet the train. Nothing today remains of this port, where ships from Cuba unloaded pineapples, sugar, and oranges, and vacationers set off on the six-hour trip to Havana. Just before the bridge today, a railroad car painted in Flagler's favorite colors, yellow and brown, is on display. It is unlikely that this particular car ever made the journey, if you're a stickler for things like that. (Flagler's luxurious private car, Rambler, which he rode in elderly triumph into Key West, was discovered in the 1950's sitting in a field in Virginia, where it was being used by a tenant farmer. It is now at the Flagler Museum in Palm Beach.)

Flagler took soundings for a deep-water harbor at the tip of Key Vaca, and Key West feared that the railroad would go no farther, that Knight's Key would become the port of entry and Key West would remain remote and unlinked. But work began on "the great one"—the Seven-Mile Bridge—and was interrupted only by a 1909 hurricane that washed out forty miles of embankment and track in the Upper Keys, convincing the engineers that more small bridges were needed, instead of filled embankments that dammed up hurricane tides. Eighteen miles of bridges replaced the originally planned six to provide a freer flow of water.

When the Seven-Mile Bridge was completed in 1911, the workers moved on. No more boats filled with girls and liquor (followed by other boats filled with preachers) plied the waters between Key West and Marathon. The population plummeted. The town became known to train passengers as a place where they were often sold colored water through the windows instead of whiskey.

Marathon remained a sprawling, wide-open outpost throughout the 1940's, when it was large enough to contain thirteen bars and restaurants but still no churches or schools. During World War II, an airstrip was installed as a training base for B-17's, or "Flying Fortresses." The 8,000-foot airstrip runs along the highway through Marathon Shores and is today home to a variety of private planes and charters. There are also regularly scheduled flights to Miami several times a day.

During the 1950's, a Detroit developer, Phil Sandowski, whose later gift to the planet was the City of Key Colony Beach, created the "instant" canals of Marathon and brought subdivisions to Key Vaca. The streets run from 126th Street down to 11th Street at MM #47.5, where the fishing and crayfish boat docks are.

Marathon has Cuban food at **Castillito** (MM #48); a breakfast hangout where an early-bird beer and big, bad biscuits are a favored combination (**Vernon's Iron Skillet** at MM #48); a big dance floor that rocks until 4 A.M. (**The Side Door Lounge** at MM #50); several liquor stores that are open all night long; and a hospital with a twenty-four-hour emergency room (**The Fisherman's Hospital**, close to MM #49). It *used* to have Fanny's, a strip joint whose sign read, Whatsa Matter, You Scared? Marathon is known for historical drinking. The first fatality of the completed Overseas Railroad was a local man, Tom Jones, who, when he saw Flagler's special train pass through at 9 A.M. on January 22, 1912, began celebrating and didn't stop until seven days later, when he was pronounced dead of alcohol poisoning.

WHERE TO STAY

Marathon has an astonishing turnover in motel and resort ownership, with places continually going in and out of receivership. Mushroomlike "villas" sprout up overnight with realtor flags flapping beseechingly for your attention. The prettier, palmier places are up-Keys a way. **The Gulf View** at MM #58.5 (289-1414) is bright and pleasant, as is **The Golden Grouper** with its little beach at MM #57.5 (743-5285). Rates are about $50 a night in season.

The Bonefish Resort (743-7107) close by is *troppo* shacky and friendly. Tiny rooms with kitchens run from $35 to $60. If you can diet your dog down to thirty pounds or less, he can stay here with you too. Be prepared for more seaweed than beach at any of the oceanfront motels much of the year.

Particularly charming are **Conch Key Cottages** (289-1377), off the road at MM #62.3. Pine walls, big porches, hammocks on the secluded beach. You can actually hear the birds back here. All the cottages have full kitchens and are $155 a night in season, $120 in summer. There is also an assortment of apartments and efficiencies that go for $87–$120. Many people like to settle in for the week in this cozy place.

In Marathon, one of the oldest and most established resorts is **Faro Blanco** at MM #48. Built in the 1940's, it has a four-story lighthouse where rooms can be rented for $175, $135 in summer. The pleasant cottages on the grounds run from $70 to $120 a night. The cottages take kids; the condos ($225 a night) do not. There's an Olympic-size pool, a bar, and a big marina. There are also permanently moored houseboats that cost $95; and lots of information from both **Hall's Diving Center** and the tackle shop **The World Class Angler**. Telephone: 743-9018. People are fond of the restaurant here, **Kelsey's**, which serves up expensive portions of chateaubriand, rack of lamb, and shrimp scampi. They'll also cook your catch for you for $10, but only if you fillet it yourself. Their more casual restaurants are **Crocodile's** down 15th Street on the oceanside and the **Angler's Lounge**.

The **Buccaneer** at MM #48.5 cannot decide if it wants to be a "resort" or a "lodge." There are older cottages on the grounds as well as new round "villas" with Singapore hat–like roofs and Jacuzzis and microwaves. There are also tennis courts, pools, charter boats, and a circular bar facing inward, away from the water and its array of rental craft. A wandering crooner with a guitar sings Elvis Presley ballads, and there are a great many large guests wearing many gold chains and drinking triple Red Labels lounging about. Dinner in the restaurant is served by waiters and waitresses in pirates' garb, plumes and frills and so forth—a Miami fantasia of pirates. Maybe it's *just* what you want. Cottages in season are $80 a night. Villas (two-bedroom, two-bath) are $200. Sometimes if you stay three nights you'll get the fourth free. Telephone: 743-9071.

The **Coral Lagoon** (page 66) at MM #53 is a reasonable and comfortable find with its plantings and hammocks, and **The**

Coconut Grove MM #50 (743-5312) is simplicity itself with its shuffleboard and outdoor grilles. Rooms at the latter run about $50.

WHERE TO EAT

Most people drive up to the Grassy Key Dairy Bar (see page 64), but there are others who rave about the Mexican food at **Pancho Villa's** at the Faro Blanco resort. Open 7–10. If you're flush, try the **Hideaway** (see page 65). You don't have to drive as far as the people from Miami. It's open from 5 to 11 and requires reservations.

In Marathon, **Herbies** at MM #50 is an eternal favorite. An old-time breezy place of screens and picnic tables. Lots of fish, draft beer, and badinage. Good desserts. Always crowded. It is so popular that you are often discomfited by the hordes waiting outside, balefully regarding you as you eat. Open 11 A.M.–10 P.M. Closed Sundays. Telephone: 743-6373.

The Quay at MM #54 is prettily lit and formal, with nice views of the water. The menu is elaborate and reaches for the extraordinary, like the alligator steak, which is seldom available to the chef. If it were made available to the chef it might be for reasons you would prefer not to know about—for example, the occasion of a marine patrol officer being recently called upon to dispose of a gator for swallowing yet another someone's dog. Open every day from 11 A.M. Telephone: 289-1810.

The **Cracked Conch Cafe** at MM #50 has a bar and serves lunch and dinner all day long, from 11 A.M. until midnight. Casual, with a little outside patio and reasonable, well-prepared soups and dinners. Telephone: 743-2233.

The **7-Mile Grille** at MM #47 is another favorite open-air restaurant, although it's not open early and it's not open late and it's closed Wednesday and Thursday. Very authentic it appears, set back on the dusty access strip a little below the highway. Beer, grouper chowder, and uncomplicated fish baskets. Open 11:30 A.M.–8:30 P.M. Telephone: 743-4481.

At **Shucker's** at MM #47.5, down 11th Street, you can eat either inside or out on the dock with one of Marathon's nicest

views. A very good selection of fresh seafood dishes. Lively bar.
Food is served from 11 A.M. to 10 P.M. Telephone: 743-8686.

FISHING

Marathon is obsessed with fish. It has been said that there are
450 species of fish in the waters off the Keys, and Marathon is
desirous of every single one of them. Here, too, there are tournaments—tarpon tournaments, sailfish tournaments, dolphin
tournaments, and bonefish tournaments. There are derbys and
slams and roundups as well. There is no kingfish tournament,
that variety having been virtually wiped out by commercial
netters. Occasionally the severe depletion of a species is noted,
and bureaucracy lumbers into action, but gross overfishing of
certain varieties can go on for years with the only complaint
being that there aren't as many fish as there used to be.

Stone crabs and Florida lobsters have diminished greatly in
number—there are three million crayfish traps between Key
Largo and the Dry Tortugas, according to *National Fisher-*

A marlin

man—and there is also a decline in the once abounding popula-
tions of grouper and snapper, fishes taken intensively commercially, as well as being the staple of party boats.

Tournament fishing is now encouraging releases, but a visit
to the charter boat docks or a glance at local tabloids, particularly the monthly *Florida Keys Angler,* published in Islamorada, will show you that many visitors have a deep desire to be
seen standing beside large dead fish hanging from hooks,
touching possessively the thing they have hauled up from the
deep—a thing of once-remarkable colors turned gray, a thing
with poundage numbers scrawled in white paint upon its sides.
Deep-sea hunters will say that the killing of a big fish after a
long battle is an emotional necessity (although battle time has
been shortened considerably by the handling capabilities of
modern sportsfishing boats, which can back up and maneuver
quickly). Otherwise, anglers kill gamefish apparently for two
reasons—photographic confirmation (although dead fish of a
given species tend to bear an uncanny resemblance to one
another) and possession of a mount or "trophy" (a trophy being
a painted replica of the caught fish that can be hung in the living room or wherever). It is now known, and even grudgingly
acknowledged by taxidermists themselves, that there is very
little fish in a mounted fish. The taxidermist is a colorist who
works with a little skin and a lot of plastic. But what is reality,
after all? Reality is a funny business. In any case, memories are
bigger and prettier than a dead fish. Go out with the guides who
encourage trophy releases and, just as important, who know
how to do it so the fish will survive.

Tarpon fishing is popular here in the spring and through
July—a little too popular for the beleaguered dolphin—particularly under the bridges where schools of "silver king" congregate to run through the deep channels back into the shallow
flats, where they spawn and feed. You can't eat tarpon, but people love to catch them because of the fish's extraordinary per-
formance when hooked. For the first five minutes, before they
sound and "dog it out," a hooked tarpon jumps, shakes, and tail-
walks. He then, it is said, feels to the fisherman like a falling
piano.

The terms you will hear used to describe types of fishing are
Gulf Stream, back country, reef or *wreck,* and *flats* or *bonefish-*

ing. For a brochure on local guides, write to the Marathon Guides Association, Box 65, Marathon, FL 33050.

Gulf Stream fishing is done by charter. The fighting chairs are for marlin and sailfish, and the bait is constantly trolled. Dolphin is also found in deep water in the summer. Usually four or fewer people make up a charter, and the cost runs around $300 a day. Cobia, shark, wahoo, and bonito are often caught.

Back country fishing is done bay-side and is for "bottom fish"—trout, grouper, snapper, and jewfish. Grouper is the fish that most unerringly finds his way into your fish sandwich or your "all you can eat" fish fry. A fish of fickle history, the grouper begins life as an egg-producing female, then changes sex later on. It also completely changes color when frightened. Jewfish are its speckled, obese, large-mouthed cousins, a type of giant sea bass that can weigh up to seven hundred pounds. Shark and barracuda are also fished for in the back country.

Reef and *wreck* fishing are done most often by party boats. These large boats take out fifty to seventy-five people at a time and charge around $25 a day per person, usually less for children. All bait and tackle are provided. Again, grouper and snapper are called upon and frequently answer. Some boats take two- and three-day trips to the Tortugas for even more extensive catches of bottom-feeding fish, returning to port with ice chests full of fish, floorboards covered with fish, fish blood, fish slime, gaping fish mouths, and staring fish eyes. Fish lust is a definite requirement for these Tortuga trips. Prices from Marathon are around $150, slightly more with rod rental, and the coveted stern spots are extra. Party boats can be found at the **Winner-Sombrero Docks** down Sombrero Road at MM #50 by bearing right at the golf course. Charter boats can be found farther down this road or behind the big motels such as **Faro Blanco** and **The Buccaneer**, as well as at the big marina at Key Colony Beach, where bareboat charters and sailing trips are also offered. Or, again, ask around. Some charter boat captains work out of their backyards.

Flats fishing for bonefish and permit has more mystique connected to it than any other type of fishing in the Keys. This is not a blood-riot of hauling up creatures from the black depths, but a ghostly stalking through crystal-clear sands and turtle-grass flats. Zane Grey called the bonefish "the wisest, shyest, strangest, wariest fish," possessing "baffling cunning." The bonefish comes into the flats when the tide is low to feed on clams buried in the bottom, at which time it is prone to sharks, barracuda, and clever bonefishermen. It is a slim, furtive fish built for speed. It never leaps when hooked, but makes a long and astonishingly powerful run. Three to five pounds is the average size, eight to nine pounds is a big one, and anything larger is a trophy catch. The world record is twenty-three pounds. Its Latin name is *Albula vulpes*—white fox. Permits are easier to see than bonefish. They are larger and more vertical—like large silver dimes with black fins. Their eyes are the most sentient of any fish and their bodies are clean and silken. Flats fishing for bonefish and permit is done in an outboard with the engine stilled, the guide standing on a spotting platform and poling across the flats. It is a silent sport of considerable skill and even delicacy. There are guides who specialize in the flats, and most of them are booked solid in the bonefish months—May is considered the best month; the season runs

LIGHTHOUSES

From the Seven-Mile Bridge, four miles south of Marathon, you will see **Sombrero light**, one of six spidery, graceful lighthouses that mark the reef off the Keys. All were built between 1852 and 1880 and have an iron-pile construction, the pilings of the foundations driven deep within the coral on which they stand. They are the **Fowey Rocks light**, the "Eyes of Miami," which replaced the ineffectual Cape Florida light on the mainland; the **Carysfort Reef lighthouse** off Key Largo; **Alligator Reef light** off Lower Matecumbe Key; **Sombrero** off Marathon and the tallest of the reef lights at 140 feet; **American Shoal light** off Cudjoe Key and six miles west of Looe Key; and **Sand Key light**, eight miles southwest of Key West.

Vessels once ran aground regularly on the reef—there was at least one "good" wreck a week—supporting a flourishing salvage industry that made Key West, where the admiralty court was located, a very wealthy little town. "Everything that the commerce of the world afforded reached Key West," Jefferson Browne wrote in his 1912 book, *Key West: The Old and the New*. "The wrecks not only threw on these shores rich cargoes, but many valuable citizens were thus furnished. . . . Several of our prominent families owe their residence here to the fact that their ancestors were wrecked on the Florida Reef."

Keys people relished their wrecks, certainly, but however beneficial wrecks were to Key West, they did not appeal to ship owners, who demanded that the government erect navigational aids along this treacherous and much-traveled route. It seemed impossible at first to build lighthouses on the reefs, so lightships were used. The lightships were a dismal failure. They were unseaworthy, they blew off course and were sometimes grounded on the very reefs they were supposed to warn about, and their lights were scarcely discernible, erratically lit, and badly placed, so that mariners were deceived more often than assisted. Open-skeleton wrought-iron lighthouses were originally designed by Alexander Mitchell in 1836. The Carysfort Reef light was designed by I. W. P. Lewis and was built in 1852, the first of its kind. The lighthouses were erected on as few pilings as possible, in order not to obstruct the free flow of water, and their webby, open construction offered less resistance to wind and water during hurricanes. Another benefit of the iron-pile design was that it could be manufactured, assembled to make sure that all the parts fit, then broken down again and shipped to open water. The Carysfort Reef light was manned until 1960, but now a solar panel charges the battery powering the flashing light.

The second light to be built on the Keys was Sand Key, off Key West. There was originally a 60-foot brick lighthouse here which was destroyed in an 1846 hurricane, killing the woman tender and her children. The new structure was the first of the reef lights to be installed with a Fresnel lens, named for its inventor, the French physicist Augustin Fresnel, a lens which increased by many times the ability of lamp light to be concentrated and magnified. Hurricanes and storms have rearranged the sandy beach here or made it disappear altogether, but the rust-red, square, pyramidal tower, screw-piled into the coral beneath, has been unharmed. The Fresnel lens was recently removed and replaced with a flash-tube array, the battery again powered by solar energy, which projects the light for nineteen miles.

Sombrero reef was first charted and named by the Spanish, and a light was placed here because it was midway between the Carysfort and Sand Key lights. Like the earlier lights, it was built under the direction of George Gordon Meade, who later became a major general during the Civil War, commanding the Army of the Potomac which defeated Robert E. Lee at Gettysburg. The octagonal, pyramidal skeleton tower of Sombrero was completed in 1858; its original Fresnel lens is displayed at the Lighthouse Museum in Key West.

Ships continued to run aground in the dark interstices between the lights, but the Civil War delayed further construction of lighthouses. It was not until 1873 that Alligator Reef light was constructed off the Matecumbe Keys, on what was considered the long reef's "elbow." This beautiful black-and-white structure, considered by lighthouse historians to be one of the finest iron lighthouses in the world, was named for the USS *Alligator,* one of the eight schooners of the West India Squadron, which hunted pirates off the coast of Florida and went aground on the reef in 1821. She was blown up by her own crew so that pirates wouldn't salvage her. Alligator Reef light survived the 1935 hurricane, undamaged by the 20-foot tidal wave that surged past the light on its way to annihilate the shore.

The northernmost of the reef lights was built in 1878 on Fowey Rocks off Key Biscayne. During its construction, workmen were often terrified by ships bearing down on them and wrecking on the reefs only yards away.

American Shoal lighthouse was the last to be built, completing the system of reef lights in July 1880. Again, it was a pyramidal skeleton tower enclosing a lightkeeper's dwelling. Looe Key and the Sambos were reefs upon which ships continued to wreck in the cavernous darkness between the Sombrero and Sand Key lights. American Shoal realized the Keys' "band of light" and brought to an end the days of the wreckers.

All the lighthouses are automated now, the lights powered by batteries that store solar energy. No keepers are needed to trim the wicks and keep the lamps clean and full of oil, nor to draw curtains over the lens at sunrise to protect it from the glare of day. The structures are massively graceful, and through their skeletal forms, the reef waters glitter and dance. They seem abandoned and improbable by day, vaguely stirring the spirit, beneficent and speechless icons that at night send messages of warning and comfort.

until November. Almost all guides require the release of these fish caught during a charter. Costs run around $250 a day. When former president Bush comes to the Keys to fish, he stays at Cheeca and goes bonefishing with guide George Hommell, who runs the tackle shop **World Wide Sportsman** in Islamorada. George, the guide, describes actually hooking a bonefish as "happiness." He also says that the other George "often gets quiet when he fishes," and that when he catches a fish, "he gets excited."

THE SEVEN-MILE BRIDGE

It is said that Henry Flagler loved concrete with a passion. He was seventy-eight years old when his workmen began construction on the Seven-Mile Bridge (MM #47 to MM #40), which, when finished, was considered the Eighth Wonder of the world. His young construction engineer, J. C. Meredith, literally worked himself to death on the project, collapsing a year after work on the span began.

The bridge was built in four parts. The first three spans— Knights Key Bridge, Pigeon Key Bridge, and Moser Channel Bridge—were made of steel-girder sections laid on top of concrete foundation piers. The entire bridge had 546 of these piers, more than any other bridge in the world. The piers, all made of a special cement that was imported from Germany, were secured to bedrock that in some cases was 28 feet under water. The Moser Channel swing span was 253 feet long and opened for any boat that required more than a 23-foot clearance. The last, westernmost part of the bridge consisted of 210 concrete arches similar to those used on the Long Key Viaduct.

The Seven-Mile Bridge, like all the bridges of the Keys, withstood all hurricanes, even the 1935 one that meant the end of the railroad. A year after that disaster, work began on converting the railway into a highway, and the 14-foot width of the bridge was widened to 22 feet with I-beams. Much of the old track was used as guardrails for the road. This highway served travelers, often harrowingly, for more than forty years, until a new bridge was constructed and completed in 1982. The new

The beach at Bahia Honda Key

bridge is wider and higher than the old and has eliminated the need for a drawspan by rising 40 feet higher over Moser Channel at MM #43.5, providing a 65-foot clearance.

A portion of the old bridge runs to **Pigeon Key**, once a community of railroad workers and their families. There was a school and even dairy cows. Later it became headquarters for the toll district operation when the highway was briefly a toll road in the 1930's. During World War II, it was used as a tropic zone GI training center and is now leased by researchers conducting a number of experiments, one of which is raising a sewage-eating fish. An African freshwater species, the blue tilapia, a pushy exotic that has driven many native species out of the Everglades, loves to graze and grow on pollutants and agricultural runoff. The researchers are excited about this protein-packed fish as a potential "new industry for parts of South Florida."

The old bridge is now used by fishermen, campers, runners, and roller skaters. Each April, there's a seven-mile sponsored run on the new bridge while in the waters below, "superboats" race, sponsored by the American Power Boat Association. Beneath the waters, in the spring, the tarpon make their far more silent, silvery run, frequently followed by large sharks, including the bizarre and voracious hammerhead.

Beyond the Seven-Mile Bridge—the "great one"—at MM #40 is **Little Duck Key**, a filled area with a public boat ramp and several cement picnic shelters. This little duck is many, many miles away from the big Duck (once touted as a fairyland playground for millionaires at MM #61). Then come **Missouri** and **Ohio** keys, named by homesick railroad workers one would imagine, but they are more filled causeway than island. An extremely large American flag flies from Ohio Key as if to assure the traveler after all these watery miles that it is still the U.S. of A. An elaborately appointed campground follows Sunshine Key, for those campers who don't want to get away from it all, and then there is **Bahia Honda**, a state park which has the finest beach on the Keys.

BAHIA HONDA KEY

The Spanish name means "Deep Bay," and this marks the geologic transition from the Upper Keys, which are coral, to the Lower, which are limestone. As it is transitional, it is unique in many ways, its coral skeleton supporting sand beaches, dunes, and a coastal strand hammock in which a number of rare plants grow, including the yellow satinwood, the only tree of its kind in the Keys, and the Jamaica morning glory. The seeds have all been brought here from the Caribbean and the West Indies by birds, wind, and water. There is a nature trail that winds around a lagoon at the northeastern end of the park where you can wander through this subdued exotica—you will see quite a number of the slender silver palm, pale as the silvery raccoons that forage here under the hot sky.

The beach sand is fine and the swimming excellent here. There is a boat ramp for trailered boats as well as a marina and small dive shop. You can also rent Windsurfers. Bahia Honda costs $3.25 for the driver of the car, 50¢ for passengers. Camping runs around $25 a night. The phone number at the park is 872-2353. As with other state parks, half the sites are unreserved on a first-come first-served basis. Stop by in the morning and have your name put on a waiting list. Names are called at three in the afternoon. Some handsome rental cottages on stilts have been built by the park service on the bay side which can be

SHARKS

Men hate sharks. They hate them a lot, as they do any creature whose existence cannot truly be confronted. The shark is not in the Tarot. It is not in the signs of Heaven, nor certainly was it invited onto the Ark. Its strict reality remains beneath the waters of the world, but it also seems to inhabit some other, deeper, less comprehensible depths.

When men catch sharks, they do not simply kill them, they mutilate them as though in the grip of an ancient rite. They hatchet fins, chop out jaws, pry out teeth, slit open bellies, and grind up claspers or ovaries beneath the heels of their boots. Scientists and fishermen alike seem to be always stomping and skidding around in the blood and viscera of a ruined shark.

This is how you go shark fishing. You usually go out at night. You chum the waters heavily with garbage, offal, the bloody remains of fish. You fish with very heavy tackle, stout leaders, large hooks. When a shark hits the line, lights are struck, and when the shark is reeled in alongside the boat your companions blast at him with shotguns, taking care not to strike each other or the boat. Winched up, the shark is then battered with clubs for a time, for a prevalent belief is that dead sharks often come back to life. Hauled aboard, the belly is then cut open and the contents of the stomach examined and marveled at. It was particularly intriguing to see a mangled shark, when thrown overboard, have the temerity to try and swim away.

Shark can be eaten, but most people don't bother, for acids build up in the flesh if it is not cleaned and iced immediately, and the meat spoils quickly. Those who go shark fishing usually just go for the ambience.

At least that's how you fished for shark in the '70's and '80's, those innocent days of recreational "monster fishing." In the '90's, with its glum and continuing message of diminishment, things are different. When they throw a shark tournament, the sharks don't come. It seems that drift nets, fish finders, and 600-hook long lines have drastically reduced their numbers, as has the commercial fishing habit of "live-finning," where the fins are sliced off and the animal is left to die right at home.

There are hundreds of species of sharks, and until recently most of the big species—the great white, the tiger, the hammerhead—seemed pretty indomitable. But sharks are slow-growing and give birth to a relatively small number of young —pups—each year. Encouraged ruthless destruction has taken out huge numbers of adults.

The rules for shark fishing are different now. There are limits—one per person or two per vessel—and sloppy slaughter is frowned upon. Newspaper photos of toddlers at dockside crouched beside the gaping head of a shark that Daddy just bagged is no longer considered cute news, and when a tourist killed a well-known, often-spotted resident hammerhead off a Key West reef this year, there were cries of pretty much total disapproval.

seen from the highway at MM #37. The access road is only available through the park. These are $110 a night. Mid-September through mid-December they're $85 a night. There is boat access, and all dishes, cookware, and linen are provided. Each of the six cabins has two double beds, two bunk beds, and two cots. There's a minimum two-night stay required. And even if you're having the time of your life, which you very well may be, you can't stay longer than a week.

To read the histories of the Overseas Railroad, engineers and workers were in a continual state of amazement. Here, it seemed, they did not realize the significance of the Spanish name for the channel. Bahia Honda was far more difficult to build than the Seven-Mile Bridge because the waters were so deep. When trying to locate bedrock for the foundation of the center span, workmen found only water, more and more water in a hole that seemed, for weeks, to be bottomless. Since the water was so deep, tide surges would be higher in a storm, so the bridge, as well as being the hardest to build, was the highest. When the Overseas Highway came in 1936 to remodel it as a road, they could not widen its enclosed structure so they built their road over the top, and it resembles nothing less than a roller coaster. The four-lane bridge you're traveling on today is a recent construction, and, of course, not nearly as nice.

A bull shark with pilot fish

Diving is good near the bridge pilings, which provide mini-reefs replete with corals, lobsters, sponges, and fish. However, bridge diving can be dangerous both because of rapid and abrupt tide changes and a superabundance of sea urchins and stinging fire coral which seems to flourish in areas of swift currents. The current that flows through Bahia Honda Channel is the fastest in all the Keys.

A phenomenon occurs here each year around the last full moon of May. Small reddish palolo worms hatch from rocks and sponges, and the tarpon come in great schools to slurp them up at the surface. At this time, tarpon can be caught on a small fly instead of the large live mullet they prefer as bait.

After the Bahia Honda Bridge come the **Spanish Harbor Keys**, including **West Summerland** which is marked by a sign, a sign that may bewilder you as **West Summerland** is 10 miles *east* of **Summerland Key**. Two coral rock storage sheds for dynamite from the time that the railroad was being pushed through were found on West Summerland years ago, but they have been misplaced again in the overgrowth.

There are several places to pull off the road during these few miles to rest or picnic or walk along the damp, curving shore. You can sometimes find old bottles along the swampy shoreline of both Summerlands, and farther down on Sugarloaf Key.

THE
LOWER KEYS
Big Pine Key
to Key West

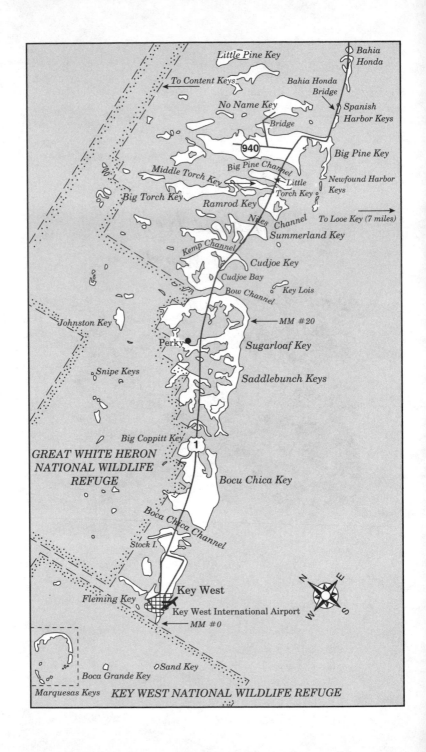

THE Lower Keys are dark and wooded, and though settled, seem lonely. They are not fabulous, nor are they lush or exotic or breathtaking. They are too modest for superlatives. They are subdued, sometimes eccentric, even secretive. And some dirt roads that lead farther and farther back into the mangroves toward unnamed flats and channels are better left unexplored. It's said that when Fat Albert, the Naval surveillance blimp, is brought down for a checkup or because of bad weather, the air springs alive with the chatter of drug runners, and the sound of outboards popping into action is heard far and wide across this watery and muddy frontier. There are those who live simply here and those who live well, and those whose privacy is the best-known thing about them. The land is scrub, cactus, slash-pine. Big Pine has trees of uncommon size for the low-lying tropics, and Cudjoe even has a stand of cabbage palms. In the old days, these keys seemed always to be burning. Settlers burned the trees to make charcoal and deliberately set other fires to flush out the tiny Key deer. Sparks from the passing railroad also set the Keys aflame. Even so, the land is low and wet, which makes great tracts of it uninhabitable. When the old iron water pipeline was laid alongside the road, it had to be raised on pilings so it wouldn't disappear into the muck. On a chart, the area is sprinkled with bays, bights, harbors, lakes, and sounds. Offshore is **Looe Key**, a reef known for the clarity of its waters, which are cleansed constantly by the waters of the Gulf Stream. The land moves back and forth upon itself, the woods rustle with palm warblers. Birds of prey like this land-scape—eagles, falcons, red-tailed and red-shouldered hawks. A frequent sight along these keys is osprey nests on telephone poles on the south side of the highway. The osprey nests for life, and the nest grows larger and larger over the years, an indication of how long the couple have flown and hunted together. In March and April there's great activity around the nests and

A nesting osprey

you'll probably see an osprey returning, a fish hanging heavily from its talons, or perched hunched, carefully dissecting the meal for its young. These keys, too, seem to abound, even specialize in, quiet water trips, conducted leisurely by naturalists in a variety of craft ranging from kayaks to Chinese lug-rigged trimarans to roomy wooden sailboats. The Great White Heron National Wildlife Refuge encompasses the waters of the Lower Keys and Key West, and to explore these waters is to realize the essence of the Keys. Take care in respecting this essence. You're going into nurseries back here. For the safety and survival of wild things, don't anchor within 200 feet of islands, and keep speed and noise to a minimum when passing. The approach of a boat can frighten a bird from its nest, leaving the eggs or nestlings exposed to the frying sun. As well, avoid boat wakes around islands. Some ospreys nest low and a wake can wash right over the young. Jet skis have now been banned in the back country, and you should not support any business that promotes "a mangrove safari" on them. If you see anyone behaving irresponsibly or harassing wildlife, don't ignore them, report them. Call the National Key Deer Refuge at 872-2239, or the marine patrol.

For a unique high-quality adventure, sail the back country with Capt. Bill Schwicker on his beautiful 28-foot wooden boat, *Egret*. He designed and built this boat himself in 1980, and with its 10-inch draft, it's a perfect vessel for the waters. No engine, it glides over the meadows and among the mangroves. A nice day for two at $185 (872-2607).

The Chinese lug-rigged trimaran belongs to Earl DeTurk and is called the *Water Spyder*. She's 41 feet, and you can have a lovely day on her picnicking, snorkeling, or fishing. A full day costs $200, a half day is $125 (872-3907).

You can rent your own boat from **Bud Boats**, off Watson Boulevard on Big Pine, near the Old Wooden Bridge Fishing Camp (which sounds much nicer than it appears) on the way to No Name. They have a variety of craft, from 13-foot Boston Whalers to Makos and Aquasports. A 17-foot Whaler with sunroof and VHF radio will cost $95 a day or $425 a week. If you have a dock where you're staying, they'll deliver. Telephone: 743-6316.
    You can also rent from **Newfound Boat Rentals** (872-1204) at MM #28.5. You can see their boats coming off the bridge from Big Pine. A tri-hull with a 50-horsepower engine is $70 for a half day. A roomy 22-foot boat with a 120-horsepower engine is $145, $175 for a full fun day.

Coming off the Spanish Harbor Bridge, **Big Pine Fishing Lodge** with tent and trailer camping and a few motel efficiencies (872-2351) is to your left and the restaurant **Island Reef** is to your right at MM #31, behind several gigantic date palms. It's a harrowing turn-in from either direction, but once there, you'll be happy. They have a variety of pot pies, steaks, and a few fish dishes. On Sundays they have roast lamb and chicken and stuffing. They may be overly prideful of their homemade breads, but it's a nice place, casual, with the good Keys "feel." Wine and beer only. Open for breakfast and lunch from 6:30 to 2:30 and for dinner at 5. But they close early—9:30—and are shut on Tuesdays (872-2170).
    Other good places to eat in the Lower Keys are the tiny **Big Pine Coffee Shop** at MM #30, open from six in the morning

until nine at night, **Mangrove Mama's** at MM #20, and the **Sugarloaf Club Restaurant** at MM #19.5, which has a pool, tennis, groves of beautiful native silver palms, and a Sunday brunch. They also serve lunch and dinner. For a small fee, you can use all the facilities here, and many people like to arrange parties and cookouts on the palmy, unmanicured grounds. It has the feel of an old, comfy summer camp. It's down Crane Boulevard and Bad George Lane. Be sure to ask about *him*. Telephone: 745-3276.

Best places to stay are **The Sugarloaf Lodge** (745-3741) and the dive-oriented, canal-side motel **Looe Key Reef Resort** (872-2215).

BIG PINE KEY

Big Pine, eight miles long and two miles wide, is second in size only to Key Largo. It is known primarily for its herd of tiny Key deer, a distinct subspecies of the Virginia white-tailed or a full species, *Dama clavia,* of its own, depending on which biologist you talk to. The deer stand only two and a half feet tall and weigh less than seventy-five pounds. Fawns weigh only two to four pounds at birth, and their tiny hoofprint is the size of a thumbnail. By the late 1940's, hunting had almost exterminated them; there were less than fifty animals left. The publicized plight of the "toy" deer of Big Pine and that of the ivory-billed woodpecker in Louisiana sparked concern over endangered species and began the conservation movement in this country. The efforts to save the woodpecker were unsuccessful when one of the last nesting areas of the ivory-billed was bulldozed to plant the magnificent soybean, but the habitat of the deer was saved and, through rigorous law enforcement, their numbers have increased. "Rigorous law enforcement" is a pseudonym for Jack Watson, a former hunter turned militant environmentalist and the refuge manager through the 1960's and '70's. Watson's war on poachers is legend. He was known to have burned the cars and sunk the boats of those in that gross fraternity. He even made house calls on those he heard were jacking deer. One famous incident concerned a poacher who was out and up repairing his roof when Watson confronted him.

A Key deer

"Sure," the man bawled, "I've been shooting 'em, and I'll keep shooting 'em if I want until there ain't any left!" So Watson shot him, unfatally I must unhappily add, right off the roof.

Big Pine Key doesn't look very Keys-like. It has pine trees and subdivisions and shopping centers. The Winn Dixie's aisles are jammed with "moribundis" just like the rest of Florida. In the summer, the moribundis leave for the mountains, and the aisles are jammed with sweaty locals cooling off by the frozen foods. Big Pine has scant human history. It has always been sparsely settled, even in the railroad days, and though there were various schemes to make use of the land—dairy farming for one (the cows keeling over under the weight of mosquitoes), and a shark processing plant—nothing was profitable, and so the land was inevitably bought up for development. Now it has a vociferous go-growth population led by retired colonels who can't understand why wetlands shouldn't be filled, particularly if they're not near the shoreline, and why marinas can't be carved out of three-foot-deep waters. They are determined to reap the monetary rewards from the land they bought for $200 an acre a few decades back.

Big Pine is formed of oolite, which means that the limestone cap rock is honeycombed with sinkholes. The sinkholes are caused by the underlying rock being dissolved by water, causing the surface rock to form pockets. Small, shallow sinkholes are called solution holes. Farmers called them "banana holes" and used them to plant what they could. Ferns take advantage of the moist soil that accumulates and flourish in the rock. The larger sinkholes are dearly loved by gators, who move along the labyrinthian corridors beneath. If you see a largish snout poking from a medium-sized hole, you'll know that a considerably large gator resides below.

There are two basic biogeographic rules concerning plants and animals. One is that islands have fewer species than a comparably sized piece of mainland, and the other is that peninsulas support less and less diversity the farther they are from the land mass. These are perfectly good rules in general as they apply to the rest of the state of Florida, which, of course, is a huge peninsula, but they have no relevance at all in the Keys. As well as being the only truly tropical area of the continental United States, the Keys have the most diverse terrestrial and marine ecosystem in the country. What this means on Big Pine is that you can enter the National Key Deer Refuge (passing churches, ball field, houses, and For Sale signs along the way, as well as many, many signs alerting you to the deer's presence—there appear to be more signs at this time than deer), walk through a pine-and-palm forest into a tropical hardwood hammock, and continue toward a tangled mangrove shoreline of small sandy beaches and coral outcroppings facing Big Pine Channel . . . which will lead you eventually into the deeper waters of the Straits of Florida, beyond which is the clear wild blue of the great Gulf Stream.

Fascinating to the biogeographer, and certainly interesting to anyone with a little time and some imagination or even just the luck to see the gators, little deer, hawks, herons, and orchids of this place.

To get to the refuge, pass MM #31 and turn right at the light on Route 940, Key Deer Boulevard. Bear left toward the Big Pine Key Road Prison. Up a ways you'll see a sign to the refuge. About a mile and a half up the road, Watson Boulevard intersects. To the right is the road to No Name; to the left, the refuge headquarters. Continue on another mile and a half to the **Blue Hole**, a small freshwater sink which was blasted out to make larger and provide fill for a parking lot where you can park your car and look at the Blue Hole. The pond ranges in depth from a half foot to twelve feet and has several resident alligators. Up until 1994, the biggest gator there was "Grandpa," who was eleven feet long and 400 pounds, but he was removed after he was seen eating a full-grown Rottweiler. People had been feeding Grandpa long before this incident, and he had taken to approaching them fearlessly and with increasingly disconcerting speed. Nonetheless, Grandpa had a lot of supporters on Big Pine, and they were sad when he was captured and carted off to Homosassa Springs State Wildlife Park near Tampa where, it is said, he has become shy because there are gators there bigger than him.

To the immediate left here is Higgs Lane. Walk down this road until you see the refuge sign, then bear to the left and go around a gate bar to take the trail that will go through pine lands to **Watson's Hammock**. The neatly constructed cement canals you see are mosquito ditches. These are connected to the Gulf and filled with tiny fish—gambusia—who do nothing but eat mosquito larvae night and day. This was the government-approved mosquito control for the Keys for decades, and a slippery concept to grasp. The back country is latticed with these ditches in which the mosquito lays its eggs and the mosquito fish eats them. Before the Navy built the water pipeline down the Keys in the 1940's, health authorities would come to individual homes and dump a handful of gambusia into private cisterns.

Watson's Hammock is a hardwood forest, dappled, lovely, cool, and quiet, with a fifty-foot canopy. There's a huge gumbo-limbo tree here. With its peeling red bark, it is lightly called the "tourist tree" because the limbs look tortured with flaking sunburn. The tree is peculiar in a number of ways. Posts made of the stout limbs sprout roots and become living fences. The sap of the tree is very gummy and was once used to catch birds. The Caloosa Indians (of which little is known except that they were very tall and feared their dead), and later the white settlers, boiled down the sap and spread it on the tree limbs. The birds would alight and their little bird feet would *stick* to the

BAD TREES

There are three trees that have really become pests in Florida—the punk, the pepper, and the Australian pine. Some people like all three because they're fast growing and good screening material, and they like the punk (the *melaleuca*) because it reminds them of the eucalyptus, and the pepper (euphemistically called "Florida holly") because of its little red berries, and the pine (*casuarina,* not a true pine at all) because of the pretty sound the wind makes coursing through its branches.

But *you* should not like any of them and should never plant the punk, the pepper, or the Australian pine. All three, of course, are easily seeded and require no care whatsoever, and all grow like mad and crowd out indigenous trees. The punk is ugly with its thick, spongy, white, shredding bark, and many people are allergic to its blooms. Plus, bees make lousy honey from its blossoms. Unfortunately, bees make good honey from the blooms of the pepper, and beekeepers have been known to encourage the spread of this bad bush just to keep their bees busy. (Bees *are* terribly busy. Each lives but six weeks, works demonically, and gathers only a half teaspoon of honey.) The *casuarina* is the nicest, with its susurrant voice, a pretty sight on a white-sand beach swaying green against a perfect sky, but it too is a pushy pest. Its needles and roots put out a toxin in the soil that prevents other types of plants from growing around or beneath it. Also, with its shallow, spreading root system, it flops right over when a vigorous wind comes up.

Another bad tree is the poisonwood, which is the Keys' poison ivy except that it is a tropical hardwood which grows up to thirty feet tall. It has large, shiny, limp leaves. Its small, yellowish green flowers are arranged in sprays, and it bears an orange fruit in the fall. Its leaves and bark are often splotched with dried black sap. It has that *look* of being a no-good.

branches. Even in the 1930's and 1940's trapping wild birds on the Keys was a lucrative business.

You'll also see the Jamaican dogwood, or fish-fuddle tree, the branches of which those mysterious Indians scraped and lay on the water, causing fish to rise, insensate. There are also century plants, orchids, bromeliads, and the huge webs of the gigantic golden orb spiders.

Another nice walk is a few hundred yards beyond the Blue Hole. This is the **Jack Watson Nature Trail**, a well-marked loop trail less than a mile in length. There should be pamphlets available in a box at the beginning of the trail, but usually the box is empty. The numbers on the trail direct your attention to various palms, including the thatch and the elegant silver; poisonwood trees, highly toxic but with fruit prized by the white-crowned pigeon; and sinkholes, large and small.

The best times to see the Key deer are at dusk or very early in the morning, in either the ferny parts of the forest or in the lower-lying buttonwood sloughs where there might be water. They also browse on the lawns of the burgeoning developments of Big Pine, their habitat being increasingly "shared" by humans. Now they're threatened by, of all things, schoolchildren. Since everywhere else has been built up, with no site for a school set aside, a big and raucous push is on to build the school right in the refuge. A commensurate, commemorative statue in honor of the displaced animals will most surely be erected if this comes to pass. Perhaps the children themselves will be called the "Dearies." In May and June you might see fawns feeding with their mothers on the mowed shoulders of the roads, in terrifying proximity to traffic. Slow down, slow down, slow down, less than three hundred deer remain.

The most comfortable time to tramp around the back country is the dry, mosquito-free winter, but the trees are not in flower then and there is little bird activity. "Chuck" at **Reflections Nature Tours** on Big Pine offers a gentle, knowledgeable kayaking tour for $45 a person. Telephone: 872-2896.

NO NAME KEY

A Russian is said to have been No Name's first resident. He homesteaded almost two hundred acres, setting trip-wired guns in the underbrush so that visitors were offered the opportunity of being shot. Little was known about him except that he grew very large sapodillas. (The sapodilla is a large shade tree that provides brown, baseball-sized fruit in the spring. The fruit of the "dilly" is coarse and pink and tastes rather like candy that fine sand has been sprinkled over.)

A small village with a school and post office sprang up in 1922, when a car ferry ran between Marathon and No Name. The railroad had bridged the gap in 1912, but there was no land route. Automobile travelers had to take two ferries to traverse the Keys, the other running between Lower Matecumbe Key and Grassy Key. The ferries, *The Florida Keys, The Pilgrim,* and *The Key West,* operated until 1938, when the Seven-Mile Bridge and the Bahia Honda Bridge were rebuilt to accommodate cars. The 15-mile trip to No Name took about two hours. At that time cars drove on a marl road to Big Pine, then south across Big Pine Channel to the north corner of Little Torch. Wooden bridges connected the Torches, Ramrod, and Summerland keys. Once the ferry service was disbanded, the village by the landing disappeared.

During 1962, a Key Wester, sympathetic to the Cuban refugees, allowed a group training to be guerrilla fighters to use his shack as headquarters on No Name. The key was fairly inaccessible, the bridge leading between it and Big Pine having both rotted and burned. The revolutionary experiment ended when one guerrilla shot and killed another, mistaking him, he said, for a raccoon.

A new cement bridge crosses Bogie Channel and connects No Name to Big Pine today, used mostly by fishermen. The road runs straight to the vanished ferry landing and stops at some very impressive rocks. There is absolutely no way you can make the mistake of running off the road into the water without annihilating yourself on the boulders first. Deer appear at the end of the afternoon and congregate on the road. Drive slowly and never feed them. A deer who is fed from a car will eventually be run over by one.

Right on Bogie Channel is **The Old Wooden Bridge Fishing Camp**. Pleasantly funky old cottages somewhat compromised by newer drab funk environs. Kitchens and dockage. If you want a TV, you're welcome to bring one. One-bedroom cottages are $60 a night or $350 a week. Two-bedroom cottages are $80 and $475 (872-2241).

The **No Name Pub** is on Big Pine just before the bridge and

A REALLY BAD TREE

A really bad tree is the manchineel, one of the most poisonous trees in the world. It is not common, but does grow wild
on the Keys, particularly Big Pine. It is a small, sprawling
tree with a spreading rounded crown and alternate oval
leaves that narrow to a sharp point. It produces green and
yellow flowers and a crab-apple-sized fruit which is deadly
when eaten. Some people confuse the tree with a guava, and
it is said, although it's difficult to imagine by whom, that the
fruit is sweet.

Poisonous apple aside, the tree itself is vitriolic. The copi-
ous sap is caustic, and even rainwater runoff from the leaves
can burn and sear the skin. Almost any kind of behavioral
abnormality can be attributed to extinct tribes of Indians,
which is why you should not be surprised when you hear that
the Caloosas employed the manchineel as Grand Inquisitor,
tying their luckless victims to the tree and letting the milky
sap run where it wished over them, the sap pickling and flay-
ing the flesh as it went.

Ponce de León was one visitor to the Keys who probably
wished he'd never come. He was struck by a Caloosa arrow
dipped in manchineel juice, and though he managed to escape to Havana, he found only his deathbed there.

is open to midnight, serving beer and good pizza. Its only ambience is that it's hard to find.

THE TORCH KEYS

Big bad parties have been taking place on No Name and the
Torches recently. Sometimes they get really bad and someone is
found murdered after them. Three particularly gruesome mur-
ders remain unsolved. All that the police know is that the vultures didn't do it.

The Torches have always been a little strange. Just beyond
the bridge crossing Big Pine Channel and linking Big Pine with
Little Torch was once the Island Woman Bar, known princi-

pally for its owner's global economic views (the world's problems began with the invention of money). It is now out of business, perhaps because he gave free beer today rather than tomorrow. A succession of restaurants followed, but it would be chancy to stop by for a meal these days as it has become a Jehovah's Witnesses meeting hall.

Down this road a half mile is **Parmer's Place**, a friendly complex of apartments, cottages, and trailers named after birds and fishes. You can stay in the Grunt, for example, for $75 a night, though you might prefer the more elegantly named Egret at $105. July and August are in-season rates, but prices go down $25 in the fall. There's a pool and free breakfast, boat basin and dockage, and many people trailer their boat down and rent by the week. Or you can rent from Bud Boats on Big Pine and cruise around these unparalleled fishing and diving waters. Weekly rates at Parmer's are around $500. Telephone: 872-2157.

The Torches—Middle, Little, and Big—got their names unsurprisingly from the resinous torchwood trees that grow there. The wood burns when green and was used for kindling by homesteaders. It may also have hallucinogenic properties. Woodcarvers working with torchwood admit to getting a kick out of it. The rare Schaus swallowtail butterfly, who might know something, feeds exclusively on it. The butterfly was thought to be extinct at the turn of the century but was found on Matecumbe Key, only to disappear again after the 1940 hurricane. There are some on Lignumvitae.

Buttonwood trees, an upland mangrove, were also cut and burned to make charcoal for cooking fires. The habit in the Keys was to cut the hardwood and plant coconut palms, pineapples, and limes. None of these farming ventures was successful and all were abandoned. One can still find Key limes growing wild in the Torches. The trees, which are not indigenous but were introduced from the West Indies, are fiercely thorny and bear a small tart and juicy fruit which is yellow when ripe and falls into your hands nicely at a touch. One of the reasons Key limes were never successful commercially was because they were too thin-skinned and therefore too fragile to ship.

The Torches were most populated in the 1920's, when the old road ran down the western side of Little Torch. When the Over-

THE LOWER KEYS

SNAKES

The Keys have all the varieties of snakes found in Florida. Yes. All the harmless snakes, the *rat,* the *water,* the *indigo,* the *black,* the *corn,* the *green,* and the *king*—as well as the poisonous ones—the *cottonmouth,* the *rattlesnake,* and the *coral.*

You may understandably be interested in the poisonous snakes. The *cottonmouth* is rather difficult to identify because he changes color as he grows from a baby to an adult. He can even resemble the gentle, huge indigo snake. But the cottonmouth has a big thick triangular-shaped head which is flat on top, and if you get very close he will probably show you what he is by opening his mouth to display the whiteness of his jaws. The *diamondback* is the heaviest poisonous snake in the world, although at eight feet it is not the longest. It is found in piney and palmetto woods, sandy areas, and hammocks. *Coral snakes* are the most intriguing because they're small and pretty as well as being the most deadly. They grow only to a length of around two feet, and their black bodies are brightly banded in orange and black. The harmless *scarlet king snake* is often mistaken for the coral snake, but the *scarlet king's* nose is red, while the coral's nose is black.

Proper snake identification depends upon considerable calm.

Snake experts tend to have three maxims:

In identifying the coral snake, they say, "If his nose is black, he's bad for Jack."

They say that all snakes are nonaggressive and will not go out of their way to bite you.

They say that snakes are where you find them.

seas Highway was built after the 1935 hurricane, utilizing the railroad's bed and bridges, many of the old roads were abandoned, along with the communities that had flourished beside them.

There is little here now, certainly—houses, trailers. . . . There is a biologist on Middle Torch who keeps his six acres as a "habitat for snakes," which sounds nice, at least it sounds natural, until you realize that because his specialty is snakes and he wants to find snakes when he's looking for them, his six acres is a "Dixie farm" covered with trash. Old boats and flattened gasoline tanks, rotting boards and fabric, rusted metal of all sorts. All the kinds of snakes that exist in the Keys from the black racer and endemic little ring-necked snake (weird in that it has no ring) to the huge indigo and diamondback rattler can be found here. Except they couldn't be found the hot winter morning we spent turning over the trash. Perhaps they had been dined on too vigorously by predators the previous fall. Or perhaps they were offended by their littered home. Or worse, they were tired of the old funky litter and wanted new funk! In any case, there were no snakes, in what had once been a lime grove.

A road that runs the length of Big Torch is called a "scenic drive." Historically, Monroe County has been madly successful in using taxpayers' money to build roads and bridges that go nowhere. Condos, marinas, and golf courses are but a gleam in a speculator's beady eye when these projects are pushed through, and this "scenic drive" is no exception. There is nothing here. And after about eight miles of zigzagging blacktop over swampy land, it ends. Those who make the trip appear bewildered, but they dutifully emerge from their cars and look. What is here is mangrove, and yet more mangrove—more and more of that splendid, hardworking, giving tree, nursery to nestlings and fishes, busily making land all the while it nourishes. Look upon it, this tangled swamp, and be both respectful and glad.

Off the humble Torches at the western end of the Newfound Harbor Keys is **Little Palm Island**, a five-acre sand-covered rock owned by a succession of millionaires and now run as a precious thatch-topped luxury resort. A millionaire-style pool-lagoon conception runs through the island. Suites in the bungalows are $501 per couple per night. (Five hundred and one!) It's $621 per couple per night with meals. You can bring your own watercraft, and yachts are welcome. If you feel you can't afford $501 for an evening at this time, you can still go over to the restaurant for breakfast, lunch, or dinner. There are certain regulations, however, involving lunch that might make you

Egrets in the mangroves

think twice. The minimum for lunch is $25 per person and this does not include taxes, tips, and whatever you would spend at the bar. Men must have "collars"—have to leave your Hog's Breath shirt at home. If you want to go swimming, you have to have a beach club membership, which is extra too. There are no children in your party, they hope. At night, entrées run between $18 and $25. The menu also offers *Les Desserts*— ("Desserts") they add helpfully. *Les Chocolats* (Chocolate) and *Les Café et Thé* (Coffee and Tea). A launch leaves the **Dolphin Marina** at MM #28.5 every hour on the hour from 8 A.M. to 10 P.M. For dining reservations call 872-2551. Resort reservations: 872-2524. (You're really going to do this??)

RAMROD KEY

This key bears no resemblance whatsoever to a ramrod—it is shaped more like a helmet. In the days when the railroad passed through, Ramrod claimed a post office, although the train never stopped here. It merely slowed down while mail was tossed on and off.

The most interesting thing about Ramrod is **Looe Key**, which is seven miles offshore. Looe, named for a frigate that ran aground here in 1774, is a National Marine Sanctuary and perhaps the most beautiful reef in the Keys, certainly the most varied and interesting reef in the Lower Keys. The Sanctuary covers five square miles; the reef itself is roughly Y-shaped, 200 yards wide and 800 yards long. Parts of the reef are awash. Other sections have gullies plunging down to 35 feet between the coral heads to a pristine sand base in what is called a spur and groove system. Looe is a lovely and lively community with exceptionally clear waters, so it is wonderful for the snorkeler as well as the diver. You'll see thousands of fish here, lobsters, octupuses, and rays. Long tongues of pillar coral rise within three feet of the surface, and there are massive brain corals as well as an array of "soft" corals—the undulating gorgonians, sea fans, and sea whips. Looe, with its winding coral corridors, its deeply carved caves, and diversity of life, is a spectacular

A brain coral gives lobsters shelter from a spotted eagle ray

reef, the jewel of the Keys. In the summer of 1994, a 170-foot University of Miami research ship carrying 21 marine scientists and practically every antenna known to man, ran hard aground on the reef. Many of the scientists were from NOAA, the federal agency that runs national marine sanctuaries. The vessel's name was the *Columbus Iselin*, though it might as well have been christened *The Ironic*.

As for what you can do (any marine researcher would agree), never anchor on coral, and when diving, never touch it or stand on it. All life is protected in the sanctuary. Spearfishing and collecting are not allowed. Dive shops offer full and half-day reef trips and night dives.

Underseas Inc., MM #31 on Big Pine, rents all equipment, including cameras. A half day is $25 per person. It's always a good idea to rent a wet suit for a few dollars more. Telephone: 872-2700.

Innerspace Dive Shop, MM #29.5 on Big Pine, makes trips on its 35-foot dive boat *Innerspace I*. Their snorkel package, which includes equipment, is $30. A scuba package, including two tanks, weights, and belt, costs $40. Telephone: 872-2319.

Reef Divers on Ramrod is located at the **Looe Key Reef Resort**, just past the Torch-Ramrod Channel at MM #27. The resort is a small motel on a canal with boat dockage. It's inexpensive and very popular. They seldom have rooms available during the season if you just drop in, so reservations are necessary. They offer a diver package, which is a room for two plus a half day scuba-ing on the reef for $150. A snorkeling package is $125. There's a pool, a crowded tiki bar, and an unhurried restaurant which serves an "early bird" special until two in the afternoon. Instruction, equipment, and two tank dives on Looe costs $75. Telephone: 872-2215.

Crossing pretty Niles Channel, where the generous sky allows you another opportunity to pick out a favorite cloud, you come to **Summerland Key**, where the outlines of some impressive housetops can be seen on the western shore. A road off to the right runs along the channel and ends at a dismantled dock leading to a small island with a familiar sign, Keep Out, with a perturbing twist—Be Aware of Caretaker. Enigmatic Summerland is developed with a series of canals on the eastern end, and it has a dusty main strip of billboards which is a tiny, hopeful version of something larger and even more dusty.

CUDJOE KEY

The best crayfish in the Keys are said to be found off Cudjoe. The second and last most interesting thing about Cudjoe is its name, about which there is much dispute. There is the slender

KEY LOIS

Off Cudjoe, in the Atlantic just before Hawk Channel, is Loggerhead Key, recently named Key Lois. Lois isn't visible from the highway, although it is, clearly, from haute Little Palm. Lois looks a little odd, as well it might since its only occupants are monkeys. One half of the key is gray, as though in shadow; the other half is a healthy, mangrove-wooded green. A narrow tidal river separates the two, a river which, it is said by those who put the monkeys on the island in the first place, they could cross but prefer not to. The monkeys, about 1,600 of them, inhabit the gray half, which they have denuded with their climbing, scrambling, swinging, and clinging. They are 70-pound, dog-faced, Rhesus monkeys, bred and raised here for laboratory research. As with the cattle one sees grazing in green pastures, they probably lead a very happy life until they don't. There is no natural food for them on the island and no fresh water, so someone arrives daily by boat with water and hundreds of pounds of Purina Monkey Chow. At other times a boat will arrive, collect some of them to fill an order from a laboratory, and take them away. Boats also arrive upon occasion to lug off the monkey feces accumulating there. It's a very clean island, and the monkeys are purportedly the biggest, blondest, and healthiest in the world.

The original colony of 100 was captured in India in 1972. The descendants are now a multimillion-dollar business for the owners of the Massachusetts supplier of lab animals for the U.S. Food and Drug Administration. The veterinarian owner of the island, Dr. Henry Foster, wanted to rename Loggerhead Key Key Lois, as a tribute to his wife, although why Lois would want an island full of yowling, scratching, gibbering monkeys named after her is not known. The state, however, apparently not liking to have places renamed willynilly for uxorial reasons, refused. The doctor got his way nevertheless with the acronym Laboratory Observing Island Simians, and Loggerhead Key became Key Lois, even though it might be more accurately called Mon Key.

No Trespassing signs are posted around the island, but there is no caretaker here, the monkeys apparently being their own best protection. So one probably will not see them, but if one did, it would be across a great distance. And the monkeys would be watching from a great distance too— across that far distance that separates monkeys from men.

Key Lois, like the holy, ruined Indian city of Galta, but with nothing sacred here—no temples, no priests, no pilgrims. Just the monkeys, monkeys, monkeys.

"joewood" theory, the joewood being a common little tree with fragrant blossoms. There is the slenderer yet "Cousin Joe" theory—an early homesteader from Key West, Joe by name, cousin to someone, who first settled here. There is also the more thoughtful explanation that the name Cudjoe was a customary African name given to a male child born on the first day of the week. The Africans, brought to Florida as slaves, then freed, often went to live among the Seminoles, by whom they were enslaved once more. It would not be unlikely for one of these men to leave the Everglades and migrate to an isolated key where he could lead an independent life. Nor would it be unusual for a freed black man to come up from Key West and, using the name he was born with, work one of the "outside" keys.

Be that as it may, Cudjoe is rather an orphan. Since it has no post office, it has no zip code, and since it has no zip, any person

FAT ALBERT

Fat Albert is a 1,400-foot, ground-tethered blimp, a radar-stuffed aerostat that floats benignly over Cudjoe, keeping its eye and ear on everything, druggies mostly, with its millions of dollars' worth of fancy electronics. Fat is a fine sight, but it crashes frequently, victim of storms and other mishaps. Once, it even had to be shot down deliberately because it had "escaped." What you see today is Son of Fat. Perhaps even Son of the Son of Fat. Fat's twin, also known as Fat, beams TV Marti to Cuba, though there are few TV's there to receive the early morning transmissions.

It required millions of very heavy bricks to construct Fort Jefferson, which was built to oversee all activities in the Florida Straits, Havana, Pensacola, Mobile, the mouth of the Mississippi—in short, all of the Gulf of Mexico. Now the dainty Fat, lighter than the air it bobs in, does the job, although he may not float forever. Cute Fat is expensive to maintain.

or establishment thereon is considered part of Summerland Key, which, as we recall, seems to the jaded eye to consist primarily of real estate offices.

Cudjoe is damp and low for the most part. Most of the development is on the eastern side, with small concrete-block houses crouching on man-made canals.

Just over the bridge that crosses Bow Channel at MM #20 is **Mangrove Mama's**, open 11:30–3 for lunch and 5:30–10 for dinner in the winter. When it's closed for the month of June, the place looks as though it's been shuttered for years. But this place jumps! Classic tacky Keys. Fireplace, wine, and beer served in mason jars. The food isn't that good, but it doesn't seem to matter. On seasonal Sundays there's barbecue and a band. You can run into anyone here, even a guy in an FBI cap on holiday. "Are you really in the FBI? I'd like to join the FBI," a girl says. "Oh, you should," he says, "it's a lot of fun." Telephone: 745-3535.

SUGARLOAF KEY

Sugarloaf was settled at the turn of the century when a sponge raising station was built here. The farming venture consisted of cutting off bits of live, large sponges, attaching the bit to a piece of concrete, and allowing it to grow in a pen in the water. Charles Chase, an Englishman, created the Florida Sponge and Fruit Company in 1912 and built a town, which he named for himself, complete with watchtower and guard to chase off sponge poachers. The company went bankrupt on the eve of the First World War when Chase's assets were frozen in a London bank. He sold his holdings, which comprised almost all of Sugarloaf, to R. C. Perky, a Florida real estate salesman who quickly changed the town's name from Chase to Perky and set out to subdivide and develop it. Perky's town was never built, but the man is responsible for the key's weirdest and most winsome construction.

The Bat Tower

The bat tower, shingled brown and elegant, is about thirty-five feet tall and is to be found down a dirt road just past the Sugarloaf Lodge, to the right of the road that leads to the Sugarloaf Airport. People bounce down the road to view it, circle it warily in their cars, then look a little embarrassed because they've gone out of their way to see it. The bat tower, standing there quietly batless, suffers these visitations with dignity.

Dr. Charles Campbell, a former health officer for the city of San Antonio, Texas, wrote a book in the 1920's entitled *Bats, Mosquitoes and Dollars*. It was Campbell's belief that the bat was one of man's best friends, both because of its insatiable appetite for mosquitoes and its valuable excrement, which makes great fertilizer. The bat towers or "roosts" of cypress lath which he designed were condos for thousands of bats, and the chute in the center of each structure collected guano, making each bat tower "a little gold mine."

It had not been that many years since malaria and yellow

The Perky Bat Tower as envisioned by Mr. Perky

fever were found to be transmitted by the mosquito and that those diseases could be eliminated by mosquito eradication. Dr. Campbell's theories were well received. San Antonio, upon his urging, even passed an ordinance which made it illegal to hurt a bat. Sixteen bat towers were built according to his plans, which he did not charge for, charging only for the bait, which cost $175. This secret formula was said to be indispensable in attracting bats. Campbell never disclosed the formula, but it almost certainly consisted primarily of batshit. One of the towers built in Texas was called the Asylum Bat Roost and was built on the grounds of the Southwestern Insane Asylum. Six of the towers were built in Italy and many were adorned with a crucifix.

Perky, frustrated in his attempts to develop his key into a huge resort—he had already built a gambling casino, restaurant, and cottages—because of a considerable mosquito problem, read *Bats, Mosquitoes and Dollars* and grew hopeful. He sent away for the plans and bait, built his bat tower, and dedicated it at a party on March 15, 1929, to "good health in Perky, Florida." The box of bait did not arrive in time for the party, but when it eventually did it was opened, water was sprinkled upon it, and it was installed in the recesses of the tower. It was noted by someone attending the event that "a smell like that ought to attract something," but sadly the bats never came. Never did a bat visit the bat tower. After a year, when it was believed that perhaps fresh bait was needed, Perky sent away for another box, but Campbell had died, and with him the formula for success. Perky shortly afterwards went bankrupt. His fishing camp burned and he himself passed on. Only the bat tower remains, still pristine and expectant.

The **Sugarloaf Lodge** at MM #17 is the only lodging of note between Sugarloaf and Key West. The lodge has tennis courts, a 3,000-foot airstrip, a swimming pool, and a marina with fishing guides and boat charters available. Some of the Key West–based kayaking tours push off from Sugarloaf to explore the tidal streams and mangrove islands of Great White Heron National Wildlife Refuge, such as Snipe and Mud keys. **Adventure Charters** (296-0362) offers half-day and full-day trips as well as overnight camping trips on a catamaran. They provide the food, you the bedroll. Everyone has a great time in a kayak: $35 per person for a half day, $150 for the overnight, star-filled-sky experience. The Lodge also has a pond in front of the glass-walled restaurant where a porpoise named Sugar has lived for almost twenty years. Sugar is fed Spanish mackerel three times a day and performs a few tricks with cups and saucers and dimes. She also has an inner tube and a palm frond that she's *very* fond of. One can believe that Sugar is very happy here, although sometimes she has to go on a diet and doesn't get all that lovely mackerel. This annoys her a little, and she is loath to do all her tricks. Sugar is a lady, and a lady of a certain age at that, and she is not going to do all that clicking and kissing and *ohh*-and-*ahh* jumping for a mess of smelt. A 37-year-old dolphin named Molly was brought down in 1994 from the Ocean Reef Club to be a possible companion for Sugar, though heaven knows how the two ladies will get along. The restaurant serves huge cuts of roast beef as well as a variety of fish dishes, the entrées running around $18. Sometimes the meat is not very good at all. The bar, however, remains a classic. So too are the wonderful rooms, with their individual murals, sleek '70's decor and weird lamps. They all have a view of the water. Rates run about $100 in winter and drop to $75 during the summer. Efficiencies are $10 more. Telephone: 745-3211.

During the season, December to May, **Fantasy Dan's** at the

Sugarloaf Airport gives sight-seeing airplane rides. A ten-minute trip costs $20, while a half-hour trip takes you around Key West for $40. Telephone: 745-2217. If you feel the need to jump from a plane, you can do that too. For only $200 you can get truly terrified. Call SkyDive Key West: 745-4386.

One of the last vestiges of the old road is on Sugarloaf. The new road is built on the former railroad bed, but before the hurricane of 1935, automobiles traveled a meandering westerly route along the Atlantic. The road is overgrown and quiet, good for bicycling and bird watching.

Take Sugarloaf Boulevard, directly across from the lodge, and follow it through a subdivision until it dead-ends. To the left are the "nude canals," an abandoned development which has been taken over by three rather distinct groups of sunbathers. There appears to be a rather overweight, if not obese, heterosexual section, a more comely heterosexual section, and a homosexual section. The water in the canal is an unusual robin's-egg blue and is dotted with rafts and inner tubes. Pickups and vans are parked on the barren, platted lots beside it. The road used to curve northward up to the famous old fishing camp Pirate's Cove, a rich man's retreat which was wiped out by a hurricane in 1945, continuing to a wooden bridge which paralleled the railroad bridge to Cudjoe. This road is unpassable now, a small bridge which once crossed Tarpon Channel having been destroyed.

If you choose to avoid the nude canals (and who could blame you) but still want to explore, take the right fork off 939. This, however, will only lead you, after three miles, to the wooden remains of another missing wooden bridge and a rusted Ford Landau with a Go Gators sticker that has toppled grille-forward into the warm, quiet waters, bringing to mind the words of one of Thomas McGuane's characters—"I didn't know what I was, not a Southerner certainly. A Floridian. Drugs, alligators, macadam, the sea, sticky sex, laughter and sudden death. . . ."

It is customary to say good-bye to the bat tower before resuming the plunge to Key West, for now the pace picks up, the land crouches flatter. **The Saddlebunch Keys** are low and pale, the mangrove, growing on just a few inches of mud above coral rock, stunted. This is the "heavy dew" of the Keys, not quite land and not quite water.

Big Coppitt is the suburb for the Navy air base on **Boca Chica Key**. Boca Chica used to be Key West's favorite beach, and there were fishing camps and restaurants here in the 1930's. The military condemned the property during World War II, the Army built airstrips here, and the Navy later took it over to train pilots. The Navy has gradually closed off much of the area over the years (there's still a bit of abandoned beach road you can walk at the end of State Road 941), and now the glum sight of old missile silos (the *new* missile silos are on Fleming Key), complete with buzzards brooding on top, is affordable only by boat. Our own American vultures congregate on Boca Chica bunkers. It is a sight that certainly can be missed, but it wouldn't hurt to remember it.

In March of 1991 the Navy was most surprised when a Cuban major landed his Soviet MiG on the airstrip. They had never seen him up there. Another MiG slipped in two years later. NORAD (North American Defense Command) admits that by the time anything from Cuba appears on their radar, they're already "here."

You will probably be driving faster now, for here the land turns ugly. Everyone is driving faster. Even the cormorants, those worried birds, fly hurriedly across the flats, or, appearing more worried still, stand on pilings or wires, drying their sodden wings. **Shark Key** is a brand-new creation for the rich, with a gate and big new palms for the instant "look," but **Rockland Key** is industrial, little more than a borrow pit, the mangroves all gone, steam shovels moving the marl around, a concrete factory to come—Flagler would have been smitten.

STOCK ISLAND AND APPROACHES TO KEY WEST

Stock Island has always been a service island. Originally cattle were penned here to fulfill the dietary desires of those sick of fish in Key West. Today on Stock Island there is the dump—popularly called Mount Trashmore, looming over the almost always bankrupt but well-groomed Key West Resort Golf Course. The Florida Keys Hospital is here, and the Tennessee Williams

Fine Arts Center, which puts on a variety of plays and musicals and brings classical music and jazz ensembles to town. Call 294-6232 for their schedule. Florida Keys Community College, beside the Fine Arts Center, offers some interesting short-term courses for the long-term visitor—plant and bird identification, crash courses in Spanish, and the like. If you continue along this road, Junior College Road, looping back toward Route 1, you will also find the **Key West Seaplane Service**, which has several flights a day to Fort Jefferson in the Dry Tortugas (see pages 233–37). On the other side of Stock, to the south of Route 1, at Junction 941, are trailer parks (which even the police take pains to avoid after dark); most of the shrimp fleet; **Oceanside Marina**, where some excellent charter boat captains can be found (the marinas on Stock had previously been best known for the "mother ships" of cocaine that found safe harbor here); and the infamous, recently closed dog track. (Many people in the Keys have adopted greyhounds, well aware that otherwise these intelligent, elegant dogs would end up in the Gulf Stream or the landfill after their last race. Greyhounds make great pets and come in every color but gray . . . and why should that pose a problem?) Stock Islanders enjoy their sunsets, as capable of staring in crazed fascination at the clouds as anybody, and are fond of their beer—the down-and-dirty bar at the **Cow Key Marina** being held in special esteem by many.

But you do not dally on Stock Island, now you move on. Behind you is the big billboard that says Paradise Welcomes the U.S. Armed Forces. You hang on to the wheel as pickups with huge tires and bumper stickers—I Love My Cockatoo, Fly Navy, Easy Does It—and small fierce Hondas rush past you. You plunge over the Cow Key Channel at MM #4, where a tumultuous division greets you.

To the left is South Roosevelt Boulevard, or A1A, the road that goes past little "Houseboat Row," the airport, the beaches, and the condominiums. The condos are all familiarly banal, one at 1800 Atlantic being particularly contemptuous of the passerby by taking a fascist command of the view.

To the right, and what most naturally sucks you down along it, is North Roosevelt Boulevard, the continuation of Route 1, and of course your heart will sink when you see the sprawl of

Searstown, once a perfectly nice salt marsh, over which sea
gulls soar, still puzzled, overhead. This is the strip of discount
liquors, discount cars, discount pizzas, and Terminix Pest Control; this is the bawl of consumerism and doubtful services. Try
to dismiss it from your mind. Kennedy Drive intersects the island shortly. To the right, by the Magic Carpet Miniature Golf
Course with its elephantine conch shell hazard, the road goes to
Sigsbee Park, which is Navy housing.

Another large shopping mall, Key Plaza, as well as the *really*
enormous pink Marketplace, lie ahead. The longer you stay in
Key West, the stranger these big malls appear, for they look exactly like the rest of Florida. Beyond the city pier and the charter boats of Garrison Bight, merge into the left lane if you wish
to drop straight down Truman and into the downtown. To the
right, Palm Avenue moves around the Bight (*bight* meaning a
bend, after all), skirting the Navy yards off Trumbo Point and
the pastel congestion of Peary Court to eventually turn into
Eaton. This is, perhaps, the quickest route to the Pier House
and Mallory Square if you don't want to cruise Duval, but of
course you must introduce yourself to Key West by cruising
Duval. So take Truman (not becoming muddled by this over-
named intersection where a medley of political figures are all
given their due, Roosevelt Boulevard turning into Truman Avenue as it crosses Eisenhower Drive, which becomes Jose Marti
Drive) past Bayview Park and the tennis courts, past the big,
lemon-yellow B & F Cleaners, which can shrink the unshrink-
able, past the Overseas Fruit Market and the Margaret Truman Launderette and the old and inexpensive motels, the El
Rancho, Key Lime Village, and the Red Rooster, to the big
DOWNTOWN sign that means DUVAL.

Yet if you were to pass this temptation nonetheless, in the interest of getting to the rock-bottom end of Florida, and continue
one block more to Whitehead, two alternative conclusions to
your journey would still remain. A few blocks to the right is the
Monroe County Courthouse with its big kapok tree and its sign,
End of The Rainbow End of the Route, a sign that could be perceived as being somewhat ominous. Yet you would not think
you were at the end of anything here, even Route 1, for Whitehead continues down to the Civil War Monument (a memorial

The southernmost house, at the foot of Duval Street

to Union soldiers) and Mallory Square (named for a native son who became the Confederate Secretary of the Navy) and stops, ambivalently, there.

However, were you to travel to the other end of Whitehead, you would be at the real foot of the street, the **Southernmost Point**, which is marked by a large, odd buoy planted firmly in cement. With the water beyond, you will now certainly feel yourself to be at the end of something, even though a painted curb says America Begins Here.

KEY WEST

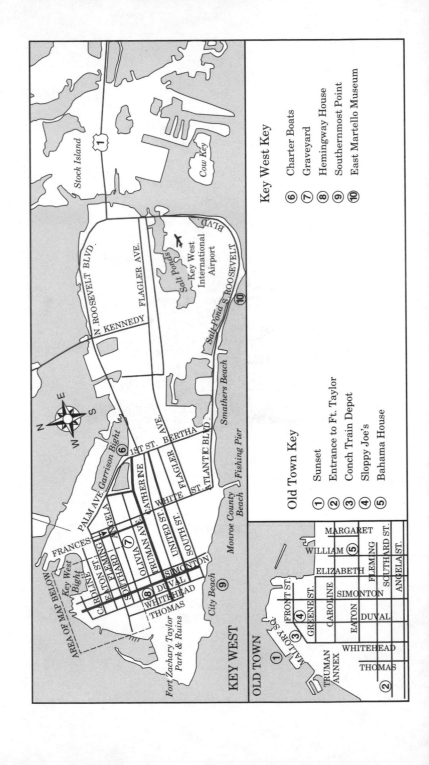

KEY WEST

Stock Island

Cow Key

N. ROOSEVELT BLVD
FLAGLER AVE.
N. KENNEDY
S. ROOSEVELT BLVD.
Salt Ponds
Key West International Airport
⑩
Smathers Beach
Monroe County Beach / Fishing Pier

Palm Ave. Garrison Bight
Key West Bight
⑥ 1ST ST. BERTHA ST.
CATHERINE
FLAGLER
WHITE
UNITED ST.
SOUTH ST.
ATLANTIC BLVD.
FRANCES
CAROLINE ST.
EATON
FLEMING
ANGELA
SOUTHARD
OLIVIA AVE.
TRUMAN AVE.
⑦
SIMONTON
DUVAL
WHITEHEAD
THOMAS
⑧
City Beach ⑨

AREA OF MAP BELOW
Fort Zachary Taylor Park & Ruins

Old Town Key

① Sunset
② Entrance to Ft. Taylor
③ Conch Train Depot
④ Sloppy Joe's
⑤ Bahama House

Key West Key

⑥ Charter Boats
⑦ Graveyard
⑧ Hemingway House
⑨ Southernmost Point
⑩ East Martello Museum

OLD TOWN

MALLORY SQ.
FRONT ST.
GREENE ST.
CAROLINE
SIMONTON
ELIZABETH
WILLIAM ⑤
MARGARET
FLEMING
SOUTHARD ST.
ANGELA ST.
EATON
DUVAL
WHITEHEAD
THOMAS
TRUMAN ANNEX
③ ④
② ①

WALLACE STEVENS wrote *her mind had bound me round*—and he was speaking of Key West. This peculiar and unlikely town does have a mind quite of her own, with attitudes and habits that can either charm or exasperate, seduce or dismay the new acquaintance. The traveler seldom wants to see what he sees, he wants to see something else. And in many respects, Key West, which is so singular in its architecture and attitude, its posturing and fancifulness, its zany eclecticism, its seedy tropicality, is a town come upon unseen, unexpected, the something else almost felt. It is an urbane, isolated, freewheeling, lighthearted, gossipy, and eccentric town. There is a sense of adventure here, of excess and individuality. It's odd. Actually odd. It is a rather dirty town and has very little dignity, but it has style. Its architecture is a charming, intriguing mélange of fine houses and shacks, painted primly white or weathered right down to the silvery bone, a mix of gingerbread grandeur and mañana collapse with an abundance of verandas and porticos, columns and pilasters and balconies. Comparison and exception are everywhere. The town can look somewhat like old New England, but with a decidedly un-puritanical cast. Jonathan Edwards would never have slept here. The Navy is a presence, certainly, owning a good quarter of the town as well as two thirds of the waterfront and all of Boca Chica, but it is not a highly visible one from land. From the air and water the extent of its holdings is clearly seen—the piers and berths, the housing, the ammunition dumps, the runways, the radar towers. In the early 1980's, when the military was, to a considerable extent, pulling out of Key West, the former mayor water-skied to Cuba in an attempt to get the Navy to stay in full force by demonstrating how close that island was to our shores. The mayor water-skied to Cuba. It took him six hours and ten minutes. Key West, being Key West, didn't even think it a particularly strange thing to do.

Homosexuals, who probably command another quarter of the

town in terms of real estate and influence, are more visible, providing a sleek and somewhat mordant glaze to the town. Tennessee Williams came to Key West in the 1940's, attracted by the sailors, who all seemed "to be walking to the tune of Managua, Nicaragua," and was influential in introducing the town to artistic gays. Now, many of the shops, guest houses, and dance halls are owned by gays, and much of the town's restoration is attributable to them.

Key West is tolerant, very tolerant. What passes for the society column in the local paper, the *Citizen,* abounds in news of gay couples and events, and a wooden pier that elbowed out into the Atlantic and was a popular lounging spot for years before it collapsed (now recrudescent) was known breezily as "Dick Dock." Gays provide much of the gloss, sophistication, and outrageousness of Key West, as well as the money which keeps the town bubbling along.

Key West is tropical. Island. Cuban. Black. In the morning one hears roosters crowing, although the sense is not particularly bucolic. Some are fighting cocks bred for the gambling pit. The birds pecking in dusty runs beneath towering breadfruit trees are a good example of the decadence and innocence that is Key West. As is the sight of a charred and blackened lot where once a fine old building stood—a lot that might remain charred and empty for years, accepting with the seasons the bougainvillea petals that fall upon the smashed bottles there.

One knows where Key West lies in a geographic sense. Forty-five miles north of the Tropic of Cancer. Closer to Cuba at 90 miles than it is to Miami at almost 150. Due south of Cleveland, Ohio. (Cleveland, Ohio!) A glittering, balmy, perhaps not terribly legitimate rock beneath vast sea skies. Key West's economy over the years has been based on a curious and volatile array of occupations—wrecking, shrimping, fishing, and smuggling. In the 1970's, certainly most of the money that came into Key West was drug money, but things have quieted down somewhat in that regard. Now the money comes from real estate. And things are changing fast.

Key West is now a tourist town—one million people visit it each year—but it is still a town of contrast and contradiction, threat and carelessness and charm. The bars should be sampled, of course, and the reef investigated. The gold should be seen, and the forts and the galleries. One should dance or stand on one of the balconies that line Duval and watch the prowl of the street. The beaches should be duly attended and a tan obtained. The yellowtail stuffed with crabmeat should be eaten, and conch fritters and, since you must, Key lime pie. Café con leche or the intense little energizing espresso called *bucce* must be bought from the window of a Cuban grocery. The flowers and trees should be puzzled over and appreciated, and their lovely names said aloud. Jacaranda. Bougainvillea. Poinciana. Frangipani. One should catch a fish. One should be in the water, and travel over and on the water as much as possible. And, when one is on land, one must assuredly walk. Stroll, linger, wander. For Key West is a walking town, and a bicycling one too. Architectural surprises are around every corner, and other interesting sights less classifiable.

THE STREETS

In Key West, "downtown" isn't in the middle of town at all but up on the northwest corner of the island, on the harbor. All the Keys veer west as they run south, and the streets of Key West, although straight, are laid out on an angle—just about on a diagonal to main compass points; the corners of intersections becoming, in fact, compass points.

Whitehead and White are the parallel boundaries of Old Town. Whitehead is where Hemingway's hoary ghost hovers, in the house where he often experienced "the black lonelies." Then there is Duval, followed by Simonton, a big street which once could have been counted on to hold the post office but no more, the new post office, landmark and comfort to the postcard laden, being built on Whitehead. The next streets, Elizabeth, William, Margaret, Grinnel, Francis, and White, can be easily recalled if you put them in the order of three friends—nice old souls who rock and converse with each other across the porches of their white, Conch houses—Elizabeth William, Margaret Grinnel, and Francis White. Actually, Francis has a middle name, Ashe, and a lovely street it is, to have as a middle name. The island's original coastline marked the intersection of William and Caroline streets until 1874.

Basically, now, you have memorized the streets paralleling Duval. Walking the other way, up Duval from the Pier House to the Atlantic, remembering the streets will be a bit more vexing. You begin at Front, nicely enough. Then there is Greene, a street named after Pardon Greene, an early settler who left his wife and children back in Connecticut rather than subject them to the rigors of the tropics, but this will probably be of little help to you in remembering that Greene is between Front and Caroline. Caroline used to be marked by the Caroline Lowe house on the corner which, unfortunately, is no longer there. There are still old Conchs in town who remember the sound of it burning. The house had been built by shipwrights, with heavy timbers that extended from the foundation to the roof. Ablaze, the timbers "were screaming." Two sequential letters of the alphabet follow next, E and F. Eaton and Fleming. Eaton has the Episcopal Church right on the corner, and Fleming has Fast Buck Freddie's on the corner. Up Fleming a bit and on the left is Fausto's Famous Food Palace, the town's premier grocery store. Fleming is easy; the only thing you have to remember about it is that it's one-way. Southard, marked by the large clock, is the next street, and that is one-way in the other direction, terminating at the entrance to Fort Taylor. Following Southard are Angela, then Petronia and Olivia (again, alternating one-way streets) and Truman. Think SAPOT. It might be best to pause here, for there is a confusing bevy of young ladies' names ahead: Julia, Virginia, Amelia, Catherine, and Louisa. In the mind of the newcomer, they seem simply United. Which is the next street, just before the last long one, South, which runs down, appropriately enough, to the Southernmost Point. (Numbers run upward from the harbor to the Atlantic and from the Navy Base and Fort Taylor northeastward across town.)

CHANGES AND CONFUSIONS

The land of Key West behaves most peculiarly. It cannot quite be counted upon to be terra firma, for its firma keeps getting changed, rearranged, created, confiscated. What used to be on the water doesn't even have a view of it anymore. What used to be water is now land, or concrete. What used to be separated by water is now joined firmly to land, like Fort Taylor, which had, in fact, almost disappeared *beneath* the land. Pine trees had grown on top of it, and the martial mausoleum had to be excavated, appearing bit by bit.

Weather moved things around a lot. After the hurricane of 1846, the graveyard was moved inland. So was the lighthouse, now one of the most landlocked in America. The military moved things around a great deal, reshaping, building, and abandoning, and playing a big role in changing the shape, direction, and accessibility of Key West. On the eve of the Civil War, the Army cut a road through the wild part of the island so that troops could be marched directly from the barracks on one end to the fort on the other, this road being first called Rocky Road, then Division, most recently Truman.

During World War II, the Navy created additional land and islands for munition dumps and housing, including Sigsbee Park, Fleming Key, and Tank and Christmas islands. For years, the reason one couldn't get to Fort Taylor, a state park and a National Historic Landmark since 1973, was because of Naval security for the Caribbean Command enveloping the land around it.

One half of the land area of Key West didn't exist 150 years ago when William Whitehead, brother of one of the four original owners of the island, first surveyed the town. He laid out lots in tiny 46 × 90-foot pieces, and the houses, built mostly by ships' carpenters, were constructed without any particular regard for their relationship to one another, and alleys and paths angled off the main streets and entered the lots at irregular intervals. Whitehead platted everything, including the bottom of a two-acre pond which existed in what was then the middle of the city. The pond was nameless, though described as a "miserable, stagnant lagoon," and was filled in by the rearranging hurricane of 1846. Land in Key West has blown in, blown away, and simply, or not so simply, been made.

Henry Flagler created 134 acres of land on what is called Trumbo Point, Trumbo being the name of the Overseas Railroad project's head engineer. After the bridges of Long, the

Seven-Mile, and Bahia Honda, the construction of the railroad approached Key West with no available dry land for the depot. When Flagler was informed of this oversight, he said, "Then make some."

All this is partly why Key West, a busy speck in an abyss of sky and distances, seems so confusing.

But the town is small. If you're invited for dinner and you become hopelessly lost, you'll still arrive only fifteen minutes late. That is, unless your hosts have moved their house. For that is another problem. Key West moves things. The Bahama houses were moved, plank by plank, all the way from Green Turtle Cay in the Bahamas. The enterprising David Wolkowsky lifted the nineteenth-century Porter steamship office off its foundations on the old Key West to Havana ferry dock and moved it three hundred feet out into the water, building first a restaurant and then the entire Pier House complex around it. The gun turret from the *Maine* was moved, all the way from Havana Harbor to an elementary school on Southard, only to be moved once more to grace the new post office on Whitehead. The Conch home that now houses the restaurant Bagatelle on Duval was moved from its site on Fleming when the library expanded—the library, the first in south Florida, having moved from its birthplace farther up on Duval where the Red Barn Theatre is today. The Oldest House was moved. And E. H. Gato was a big mover. He built a mansion on Truman in an area which is now Bayview Park, then moved it to Virginia Street on rollers. The trip took two weeks and employed one mule and a windlass. His son, E. H. Gato, Jr., built a rambling Victorian house at the end of Duval, where it intersects with South Street, but found that he didn't like the way the sun struck one of his favorite porches, so he turned the enormous structure around on his yard.

The only place that seems determined to remain exactly on the spot where it began is St. Paul's Episcopal Church at 401 Duval Street. Built here in 1838, it was blown down in the 1846 hurricane. Promptly rebuilt, it burned in the great fire of 1886, a fire which destroyed two thirds of the town. Promptly rebuilt again, it was toppled by the hurricane of 1909. It took the parishioners a little longer to get organized this time, and they did not begin rebuilding until 1914. The white concrete structure you see today has stayed put now for over sixty-five years. When you find the right rock, you stay on it.

MYSTERY AND HISTORY

There is a mystery about Key West, and it is not just behind the name the Spanish gave it in the 1500's—*Cayo Hueso*—Island of Bones. It's true the bones are a puzzle. For whose were the bones, and why were they here? No one knows if the island was actually littered with bones. If it was, they probably belonged to the Caloosa Indians, who used the place either as a burial ground or were massacred here by some other tribe, possibly the Seminoles, although how that somewhat placid group were able to extirpate the ferocious Caloosas has never been explained. In the 1700's the English felicitously altered the sound of *Hueso* to the name of *West*. But the murky etymology of the name is not the mystery. The mystery is in Key West's very self. Why does it look the way it does? And why is it still here? In 1934 the state suggested that the city, which was bankrupt, be abandoned, and that the people be relocated to the mainland. It has endured hurricane, fire, and neglect. It is the oldest city in south Florida, an area known to suffer greatly from the heavy, obliterative hand of speculation, development, and redevelopment, and yet the old part of town, the town platted out by William Whitehead in 1829 and built throughout the nineteenth century, remains startlingly, strikingly intact.

In 1822, the year that the island of Key West was sold by a Spaniard, Juan Salas, to a Mobile businessman, John Simonton, for $2,000, the only beings that frequented the place were mosquitoes and pirates—pirates at the time being a bigger problem in the area than malaria, heat, and lack of fresh water. In the same year, Lieutenant Matthew Perry sailed down to raise the American flag over the country's new possession and confirm that it had one of the largest, finest deep-water anchorages in the country. The flag was raised in the vicinity of what is now Mallory Square, the event attended by a few sweating sailors and some black and Cuban fishermen. Several months after the raising of the flag, the energetic Naval Commodore

David Porter arrived with the ships of his West India Squadron
to set up headquarters in Key West and suppress the pirates
who had been scooting around the Caribbean and the Gulf in
their shallow-draft boats for years, murdering, plundering, and
engaging in their sleazy piratical rites. Porter's depredations
caused the town more grief than those of the pirates, for he considered Key West a military post and appropriated the settlers'
livestock, buildings, and supplies. He wanted to lay out the
streets in a starlike pattern radiating from central plazas
which could be controlled by artillery in the event of civil
unrest. He even tried to change the name of Key West (as had
Perry, who wanted to call it Thompson's Island after the then
Secretary of the Navy), constantly referring to it as Allentown.

After establishing himself here, however, Porter found that
his ships, which were mostly deep-draft frigates, could not pursue the pirates over the reefs and into the winding mangrove
creeks where they hid, so he acquired several small light-draft
schooners and built five flat-bottomed 20-oared barges, which
he called the *Mosquito, Gallinipper, Midge, Gnat,* and *Sandfly.*
He also acquired a steam ferry boat that had been retired from
the New York–Hoboken service named the *Seagull.* With the
ferry towing the agile bug squadron up and down the Keys,
Porter was soon successful in the pursuit and extermination of
pirates. He had driven them from the Keys by 1830 and continued to pursue them to Cuba and Puerto Rico. Court-martialed
by America after Spain protested his intrusion into Spanish
territory—Spain being in the habit of protecting pirates as long
as Spanish ships were allowed safe passage—Commodore
Porter indignantly resigned, joining first the Mexican Navy,
then the Turkish one. Porter never cared for Key West and
urged the government not to establish a permanent station
here. After the pirates were eliminated and he was court-
martialed, the West India Anti-Pirate Squadron was trans-
ferred to Pensacola.

With the pirates gone, the only fears the captain of a vessel
had were hurricanes and running aground on the reefs, a likeli-
hood that Key West profited from, for they made the salvaging
of wrecked ships a regulated industry. Between 1832, the year
John James Audubon dropped by, and 1855, the population of
the island had risen from 500 to 2,700, most of them New En-

glanders or English Bahamians, almost all involved in wrecking. Millions of dollars' worth of salvage cases involving ships wrecked on the reefs were being adjudicated in Key West courts by the city's own Judge William Marvin, who literally wrote the book on salvage laws, *A Treatise Upon the Law of Wreck and Salvage,* the standard authority in the admiralty courts of both England and the United States. (The Judge's other work was on the internal evidences of the authenticity of the Four Gospels.) It was an educated and colorful group on this tiny island far from mainland America, this place that the poet Richard Eberhart calls "umbilically extravagant." The men wore silk top hats, the ladies served suppers on fine china—on occasion, gold plates. All the wealth was wrecking wealth. Indeed, much of the exotic furnishings that filled the houses, and the formal clothes the people wore, came directly from the foundered ships.

Ava Parks, in her book *The Forgotten Frontier,* wrote about the Key West of the time:

> There was nothing else like it; a city crowded on a small island in the middle of nowhere . . . this was it—civilization began and ended here.

By the end of the 1850's, however, the first of the reef lighthouses (pages 77–79) was being constructed, bringing the beginning of the end to the profitability of wrecking, and in 1859 the look of the town was changed when the first of Key West's two great fires occurred.

There was no fire-fighting equipment in town. There had been a small hand-pump engine, used mostly for parades, which, failing to be effective against a small fire in 1843, was carried to the wharf by irate citizens and thrown into the water. The fire of 1859 began in a warehouse on Front Street and Duval and gutted two square blocks before it was stopped when a man named Henry Mulrennon got a keg of gunpowder from Fort Taylor and blew up his own house on Greene Street. The town was rebuilt quickly, and many people felt that the fire had been a benefit rather than a liability because the new structures were more "elegant." Key West's newspaper of the day, *The Key of the Gulf,* said the new buildings were "not only an ornamental embellishment but gave an air of permanency and durability to the town."

Wealth no longer came from wrecking but from a new discovery, sponging. Cubans were also emigrating in great numbers from their country's ten-year war with Spain, and cigar manufacturers were establishing large factories here and employing thousands of men. The town was a great mélange and somewhat baffling to casual visitors, one of whom wrote in the 1880's:

> It is densely settled, and about as un-American as possible, bearing a strong resemblance to a West Indian town. The houses are of wood, plainly built, and, with few exceptions, painted white. The houses are of all sizes, jumbled up in the oddest way. . . . The interior of each block is filled up with one-story shanties. . . .

On April 1, 1886, the second and great fire engulfed Key West. It started in the Cuban patriotic club and school, the San Carlos, on Duval Street. (The building of today is the third San Carlos to be built on that site.) The town's single fire engine was in New York for repairs (it's *still* hard to find a good mechanic in Key West) and the fire quickly spread, burning the same area as before along the waterfront as well as turning inland, destroying Fleming Street from Whitehead to Bahama. Once more, an attempt was made to stop the fire by blowing up houses with kegs of gunpowder from the fort, but this time the blaze raged on and the three sailors who lit the fuse were "blown to atoms." The fire burned for twelve hours, consuming fifty acres of the town. Again, Key West was rebuilt quickly, carpenters working day and night, building homes on the outskirts but bringing them into the burned-out areas once they were cleared. The peculiar thing, of course, is that after both fires, the town was rebuilt in wood, with the wealthier citizens building even grander homes than they had occupied before. There were some commercial, military, or public buildings made of stone and well-laid brick and a few homes made of cast or "rusticated" stone, a concrete block formed in a mold—a fad of the mainland which came quickly in and out of fashion. (Several of these houses, large and side by side, can be found on South Street, near the Southernmost Point.) But Key West was a wooden town, and when the town abruptly stopped growing early in the twentieth century, wooden it remained. Silence entered the picture—a deep and sleepy silence. Nothing happened. The Florida land boom boomed but was unheard in Key West. The railroad came and the railroad went and Key West slumbered behind its vines and flowers. The trees grew and blew in the heat-thickened wind, and termites sculpted their own interior columns and castles out of porches undisturbed.

COLLAPSE AND RESURRECTION, COLLAPSE AND RESTORATION

From being the richest city per capita in America in the 1880's, Key West by the 1930's had become the poorest. The sponge industry had declined; the cigar makers had moved to Tampa; the railroad and shipping trade with Havana had diminished; and the Navy and the Coast Guard had pulled out. Henry Flagler's train chugged across the waters "carrying nothing, nowhere, for nobody." Things were so bad that the city's Economic League recommended that only bread baked in Key West be allowed to be sold here and only local orchestras be allowed to play.

On July 5, 1934, with no economic base other than fish, five million dollars in debt, and with 80 percent of its 12,000 citizens on welfare, Key West relinquished all its powers of government to the state. The governor, David Sholtz, was aghast. He immediately turned the problem over to the New Deal's Federal Relief Administrator in Florida, Julius Stone. Stone arrived in Key West and saw the abandoned cigar factories and Navy barracks, the collapsed piers and dilapidated houses. He saw the privys, the cisterns, and the trash, and learned that most of the people were living on fish and coconuts. He also learned that Key West was the only city in America never to have frost. He decided that the only way to save her was to turn her into a resort town, a "Bermuda" as it were. Key West's salvation was to be The Tourist.

Stone was a debonair fellow and a flashy administrator, using FERA funds to subsidize air service and to underwrite the rehabilitation of houses and the reopening of hotels. He organized the Volunteer Work Force to spruce up the town and in six months, four thousand people had donated a million and a half hours, planting trees, building a thousand park benches, painting murals, and shoring up houses. The beaches were cleaned of seaweed and a "smart cabana colony made available." A Maids' Training School was established, with the few remaining grande dames of Key West tutoring young girls in the cleaning and serving arts. There was also a school for fishing guides. Out-of-work musicians were recruited into the Hospitality Band, which met every arriving ship and train. The submarine base, abandoned by the Navy, was turned into a private yacht basin. (A nice and nasty description of the yachty set is in Hemingway's novel *To Have and Have Not.*)

Key West needed a lot of cleaning up. There was trash everywhere, tons of trash. There is always someone who likes to figure out the quantity of one thing in terms of the quantity of another, and trash is no exception. A writer of the time drew this picture:

Or, if someone had constructed small bungalows, say, 42 feet × 20 with a 9-foot ceiling, the garbage and trash would have filled 176 such bungalows. Figuring eight lots to each side of a city block, such procedure would have necessitated five solid city blocks of bungalows!

There was a lot of trash and it was hauled off and put somewhere, if not in five blocks of newly built bungalows.

Classes in handicrafts were organized and people set to work making hats, pocketbooks, and belts out of coconut fronds, and ash trays and buttons out of shells. A guidebook was published touting the attractions which included the Southernmost House, the Martello Towers, and the Turtle Kraals, as well as "Raul Vasquez's tame fish." The fish were in a pond at the rear of his nightclub on Roosevelt, and one could stroke them as one "would a cat." Also mentioned was the home of a retired schoolteacher, Miss Dunn:

The house, with Miss Dunn still residing within, stands as a monument to the appreciation of her students.

(Actually, Miss Dunn's house, at 420 Simonton Street, may be the oldest house in Key West. If it was built around 1823, as is suspected, it would be older than the "Oldest House" on Duval.)

Fifty-three attractions were mentioned; many of them, including various tropical parks and the magnificent Convent of Mary Immaculate, are now gone. There were also listings of fishing guides, churches, and mixed drinks.

Julius Stone even specified how long a visitor should be prepared to stay:

> To appreciate Key West with its indigenous architecture, its lanes and byways, its friendly people and general picturesqueness, the visitor must spend at least a few days in the city; a cursory tour of an hour or two serves no good purpose. Unless a visitor is prepared to spend at least three full days here, the Key West Administration would rather he did not come.

Stone's experiment in massive volunteerism, which turned a bankrupt and shabby city into a vacation mecca, was wildly successful. Tourists poured in and the demand for accommodations was so great that residents moved out of their houses and lived elsewhere in order that winter visitors might have the more desirable locations, a practice, certainly, that exists today. But only six months after the best tourist season Key West had ever had, the Labor Day hurricane of 1935 hit the Middle Keys and blew the railroad away. And tourism was forgotten for many years.

As for Julius Stone, the man who introduced Bermuda shorts to the Keys (Conchs maintained it was his underwear), in 1940 he returned to live in the city he had saved, involving himself in investment, banking, and law. In the next twenty years, as leading citizen, he had managed to represent and bilk just about everyone in town. In 1960, the master of the shady deal fled, practically as a fugitive, settling first in Cuba, later in Jamaica, and dying in 1967 in Australia.

It took World War II to bring people and prosperity back. In those randy war years, Key West became known as the "Singapore of the West." The Navy swept up the town in a dizzying, flustering embrace, but after the war, abandoned her once again, and Key West looked more dilapidated than ever. It had entered its own time zone once again—the old houses in Old Town jostling together in eccentric neglect, the roots of banyans erupting through sidewalks, the docks rotting, the streets deserted and silent.

In the late 1950's, things began to change. Action arrived in the guise of destruction. Demolition began to follow dereliction. Fine old buildings were razed and an unseemly demand for vacant lots for parking arose. The handsome Jefferson Hotel on Duval Street with its cupolas and wide verandas, built in 1886, burned and was demolished in 1958 to create the drive-up window facilities for the Southeast Bank.

In 1958, the Geiger House on the corner of Greene and Whitehead was slated to be demolished so a gas station could be put there. It was this possibility of loss, more than any other, that finally roused Key West. Jessie Porter Newton, a fifth generation Conch, invited some wealthy and influential people into her garden, and the Old Island Restoration Foundation was formed. Their first act was to purchase (with the help of millionaire Mitchell Wolfson) the Geiger House and restore and transform it into the Audubon House. Miss Jessie was instrumental in saving and moving dozens of houses, but even her energy and the increasing effectiveness of the OIRF as a lobbying and preservationist group could not prevent fire and bulldozers from leveling some of Key West's most beautiful structures. The huge Curry and Sons Ship's Chandlery, a twin-towered landmark for more than seventy-five years, taking up an entire block on Simonton and Front streets, burned in 1963, and the beautiful Convent of Mary Immaculate on Truman Avenue was destroyed despite wails of protest in 1966. The convent is probably the most-mourned lost building in Key West, and Conchs, many of whom were educated here, still speak of its demolition with bitterness. It was made of coral rock and took years to build, first completed in 1886, then enlarged to twice its size in 1906. It was a rounded, graceful, airy structure surrounded by rose gardens and palms. The wounded from the battleship *Maine* were brought here, and it served as a Navy hospital throughout the Spanish-American War before being turned back into a school. There was a large museum inside the convent, filled with relics of the *Maine* and a number of oddities including a little wooden chest covered with seashells that Dr. Samuel Mudd had made when he was imprisoned in Fort Jefferson on the Dry Tortugas. It seemed that no one wanted the convent torn down except the Catholic Bishop of Miami, who was determined to put up more modern concrete-block classrooms. Many fragments of the convent—fanlights, gingerbread trim, shutters—can be found in various homes in Key West today, and over the convent grounds, beside St. Mary Star of the Sea Church, the after-image of the lovely structure seems to hover in the empty air.

Each year, during February and March, the OIRF sponsors house and garden tours as part of "Old Island Days" celebrations. The houses are shown in groups of five or six and there are three separate tour dates. Tickets cost $10. There have been four categories of houses established—Old Historic, Uniquely Located, Famous Occupants, and Island Living. This covers a lot of territory, so don't expect to see merely "classic" homes—the selections have a fine Key West eccentricity. The OIRF-sponsored **Hospitality House** (294–9501) in Mallory Square can give you current brochures and information on the house and garden tours and other seasonal events. The Hospitality House is the former ticket office for the Mallory Steamship Company, which used to ferry passengers to Cuba.

TOURIST TOWN

Mallory Square is difficult, perhaps impossible, to experience with style. It certainly is no place to pretend you're not a tourist. Hundreds of gallons of ice cream and piña coladas are consumed here daily, and the streets are jammed with curio shops and bad restaurants. At the newly *re*-refurbished Mallory Square Dock, enormous white cruise ships take turns in waiting out the day. Almost three hundred of them visit Key West each year. They loom above the town, making everything appear Lilliputian, including the already toylike Conch Train.

The square is named for Stephen Mallory, a prominent Key West citizen who in 1861 was appointed Secretary of the Confederate Navy, a job, it is true, grander in illusion than in fact.

The little Civil War monument is dedicated in turn to the Union. In Key West, the soldiers who died during the war died from yellow fever. There are some dignified old buildings here which seem to stand back a bit, bemused at all the bustle. The large brick Romanesque Revival **Customs House** was built in 1891 and served as the federal courthouse during the Keys' wrecking years. On the National Register of Historic Places, it has now been restored as a museum. The buff-plastered brick building beside it was built even earlier, in 1856, and was originally used to store coal. It is the sole surviving building from the earliest naval base in Key West. It is referred to as **Coast Guard Headquarters** for its last tenants, but the building also served as headquarters for the Lighthouse District when that now defunct organization administered the reef system of man-tended lights. The niche above the arch on the buttressed pier façade is filled with the bas-relief decoration of a lighthouse. Another impressive structure here, built in the same year as the Customs House, and of the same seemingly untropical brick, is the **First National Bank Building**. Built by Cuban cigar manufacturers, the decorative yellow design on red and the ornate balcony is in the style of Havana architecture.

Trinket traps fill the Mallory Market area, and there are also a number of dummies standing about; not dolts but rather statues of old sea captains and bearded fishermen holding aloft sponges or shells. Sponges abound, big drab heaps of sponges. The big ones are splendid to plant ferns in.

SPONGES

A sponge is a living marine animal of uniform structure, though varying greatly in appearance, that grows in a plant-like fashion and is remarkable for its power of absorbing water. Keys' spongers would go out in skiffs, spot the creatures in the shallows through a glass-bottom bucket, pull them up with a long-handled three-pronged hook, then beat the bejesus out of them with a paddle. A phosphorous-smelling liquid called "gurry" would ooze out of them until it didn't, then the sponges (now the skeletons of the animal) were rinsed and trimmed.

A lady named Violet Turner recalled her daddy, sponging:

"To identify these horrible looking black creatures isn't that simple," Violet noted. "They are sleeping in the beds at the bottom of the sea. An amateur would assume they were merely seaweed. It is so fascinating to see how the spongers would lower their long poles with a hook on the end to the bottom of the bed and extract the creature with many eyes. After the dinghy is filled, the men head back to the mama boat to kill their catch. They are alive and must die to become useful and beautiful."

Sponging and cigar-making were Key West's primary industries in the last half of the nineteenth century. The city provided 90 percent of all the sponges sold in the United States. There was a great demand for sponges. Everyone used them. There were hundreds of boats employing thousands of men harvesting millions of sponges for a great deal of money. When Greek divers came down from Tarpon Springs to work deeper waters in their suits and helmets in the early 1900's, walking over sponge beds in their heavy boots, the locals blamed them for the fact that there were fewer and fewer sponges to be had. There were battles between the two groups, boat-burning and hose-slashing and the like. In 1953 a movie was made, *Beneath the Twelve-Mile Reef.* Robert Wagner and Gilbert Roland were two of the Greeks. Terry Moore and Richard Boone were two of the Conchs. Robert Wagner and, of course, Terry Moore fell in love, an event which did not increase the number of little sponges one whit.

The Greeks eventually returned to Tarpon Springs, but the sponge supply remained depleted and in the 1930's a blight (some said caused by the dredging involved in the construction of Flagler's Railroad) and the introduction of artificial sponges virtually wiped out sponging as an industry.

Some of the last to buy them in any quantity were the Japanese. A sponger said in 1935 that he suspected there was going to be a war soon because of all the activity on the Elizabeth Street dock.

The price sponges bring in Key West right now is fantastic. . . . They surely must be planning a war before too long. That's always when we get our best prices, when a war is being planned. Especially sheepswool and glove sponge. They use a

> lot of those in hospitals. In a hospital they are used only for cleaning wounds, no lint to shed! They are much more sanitary and more absorbent than any other material. On the battlefield they are used for sponging and cleaning weapons. Nothing can stand that rough treatment as well as sponges. There are so many foreigners in Key West buying sponges . . . gotta be a war coming.
>
> Today, an occasional tourist buys an occasional sponge, probably one of three species—*the sheepswool* for bathing, *the yellow* for washing up the car, *the grass* for decoration. A sheepswool sponge about the size of a grapefruit costs $13.

Shopping, Warships, Time, the Conch Republic, and the Conch Train

Key West has become the T-shirt capital of the world; it is believed to have some forty-five T-shirt shops, some of them, like Beach Break at 501 Duval, being highly creative in their pricing. (There's no law against overcharging someone, of course.) Bars have T-shirts, bail-bond companies have T-shirts, even dry cleaners do. The grocery stores have T-shirts (You Can't Beat Our Meat). You can buy other things here, but it's becoming increasingly hard to do so.

On Duval at 721, **Machoti** has pretty clothes and leather bags. **Kudu** at 1208 sells flamboyant African jewelry and lovely kilims from Turkey. **Kokopelli Southwest Gallery** at 824 brings you New Mexico. **Swept Away** has three chic clothing stores, at 505, 605, and 1022. **Ocean Footwear** at 703 has a big selection of rugged but good-looking sandals. **Winter Sun** at 505 has pretty, filmy dresses and inexpensive sweaters. And **Fast Buck Freddie's** at 500 is a classic—their ever-changing display window is an event in itself.

From the Ruins at 219 Whitehead, down by the Mel Fisher Museum, has dramatically singular clothing for women. Maybe you'll find a totally new personality there. **Native Material** on Whitehead Street by The Green Parrot carries folk art, hammocks, and weavings from Guatemala.

In the Mallory Square–Front Street area, take a listen to the simple and melodious brass wind chimes at the **Shell Warehouse**, a rugged building of coral rock, part of what was once Tift's Ice House, the oldest commercial building in Key West. **Shades** at 306 Front is definitely the place for sunglasses with a hundred different styles and colors available, whereas **Sweet Mischief** (335 Duval) is where to go for the niftiest bikini. **The Cigar Factory** in Pirate's Alley is a microscopic touristic representation of a Key West industry that in 1890 employed more than six thousand workers and produced a hundred million hand-rolled cigars yearly. Two men now roll Honduran tobacco in the dim light. A box of "El Presidente" will set you back $50, but you can have "El Hemingway" for less. **Key West Hand Prints** at 201 Simonton is a silk-screening institution. The colors are mixed up in old Navy soup kettles. If you enjoy watching paint dry, you'll like seeing the printers working behind glass at 60-yard-long tables. There are a few chairs around in which exhausted men sit while their wives and granddaughters browse through the delicately colored skirts and sundresses. Lots of tea towel specials here. (A place for bolder hand-painted fabrics is **The Sign of Sandford** at 328 Simonton Street. Sandford designs fabrics for the decorating trade, but everything in the window is for sale, including the bright and witty hand-painted canvas beach chairs.) **The Saltwater Angler** at 219 Simonton is a sophisticated fly-fishing store with the best selection of reels and custom rods in town. The owner, Jeffrey Cardenas, a former flats guide, is an expert on the art and the waters. As well as gear, there are clothes and books and a bright green iguana named Emery traversing the merchandise (294-3248).

Key West Aloe at 524 Front is a Key West institution, even though the aloe, that soothing succulent, is imported from Haiti. The sights and smells in here are a bit overwhelming—so many perfumes vying for dominance—so much "White Ginger," "Black Coral," "Frangipani," and "Sexy Afternoon"—so many immaculately complexioned girls with long bright nails sweeping about in white lab coats. When one regains the street once more, the homely smells of seaweed, engine oil, and frying fish seem refreshing. There's a tiny public beach and boat ramp squeezed between the **Pier House** holdings and the high-

Bermuda design of the new **Hyatt** at the end of Simonton. There used to be nothing down here but gasoline storage tanks and the old and decidedly midscale **A&B Lobster House**. (No one's known to have gone to the A&B for years, but it determinedly anchors down this end of the island, just as the dim and dowdy **Logun's** anchors down the other end.) Things have changed, it's clear. **The Galleon** now takes up a lot of space, its dockage fees perhaps the highest in all Florida. Even sunning has become more expensive. Some locals and long-term visitors buy a Beach Club membership card at the Pier House. The club has an initiation fee and yearly dues, and the card enables you to enjoy the beach and pool and to charge drinks and food. You are also given a nice fluffy beach towel daily, towels in Paradise not being cheap.

In the '50's, the car-ferry **City of Key West** took passengers from Havana Docks (where the Pier House is now) to Cardenas, Cuba. She was later replaced by the **City of Havana**, which left from Stock Island. Many are looking forward to the resumption of ferry service to Cuba, an "exotic" destination. Things come and they go. In the '80's people lounging around the Pier House could see Navy hydrofoils churning past. Stationed at Trumbo Point, they prowled back and forth, to and from maneuvers in the Gulf, where they made their acrobatic turns and reversals and barreled about at classified speeds. Hydrofoils are agile and fast war vessels, each equipped with eight computerized surface-to-surface missiles and an assortment of rapid-fire machine guns. Because, thankfully, they had nothing to shoot these weapons at, they cruised the waters off Key West and intercepted drug boats, making the town no longer the primo port of call for drug smugglers that it once was. As a psychological weapon against a coke-laden cigarette boat, the hydrofoil was without peer. When the foils of these "flying ships" are deployed, they generate lift that raises the ship a few feet above the surface of the water, allowing it to move unhampered by the waves. A Navy commander said, "The Navy built this ship and now they're trying to find jobs it can do." They either never found out exactly what those jobs were or the hydrofoils were so expensive to operate that they became high-tech dinosaurs. In any case, all six of them were being decommissioned in 1993 and you will no longer see them passing by in their sinister fashion. They certainly were arresting-looking, but you're just going to have to enjoy your shockingly red strawberry daiquiri, mid-morning, waterside—without them.

At 512 Greene Street, a little behind Sloppy Joe's on Duval, is the handsome and recently restored **Old City Hall**. Built just at the turn of the century, it replaced a wooden City Hall that had burned in the fire of 1886. Only ten years before, that structure had been dedicated at the centennial Fourth of July celebration for which W. C. Maloney, a prominent citizen of the town, had prepared a speech. The speech, entitled "A Sketch of the History of Key West," which he later published, would have been three hours long. Midway in his presentation, however, a bar caught fire from one of the celebratory rockets that were being shot off, and Maloney's audience ran off to see the blaze, never to return.

Something called The Key West Torture Museum once had a stint here on the ground floor, and we all wish we had been around for that.

The Old City Hall has four large clock faces in its tower. Few people glance at them, though, thoughts of time being eschewed here.

A Navy hydrofoil

The Conch Republic

The Conch Republic was born on April 20, 1982, in reaction to
roadblocks set up by the border patrol near Florida City. The
federal government maintained they were screening for drugs
and illegal aliens, and everyone leaving the Keys was stopped
and questioned. After insult came annoyance at the long
delays, then protests in the form of lawsuits and letters to the
governor. Then came inspiration, the idea of secession, followed
immediately by plans for a party. On April 23, at high noon in
Mallory Square, there were secession ceremonies. A Key West
flag was invented and raised; the establishment of a new republic was marked with speeches; a loaf of stale Cuban bread was
tossed in the air as a token shot declaring war against the
United States; and then the Conch Republic quickly surrendered in order to be eligible for foreign aid from the state of
Florida. There were T-shirts of course, and flags and border
passes and passports. And there was a party which lasted a
week. "Conch Republic Days" have now become an annual
event each April, with parades, dances, powerboat races, and a
very peculiar *bed* race in which teams of five people decorate
beds which must consist of four wheels, a mattress, and themselves, and race down Duval Street with four team members
pushing the bed and one riding on it. Prizes, of course, are
awarded to the winner, as well as for the most creative bed.

The Conch Train

The Conch Train is a pretty curious number. Imagine a little
amusement park train with open cars and a fringed top, pulled
by a Jeep camouflaged to look like a locomotive, rattling through
the streets of a living town (not a theme park, not a wildlife
safari, but a *real* town), the driver babbling about trees, houses,
gingerbread, cisterns, hydrofoils, presidents, and emeralds.
The train goes past bars, and little old men rocking on porches,
and ladies watering palms in the graveyard, and mustached
cruisers wearing shorts and thigh-high black lace-up boots, the
driver babbling all the while. You don't have to imagine this, of

The Conch Train

course, because the improbable thing exists and has since 1958 been faithfully serving tourists from 9 A.M. to 4 P.M. daily.

The train was Bill and Olive Kroll's idea. They were running the aquarium, the first tourist "attraction" in town and just about the only one in the 1940's. Built in the 1930's with Federal Emergency Relief Funds, it was abandoned during World War II while the Navy used it as a pistol range. The Krolls took pictures of the way it was and put it back together again, stocking it with the funny looking fish that the local fishermen would bring them. People would pay a quarter, stare at the fish, and ask the Krolls what else they could do to wile away the afternoon. Where do we eat? What else is there to look at around here? They had a lot of questions. What is that weird tree with those *things* dangling from it? Where does Harry Truman get those shirts? What's that big pile of bricks out by the beach? Why isn't the lighthouse on the water? Such a tiny town and so many questions! Bill Kroll realized that there was a thirst for information, *accurate* information if possible, that the town's cab drivers were often loath to provide. (For a taxi today, info still not 100-percent-guaranteed, call 296-6666 or 294-2222.) He decided to get into the sight-seeing business, patterning his vehicle on something he had seen once in, of all places, Helena, Montana. The Conch Train, hauled by its little propane-powered Jeeps, proved to be far more profitable than Henry Flagler's venture. The Krolls have sold the train, but the spiel remains pretty constant after all these years. Pirates are mentioned, and cigars, and sponges, and Ponce de León. The new owner owns all the taxis too, and the Trolley. The Trolley is warmer in cold weather and drier in wet and is somewhat more nimble than the train (it can pick up passengers at certain motels and it drops them off at certain attractions) but the itinerary and route are similar. But it is not the train. It is definitely not the weird little train.

You needn't feel embarrassed riding the Conch Train. A strange cloak of invisibility is dropped over your self as you board. Once in a while a tourist will take a picture of you, a tourist on the Conch Train, but mostly no one pays the slightest attention to this contraption whirring down the streets, the driver repeating outlandish jokes without the slightest trace of shame.

> . . . on your right is the only free hotel in Key West, the county jail . . . and on your left is a famous old bar which used to be the city morgue. You'll still find old stiffs hanging out there . . .

On one modest little street that must be working out some unfortunate karma, the driver talks about crotons. Unfortunately, there is a clump of crotons growing on this street. Now, crotons grow all over Key West, indeed all over Florida, but this is the street where all the Conch Train drivers in the world, a dozen times daily, mention the croton and its medicinal properties. Its purgative qualities actually. Its use in a tiny chocolate bar called Ex-Lax. ". . . Don't laugh, folks, you didn't laugh when you needed it. . . ."

Sixty subjects are covered in the course of the tour, including a listing of all the ways in which "Conch" is used—the high school athletic teams are called Conchs, the drill team Conchettes, a Conch Cruiser is a dilapidated Key West car bought for less than $500 . . . and so on. The passengers listen, earnestly invisible. *See,* the driver states, *Ernest Hemingway's home and feel the personality of the man radiate around you.* It's hard to know how much radiating gets through. What you see as a passenger on the train are people milling in the Hemingway gardens, taking pictures, milling. After passing the airport and the houseboats nosed up to the sidewalk on South Roosevelt Boulevard, the train takes a boring jog down Flagler through the development of new homes there. There is not

much to talk about here. The driver is reduced to talking about
fill. He talks quite a bit about fill and how much of the island is
built upon fill, and what fill is. The driver never stops talking,
actually. You will deboard almost refreshed, invisibility being
quite relaxing. **Conch Tour Trains** leave from two depots—
Mallory Square and Roosevelt Avenue at U.S. #1. One and a
half hours. Frequent departures daily 9–4. Adults $11.

Sunset

In the Keys, the best place to ponder the descending globe of
gas, our sun, is just about any place other than Mallory Square,
where actually only a small wedge of horizon is visible.
Audubon beheld a few sunsets in the Keys and couldn't get over
them. "A blaze of refulgent glory streams through the portals of
the west," he wrote, "and the masses of vapor assume the sem-
blance of mountains of molten gold." The sun, as we know,
appears to grow larger as it sinks in the west. This is one of the
many illusions which nature presents, perhaps, as a children's
astronomy book suggests, "to sharpen our wits in deciding
between sights that are real and those that only seem to be." At
Mallory Square, the sunset definitely plays second fiddle to the
unreal people and events that accompany it. In order to get
your attention, a young man will lie on a bed of nails, place a
concrete block over his groin, and have someone shatter the
block with a sledgehammer. You can buy a freshly woven palm
hat and see some white cockatoos. You can't pet an iguana anymore because the Iguana Man died and the iguanas don't come
down to see sunset by themselves. You can buy a chocolate chip
cookie. You can watch a rather saucer-eyed cat jump through a
flaming hoop. You can watch fire-eaters and jugglers, some of
them quite talentless. Everything is giddy and determinedly
carefree. And everyone is there . . . breakdancers and frightful
bikers . . . little kids and deeply tanned weirdos . . . old ladies in
their Lily dresses and guests from the Casa in their tennis
whites . . . college students in their Bahama Mama buzz . . .
    The hippies began this sunset viewing in the 1960's when
they congregated here to pound drums and smoke dope. Now
the camera is king. If you don't have a camera you will probably

be elbowed away from various sights by those who do. The pier itself has been refitted for part of the new cruiseport facility. The mayor had to promise sunset devotees that whatever gargantuan ship will be docked there will have left each day before the sun goes down. The crowds mob this congested spot. Street entertainers quarrel with parking lot attendants. Merchants quarrel with street vendors. The City Commission, wanting sunset "to be maintained," has set up a committee to explore the possibility of an alternative site for sunset activities. The sunset has become something of a problem.

Key West Aquarium

Your Favorite Seafoods Alive! The oldest attraction in Key West, it was once open to the sky, with individual coral tanks for the fishes. An admission ticket is good for several days so you can wander in more than once if you're at terribly loose ends. Kids come back often. It's one of the few things available for them in Key West—the town not exactly being Toys "R" Us. There are some very wiggy fishes in here. The big-eyed, flaccid porcupine fish, for example, which has no fish enemy. If anything tries to swallow it, it just puffs up and the predator gags to death. The Atlantic guitar fish, the sawfish, the peculiar reef squid, all representing life as we certainly do not know it. The butterfly fish, with splotches of color near the tail resembling eyes, draws would-be attackers to the wrong end of itself. The coral-crunching colorful parrotfish with its big bright lips wedges itself between rocks and secretes a gelatinous cocoon of mucus around its body when it goes to sleep at night. Fish, if not exactly leading rich emotional lives, have developed some very peculiar characteristics. The old shallow coral pools are used as well as glass-wall tanks and a deep outside pen where there are turtles and tarpon. The tarpon have been here for years but are small, not growing because there's no room for them to grow. At one point there was a good-sized permit, which some selfless angler had donated, in the enclosure. Outside, there's the usual array of cats and pelicans.

There are half-hour tours four times a day, much of the talk eliciting enthusiastic "yarggghs" and "yuks" from the kids.

There's a touch tank, and the feeding of lemon, blacktip, and bonnethead sharks. You can pet a barracuda, and pick up a sea cucumber and watch it squirt—the Conchs don't call them "sea pissers" for nothing. You might be able to identify some of the fish you've seen on the reef in here, but the multitude of wild water life in the Keys is vast and enigmatic, and the number of species in here represents only a small percentage of the variety out there. People often come in and try to explain what it was they saw, not realizing how strange it actually was, or how difficult to describe. Open 10 A.M.–7 P.M. Adults $5. Kids seven and under, free.

Truman Annex

Just off Mallory Square, behind the iron gates on Greene Street, is **Truman Annex**, forty-three acres which became highly controversial when the Navy deemed it surplus property and put it up for sale. The Navy had been annexing the land piece by piece for over a century and it had been off-limits to the town for almost fifty years.

The oldest building in the annex is the **U.S. Marine Hospital**, built in 1844. It was designed by Robert Mills who was the architect for the Washington Monument. The high, steep steps which distinguish it seem ill-suited for a hospital entry, but the building originally stood directly on the water and patients were brought by boat to the rear.

In September 1986 the Navy conducted an auction of the land and all its buildings. Many came ready to bid, including a group of Eskimos, but it was purchased by a 36-year-old rich Sikh from Maine named Pritam Singh for $17.25 million. Singh seems a democratic sort, although he frequently, unnervingly, refers to his "covenant" with the people of Key West. He wears a turban and has a sparse beard even though he hasn't shaved it since he was seventeen. He razed a number of buildings that had been running down for years with Key West panache but rehabilitated the ones most important from a military or historical perspective. His plan was a mix of condos, residences, and shops, all mixed in with amazing trees (two of the most fabulous banyans in Key West live in the Annex), white-picket fences, walkways, and parks, everything architecturally correct and lavishly landscaped. He promises not a chicken in every pot but a hibiscus tree in every yard. Other plans included an 80-slip marina (flanked on one side by the town's cruise-ship dock and on the other by the Navy's port, recently expanded and deepened to accommodate warships—pleasure and war having apparently been judged compatible); the transformation of the Romanesque Revival Customs House, the most imposing structure on Mallory Square, into a yacht club; and the development of Tank Island, the 27-acre spoil island created by the Navy to hold its fuel tanks. Singh's plans were for a hotel to pop up here—a Ritz-Carlton hotel no less—all turreted white clapboardy gingerbread Victorian with a pitched roof and French door. Mullions and millions. His plans were for aviaries and croquet courts and instant jungles too. He worried that the "sleaze factor in Key West" would keep this all from happening. But it wasn't the sleaze factor that has so far prevented all this fancy development of Tank—it was the end of the boom '80's. The Customs House, restored beautifully right up to its screaming watermelon-pink roof, will be a dignified museum, and the plan for humble Tank, now renamed Sunset Island, is to fill it up with mere houses. Lovely houses, of course. In 1994 a seaplane from Chalks Airlines, which has flown people for years to the Dry Tortugas as well as to Miami and the Bahamas, crashed off here, tragically killing both pilots.

The development of the Annex property has now been pretty much completed, and it seems a bit more congested than envisioned.

The Treasure Salvors

The large raised stone building near the Greene Street gate to the Annex is an old Naval storage building, home of **Mel Fisher's Treasure Exhibit**. Fisher is a successful computer-age salvor whose most spectacular discoveries were the gold-and-silver laden Spanish galleons the *Nuestra Senora de Atocha* and the *Santa Margarita,* which sank in a hurricane in 1622.

The Spanish referred to all the Florida Keys as Matecumbe, and for some time Fisher and his Treasure Salvors searched the

THE LITTLE WHITE HOUSE

Built in 1890 as the Naval Commandant's Quarters, this comfy structure is recognizable by its symmetrical double façade and its encircling porches enclosed by wooden louvers. President Harry Truman first came here in 1946 and returned ten times for vacations during his administration, arriving at the Boca Chica air station on the presidential plane *Sacred Cow*. Truman enjoyed walking around town buying coffee with autographed dollar bills, eating coconut cake which was made especially for him by a Miss Etta Patterson, and playing a great deal of poker. His habits also included swimming (no one in The Little White House was allowed to flush during these ablutions) and being downstairs in the kitchen every morning at seven for a shot of bourbon followed by a glass of orange juice, a practice which, it was said, "always astonished" the Filipino housekeepers. The tour, including a video, is half an hour and costs $5. The guide is earnest. Truman the Human played Chopin, he'll say. Truman the Human wrote Bess every day, every day without fail when he was away from her. He and Bess were poor, humble, simple folk, he'll say. Bess wasn't poor, a woman from Independence says. Yes she was, the guide says. No she wasn't, she was certainly not poor, she was very well-off, the woman says. Oh well, the guide says. Another tourist, a boy in a Just Do Me T-shirt, doesn't know who to believe. He studies the poker table, a magnificent poker table. An alarm is supposed to go off if you sit in any of the chairs but it usually doesn't.

Another structure that more peculiarly carries the old haberdasher's name is the **Harry S. Truman Import Center** on Fleming Key, off the Trumbo Point Annex of the Naval Air Station. This considerably creepy-looking structure is a quarantine center for animals imported into Florida. Its uneasy guests have included llamas, hogs, birds, and water buffalo.

waters off Matecumbe for the *Atocha*. Wrecks which had previously been discovered were in an area between Key Largo and Long Key, and most had been salvaged by the Spanish themselves, who had mapped their locations. The correct sites of the *Atocha* and *Margarita* wrecks, 100 miles south of the area in which they had been searching, were discovered by a historian going through seventeenth-century Spanish documents in the archives in Seville. The manifests of the ships indicated that they had been loaded with over forty-seven tons of gold and silver from the mines of Potosí, Lima, Mexico City, and Bogotá. The galleons had gone down within miles of each other, the *Atocha* on a shallow reef in fifty-five feet of water, the *Margarita* on a wide shoal, an area referred to as the Quicksands. Fisher discovered some of the wealth of the *Atocha* as early as the 1970's—gold and silver bars, gold chains up to 8 1/2 feet long, coins, crucifixes, and navigational devices, the most important being the ship's astrolabe, a precursor to the sextant.

As of early 1985, however, only a small portion of the *Atocha*'s treasure had been found. The wreck had scattered, most of its cargo lying beneath twenty feet of sand and shell. Most of what had been retrieved was contraband gold, smuggled on board and not listed on the manifest at all. Still to be found too was a suspected, but unlisted, seventy pounds of raw emeralds. Almost daily, the Treasure Salvors were out searching for the "Big Pile" with their divers, ships, and planes, plotting and mapping, scanning inch by inch the ocean bottom with magnetometers, sub-bottom profilers, and side-scan sonar, and moving sand with their "mailboxes," a device of Fisher's which forces the wash from a boat's propeller down through an elbow-shaped tube aimed directly into the sand.

On Memorial Day 1985, thirteen gold bars, sixteen emeralds mounted in gold, and piles of pieces of eight were discovered, but it was not until July 20, when divers found a telltale wall of ballast stones about five feet high and began bringing up hundreds of silver bars, that it was known that the "Big Pile," the mother lode, the largest shipwreck treasure in the world, had at last been found.

The yield is enormous—large, loaf-shaped silver bars (forty-seven tons of silver alone have been recovered), gold bars, and chests of coins—and is all being cleaned by an electrolytic reduction process and catalogued on the upper floors of the Treasure Exhibit with typical Key West insouciance by a large staff. More exciting even than the gold is the recent emerald bonanza; thousands have now been found. The divers put their first discoveries in a Mr. Peanut quart jar. As for the site itself,

Pieces of eight (Spanish silver)

forty miles southwest of Key West, it is protected from possible piracy by a great deal of potential muscle. Mel Fisher says, "We have instant direct scrambled communications and on a moment's notice can have Navy dive bombers, hydrofoils, radar blimps, Coast Guard helicopters, marine patrol boats, and lots of other security on the spot."

All this is heady, even giddy, stuff, but the typical visitor to the Treasure Exhibit does not, in fact, see a great deal of the *Atocha* discovery. It is a huge building, and one might think one would be wandering around for hours viewing tons of artifacts, but the exhibit is small, all taking place in a single, curving, dark room. There is some gold and silver prettily displayed on sand and velvet and some impressive globs of silver coins fused in the shape of the mahogany boxes they had been carried in. Each chest contained 2,500 coins. There is also a gleaming exhibit of silver bars. The most interesting items are a gold bar which one can heft by worming one's hand through a small hole—a solid gold "anti-assassin" cup with handles in the shape of dolphins and space in the pedestal to hold a bezoar stone, which was meant to absorb and be an antidote to arsenic—and an $8\frac{1}{2}$-foot gold chain brought up by diver-photographer Don Kincaid. Kincaid was new on the job as Treasure Salvor when he discovered the heavy chain bright as the day it was in 1622 when the *Atocha* went down. He thought that the other divers had planted it there to tease him. Gold remains impervious to time and seawater, but silver will corrode—thin silver coins becoming big as biscuits from calciferous buildup. As part of the exhibit there is also a long-winded National Geographic film concerning the Treasure Salvors which plays all day with a

wheezing soundtrack, and a gift shop where you can buy shipwreck coins and T-shirts with Mel Fisher's trademark cry
Today's the Day imprinted on them. Most of the treasure
remains at the bottom of the ocean still, to protect the value of
what has been brought up.

Mel Fisher's Treasure Exhibit, 200 Greene Street. 10–6.
Admission: $5. Children under seven, $1.

The Audubon House

Across the street at 205 Whitehead is the **Audubon House**.
Audubon was ubiquitous, seemingly sleeping in as many places
as George Washington. But the fact is, Audubon did not sleep
here, in the Geiger Home on Whitehead Street, nor did he even
step inside the door. According to a sketch made by William
Adee Whitehead in 1838, no two-story house existed on the site.
Audubon spent only a brief time here in 1832 and probably
spent most of his time on the vessel *Marion*. There were but five
hundred people living in Key West then and only eighty-one
buildings of any note. Captain John Geiger is not so much as
mentioned by Audubon in his journals, even though he had
been a pilot for Commodore Porter and was supposed to be such
a wit that his sayings were referred to as "Geigerisms."

The Audubon House *was*, however, built by Captain John
Geiger sometime in the 1830's and possibly moved to this site.
Geiger was a wrecker who furnished his home with treasures
salvaged from foundered ships. He introduced the Geiger tree
(Cordia sebestena) to Key West from the West Indies. He must
have been interested in this tree, since it possessed the same
name as he did (no one knows who the *real* Geiger was). He
planted it in his front yard, where the much-pruned specimen
with its pretty orange blossoms is extravagantly noted today.
The captain had many children, and his descendants lived in
the house until 1956, the last one being a drunken hermit
named Willy Smith.

Audubon's host and helpmate in Key West was one Benjamin
Strobel, a doctor, newspaper editor, and amateur ornithologist.

It was Strobel who procured the Geiger twig that Audubon used in his painting of the white-crowned pigeon. In his newspaper, Strobel enthusiastically wrote of Audubon:

> It is impossible to associate with him without catching some portion of his spirit; he is surrounded with an atmosphere which infects all who come within it, with a mania for bird killing and bird stuffing.

Audubon indeed had a mania. Though his name has become synonymous with wildlife preservation, he was in no way at any time concerned with conservation. He killed tirelessly for sport and amusement as well as for his art, and he considered it to be a very poor day's hunting in Florida if he shot less than a hundred birds. From St. Augustine he wrote:

> We have drawn seventeen different species since our arrival in Florida, but the species are now exhausted and therefore I will push off. . . .

Audubon shot thousands of birds and never in his mind made the connection between the wholesale slaughter he so earnestly engaged in and their decreasing number, although in his forties he did begin complaining about the scarcity of mammals and birds for his studies. "Where can I go now," he grumbled, "and visit nature undisturbed?"

It is ironic that the Audubon Society has taken as their standard the name of a man who had no interest in the survival of the birds he so painstakingly drew and that the Audubon House, which is worthy because it began the preservation and restoration movement in Key West, was a home which Audubon never visited.

The two birds which are connected to Key West in *Birds of America* are both pigeons, although the Key West pigeon, which he named for the town, was actually a dove. The detailed background painting of Key West that is behind the great white heron, Audubon's prize find on his trip to the Keys, was done separately by George Lehman, a Swiss landscape painter who accompanied Audubon on his southern trip aboard the *Marion*.

Three of the birds done on the trip were sketched in the Dry Tortugas—the noddy tern, the sooty tern, and the brown booby.

In all, 1,065 birds appeared on 435 plates in Audubon's masterwork, the Double-Elephant Folio (so called because of the size of the paper, 40 × 30 inches, double the size of an ordinary folio sheet) of *Birds of America.* The engraving, printing, and coloring of the plates took eleven years and was done in England by Robert Havell and his son. Around 175 complete sets were published, and the Audubon House had one on display for a while but someone stole it. It was later recovered but is now being exhibited at an ostensibly more secure location in Miami.

What you do see in the Audubon House are delicate ceramic pieces of warblers, flycatchers, and wrens by the English artist Dorothy Dowdy, who was commissioned by Royal Wooster in London after World War II to produce collection sets to be sold to help relieve England's war debts; a dozen framed bird prints; and antiques "typical of the period." Upstairs, on a self-guided tour, you trip a recording device as you enter the bedroom and a voice comes booming out from beneath the mattress, talking about shaving mirrors, Queen Anne footstools, and "m'Lady's hipbath." A film describing the Double-Elephant Folio is shown on a small screen in one room. A small, very pale, and very dusty stuffed roseate spoonbill perches disconsolately on a desk just inside the door of another. Its presence here is carefully explained. It was not tracked down and shot by a bird fancier but "found in Key Largo, tangled in wires and choked to death." There is also a photograph of Audubon's shovel-jawed wife Lucy, who once wrote, "I have a rival in every bird." **Audubon House and Gardens**, corner Whitehead and Greene. Daily 9 A.M.–noon and 1 P.M.–5. Adults $6. The gardens are very lovely.

Caroline Street

Caroline begins in official pomp at the wrought-iron presidential gates on Whitehead Street, moves regally past shaded, stately homes for several blocks, turns abruptly into homely marine practicality, and dead-ends at the City Electric stacks.

Its variability is pure Key West, for here is a history of mansions and rough bars, turtle slaughterhouses and pretty little lanes.

Just opposite the gates is the old **Airways Building**, the former home of Aero-Marine Airways, which flew passengers and mail to Cuba in the early 1920's. Each flight would carry a passenger pigeon, to be released in case of trouble over the open water. As part of the operation, the trained birds were kept in cotes in the **Pigeon House**. Aero-Marine went out of business in 1924, to be replaced by Pan Am, the first international airline recognized by the Post Office. It made its first flight from Key West in 1928. The restaurant in this great old building is called **Kelly's**. It's pleasant to sit outside here on the spacious patio, though the food is about as memorable as an airline meal. Next door is the rickey-green **Heritage House Museum**. Robert Frost apparently visited at the cottage more than a dozen times. You shouldn't say, *Who cares* . . . It is said that he enjoyed it here (though not at first) but didn't talk about it much. The stately house was built by a British barroom owner in the 1850's. He boasted that his ancestors could write evenly on paper without lines, but only when drunk. The house as a museum is interesting because it is Conch shambly with lots of odd collectibles, "treasures," and antiques from seven generations of a Key West family. In one of the tiny rooms, displayed on the bed as though he were going to totter in to it at any moment, is the tiny suit of lights worn by the "Brooklyn Bullfighter," Sydney Franklin. It was a gift to Jessie Porter, the house's late, gregarious owner, from Pauline Hemingway. How Mrs. Hemingway acquired the whole suit rather than the more traditional hat, or ear, is a mystery. Look at it and ponder the fleetingness of glory. The house and engagingly overgrown garden is open from 10 to 5, and you can tour it for $5.

The second block of Caroline is perhaps the prettiest in town, with eight splendid wooden houses and one, at 529, made of brick, complete with tin roof and turret, built by a Turkish sponger in 1906. The **Milton Curry Mansion** at 511 is a miniaturized version of a Newport cottage with all expected excessive embellishments. Milton built this home in 1905 as a wedding present to himself and his new bride. He was the son of William Curry, who had come to Key West from the Bahamas as a child in 1837. It is said that the elder Curry's "capacity for making safe and lucrative investments amounted to genius." He became owner of the largest ship's chandlery in town, and when he died in 1896, he was considered the wealthiest man in Florida. More than seventy carriages accompanied his body to the graveyard, although the solid gold dinner service he had purchased from Tiffany and Company in New York over the years stayed at home. The mansion is now open to the public. Behind it is a recently built, wickered-up inn (see page 209).

At 522 is the most graceful example of Queen Anne architecture in Key West, the **George Patterson House**. It was built immediately after the annihilating fire of 1886, as were many of the grandest homes in town, including the **Richard Kemp House** at 601. This beautiful home has an elegant simplicity of style and proportion and represents the "Conch" style at its very best, employing shipbuilding techniques as well as Classic Revival and island architectural design. The house was built by John Sawyer (who also built the twin-towered Armory on White Street) for the Kemp family, who had become wealthy in the sponging business after William Kemp introduced Key West

The Patterson House

sponges to the New York market. Great care and detail was
given by the builder to the outside appearance of the house.
Inside, old odd lumber was frequently used, for wood was dear
in Key West and little of it was wasted. Many of the beams had
been salvaged from other structures and show old square holes,
caused by a previous use of pegs rather than nails. Today the
Kemp House, which is built of pine, is called the **Cypress
House**, a gay guest establishment.

The following block of Caroline offers a lovely array of Classic
Revival homes before the street opens up into the more utilitar-
ian, humble, and often raucous structures that, past and present, have served the fishing and shrimping docks. Look into the
marine hardware store at 818—a great supply store with everything for the boater. Across the street is **Land's End Village**.
The party boat *Conch Pearl* is berthed here, and the Tortugas
"fishing machine" *Yankee Cupts*. **Seasports Dive Center** goes
out to the reef twice a day. Here too is the popular **Half-Shell
Raw Bar** and the old **Turtle Kraals**, a former butcher shop
and cannery, now a restaurant where you can "drink your way
around the world" with a staggering selection of imported
beers. The Kraals is a rambly place, and nice to go to on a cold
day, for it has a pot-bellied stove, though you might find their
"turtle races" at cocktail hour a bit stupid. (**Capt. Tony's** is
another place jammed when the temperature drops, for it has a
fireplace.) The Kraals once maintained a clouded pen where a
few green turtles, those fabulous travelers, drifted aimlessly,
but no longer has the permits to keep these species. Down a
short pier is the old slaughterhouse, now a "museum" devoted
to the artifacts of what is often referred to as the "colorful"
industry of turtling, although the only color which comes to
mind is red. Here are axes, grinders, photographs, and a painting of an old turtle schooner, the *A. Maitland Adams*.

Green turtles, a species virtually extinct, were hauled back to
Key West from the coast of Nicaragua until the late 1960's,
when tourists would still gather eagerly at the docks with their
cameras to see them being butchered. The butcher would sometimes have a bit of fun with his "neat trick" of slitting the turtle's throat so that the blood would spring twenty feet toward
the insatiable observers' eyes.

TURTLES

The life of the green turtle in the vast oceans is mysterious, but not mysterious enough to insure its survival. Its behavior on land is better known and has steadily doomed it. The turtle's fate is to come ashore to lay her eggs—a hundred of them at a time, several times a year—in a deep sand nest which she covers up with her flippers before returning to the sea. She always nests on the same beach, and her female hatchlings, those that survive, will come back to the beach where they were born when it is their time to lay eggs. Male turtles never return to land. Nests are dug up by raccoons, dogs, and men. But if the nest is not discovered by the second day, the eggs are usually safe for the following sixty days; then the nest erupts and little turtles emerge en masse and make their rush to the sea, a dash which is often cut short by hordes of feeding birds. Hatchlings instinctively head for the brightest spot they see, and for millions of years this was the reflection of moon and stars on the water. Now, however, street and house lights often attract them to death on highways and lawns. If the water is reached, the first wave releases in the baby turtle its sea knowledge—it is the water that teaches the turtle how to swim—and it is then only a matter of luck how many survive the onslaught of predatory fish.

The green turtle is considered to be the world's most valuable reptile, and it is a form of life that has almost been extinguished. The United States banned the import of all sea turtle products—meat and shell and calipee—in 1979. The calipee is the gelatinous cartilage cut from the bones of the bottom shell and is used to flavor soup. Huge nesting turtles are often killed on the coasts of the Caymans, the Caribbean Islands, and Costa Rica for the sake of a few ounces of calipee alone—the rest of the turtle left for buzzards.

Hunted and harassed and exploited, protection of sea turtles has probably come too late. In remote areas they are still killed regularly and all the eggs in a nest taken. In built-up areas, tenderhearted condo dwellers guard the nests of turtles who stubbornly return to beaches now bright with the lights of development. They protect the eggs, even taking them back to their balconies where they try to hatch them in cardboard boxes. If the turtles hatch, they feed them raw hamburger for a while before releasing them into the sea. It

A shrimp boat

isn't known whether this sort of assistance raises or lowers the incredible odds against their survival. The fact is no one knows where young turtles go. They are seen only after some years have passed and they are old enough to mate, the female then making her perilous journey ashore.

A Key West newspaper of the 1890's, *The Daily Equator Democrat,* wrote:

Thousands of these monster turtles weighing from 100 to 1200 pounds are taken in these waters. They are shipped to the larger cities in the U.S. and command a high price. The turtle business is growing rapidly on the coast and seems to be, like the fish business, inexhaustible.

SHRIMPING

Nocturnal shrimp were discovered off Key West in the 1970's and for a while it looked as if the good times would never end. More than 400 boats worked the waters from November through July, dragging 65-foot-long cone-shaped nets behind them. It was a boom, it was wild. Pink gold. Now shrimping is, ah, in decline, the catch down 60 percent in the last decade. The Bight harbors no working boats—the much-diminished fleet is on Stock Island. The business has become very competitive, and the not-so-plentiful shrimp now costs around nine dollars a pound.

In 1980, during the Mariel Boat Lift, initially called The Freedom Flotilla, then Operation Alien Assist, ultimately A Disaster, shrimpers abandoned their nets and went to Cuba to bring back refugees, sometimes at $2,000 a head. "Hauling Cubans paid a lot better than shrimping," one captain said. Boats left Garrison Bight by the hundreds and returned with thousands of people, depositing them on the pier at Truman Annex from which they were sent by bus to an old railroad shed converted into a hangar on Trumbo Point, from which they were airlifted to Homestead and Miami. President Jimmy Carter, after first declaring "an open arms, open heart policy," changed his mind when it appeared that a considerable number of emigrés were deranged, or were thieves and murderers, the latter being marked by tattoos on the inside of their lips. When he declared a halt to the flotilla, Key West fishermen ignored him, preferring to continue their lucrative missions of mercy. Forced by the Cuban authorities at Mariel Harbor to take on increasingly unsavory individuals, the shrimpers returned home and had their boats seized by the U.S. government. Boats rather than people started piling up at Truman Annex. At one point, 80 percent of the commercial fishing boats of Key West were red-tagged and impounded on the docks. The seizure was later declared unconstitutional, 100,000 Cubans were absorbed into the city of Miami, and Key West's shrimp boats returned to their former occupation. There hasn't been one of those sentimental Blessing of the Fleet ceremonies in town for a long long while. At the last one, only several local boats showed up. The rest were out shrimping.

A WALK UP DUVAL STREET

One mile long and certainly no Zona Rosa, Duval stretches from
the glass-bottom boat *Fireball* docked on the Gulf to a little
beach beside the Southernmost House on the Atlantic. Perhaps
the most interesting strip in Florida, Duval has it all—emeralds and chicken wings, dance clubs and missing elks, fake but-
terflies and party baskets, lewd underwear and failed
fountains. It's got chic shops and forbidding hotels, twinkling
galleries, and bars. It hums at night and in the sun. In the rain
it appears less than electrifying. Old-timers feel they've lost the
real Duval, which was darker, danker, noisier, had even more
bars and certainly fewer postcards. The Duval Crawl is a must.
It's done in a car at any time, slowly, very slowly. Be cool now.

The street was named before Florida even became a state, for
William Pope duVal, the first governor of the territory. It was a
dirt road until the 1920's when it was paved with brick. People
bought milk from vendors who milked their cows and goats at
the door. Much of Duval burned down, was rebuilt, and burned
down again. In the 1950's it was wild, in the 1960's dirty, in the
centennial year of 1976, after rejecting a plan which would turn
it into a canal with Venetian gondolas poling people around to
the shops, it was not exactly rehabilitated—and certainly not
restored—but made more reputable. False fronts appeared.
Brick planters. Balloons and cookie and croissant shops were
invited in—particularly in the 600 and 700 blocks. Beyond this,
well into the '80's, was terra incognita to the tourist. It was a
mixture of cans, cats, old convertibles, a few Cuban groceries,
and many empty lots, as derelict buildings burned down with
regularity. Other than La-Te-Da and the cavernous old-time
Valladares newsstand, which carries more magazines than
could possibly be published each year, it seemed the big empty.
But now retail has moved in and there are malls and squares
and shops, shops, shops. Cigar makers' cottages now sell lin-
gerie, soft pretzels, and kayak trips, and the dour Holmes Auto
Body building is an art gallery. "I'm upscale and uptown," the
proprietor of Oink's Originals, a shop on Duval Square, said.
(Oink's Originals sells what look an awful lot like T-shirts.) "I

wanted to be away from the T-shirt shops." (See also Where to
Eat, pages 213–21, Galleries and Antiques, pages 171–72, and
Bars, pages 221–26.)

The 200 block is the bar block. Always carnival time here:
Durty Harry's, **Rick's Cafe**, **Bull and Whistle**—they all rock
and roll. The **Whistle** and **Rick's** have skinny upstairs porches
and do well for hollering and howling. **Sloppy Joe's** hammers
down the corner at Greene. "I'm going over to Sloppy's," you
hear from the most elderly and exhausted tourist as well as the
most energetic short-shorted youth. Everyone makes the pil-
grimage to Sloppy's—"Hemingway's favorite bar." Parachutes
billow from the ceiling. Pictures of the writer beam or brood
from every cranny. The waitresses clang a cowbell every time
the Conch Train goes by (as does the funkier **Green Parrot**).
Two Germans recently rushed into Sloppy's, then rushed off to
the library on Fleming to copy all the photographs of the interior available. They were going to open a Key West Sloppy Joe's
in Munich. What they were going to do about the Conch Train is
a puzzle. **Rumrunners** has innumerable bars squirreled away
in a shambly building. There's a psychic next door for those who
are aware they're lost.

(For jazz, go to **Isle o' Bones** at 1208 Simonton, **Captain
Hornblowers** at 300 Front, or **Two Friends** at 512 Front.
Catch the Junkanoos, who play black Bahamian calypso music,
whenever and wherever you can.)

On the corner of Caroline, opposite the Bull and Whistle, is
the **Fogarty House**, built by yet another son of William Curry,
Key West's first millionaire. The walrus-mustached President
William Taft was once entertained here as well as Henry Flagler during the festivities accompanying the arrival of the first
train into town. The Fogarty House has been reclining in its
decline for years, ever since a group of French sailors on shore
leave used the fountain as a pissoir. The restaurant here need
not be investigated.

In the 300 block, the **Joseph Porter House** on the corner of
Caroline reflects the best of Conch formidable design—taking
the architectural flavor of the Bahamas as well as New England and New Orleans. It is now apartments, and houses two
small specialty shops which are worthy of approach if only for
the opportunity of being able to linger for a moment on the wide

cool veranda. Up and across the street is the **Red Barn Theatre**. Tiny (85 seats) and terrific with skillful professional performances. Call 296–9911 for information on their seasonal offerings. At 322, next to the melancholy **Southern Cross Hotel**, is The Oldest House.

The Oldest House

As mentioned, this may not be the oldest house, but it is the one researched, restored, and made accessible, and it is old enough, certainly, having been built only a few short years after John Simonton bought Key West in 1822 and found "no living person" about. The house was built by Richard Cussons, a grocer, and probably moved here from Whitehead Street. It sits on unusually tall three-foot piers to protect it from the storm tides which used to flow unimpeded up Duval, and it has low ceilings and shuttered windows. The early scuttles on the roof were later replaced by dormers, and these are the house's most peculiar characteristic, for they are wildly dissimilar in size, the sort of dormers fairy tale bears might fancy.

The house is pleasantly askew and homely. Another house was added to the original structure early on, probably around the time Francis Watlington bought it in the 1840's. Watlington was a wrecker who raised seven daughters here. During the Civil War, when he was in his sixties, he went off to fight for the Confederacy, but returned to Key West and is one of the few early settlers buried in the graveyard.

The house is now a museum and is open every day from 10 to 4. The "Rules of Wrecking" are on display and upstairs there is a dollhouse upstairs furnished as eclectically as the house itself. On the grounds there is a cookhouse, the only outside kitchen remaining in Key West.

Anchoring the corner of the 400 block is **St. Paul's Church** with its towers from which hurricane-cracked bells peal daily. There are ten bells at St. Paul's, the largest weighing 1,800 pounds, and chime recitals are played for fifteen minutes at both noon and 5 P.M. Each Christmas a wonderful choral pro-

gram is presented where everyone from the Fabulous Spec-
trelles in their beehives to gospel choirs perform in one of Key
West's marvelously nontraditional traditions. The **La Concha**
(see page 209) has held down the other side of the street since
1924. Redone as a Holiday Inn, it's now well-run and quite elegant, pretty and tropical de rigueur pink. At the top there is
The Top, with its three-sided view of the town. (From here, a
local lawyer, Counselor B., known posthumously thereafter as
No Bungee B., jumped, having waited until the place was totally renovated.) A new restaurant on the street called "Celebri-
ties" is very black-and-white-and-mirrored handsome. Salads,
sandwiches, pizza, and a fresh raw bar in smooth surroundings.
The food makes robust literary references, though the Short
Story has been reduced to a couple of scoops of ice cream.

Here, Fleming is the cross street of the 500 block, up which is
Fausto's (a grocery store that takes Visa and has the coldest
air-conditioning in town) and the nice pink library. Commanding the corner is sleek, slick **Fast Buck Freddie's**, where in
the shimmering, heady recesses people are heard to cry out, "I
have to buy something from here!" Fast Buck's has great
clothes, toys, jewelry, kitchen equipment, and flashy souvenirs.
Nobody misses Fast Buck's. See if they still have the battery-
run, super-realistic writhing rat in a trap that was the sensation of a Christmas past. "People *love* them," a salesman said.
"Those things just *fly* out of here."

The San Carlos (516 Duval)

The original San Carlos was built in 1884 and named for Carlos
Manuel de Cespedes, a Cuban plantation owner who in 1868
cried *Cuba libre!* from the balcony of his estate. He wasn't talking rum and Coke; the cry sparked the Ten Years' War against
Spanish rule, a war which the patriots ultimately lost. (Cespedes' son, Carlos, became the mayor of Key West in 1876.)
Cubans who fled to Key West founded this political and social
club, financing it with the abundant profits of cigar-making.
The fire of 1886, which destroyed most of the town, originated

in the San Carlos, which was then located on Fleming Street. It
was rebuilt three years later on Duval and became as well a
political club, a school, a cultural center, and an opera house.
Anna Pavlova and the Russian Ballet danced here in 1915. In
1919 it was virtually destroyed by a hurricane, and in 1924 it
was rebuilt with money donated by the president of Cuba.
Designed in the Cuban-baroque vernacular of that time—spacious rooms, high ceilings, graceful arches, marble stairways,
hand-crafted mosaics, and floors of checkered Cuban tile, it was
considered the "jewel" of Key West. But Cuba ceased funding
the San Carlos after diplomatic relations with the United
States were severed in 1961. The school closed in 1973, and by
the '80's the building had been invaded by vagrants and was at
the point of collapse. A portion of the façade fell off at one point,
braining a German tourist. Shortly afterward, $10,000 was
spent on restoring the façade, most of the money being used for
an injection process which literally glued the building back
together. Later, in an astonishing display of cooperation,
wealthy Miami Cubans, the state of Florida, and many volun-
teers, from lawyers to artisans, restored the building, and it is
now proudly open, providing today's "veladas." Stop by and see
the historical displays, the wonderful prints of Cuban birds, the
theater with its intriguing backdrop painting of the tree on the
farm of de Cespedes. Concerts, recitals, and other events are
presented at the San Carlos frequently.

The Strand (527 Duval)

A movie house built in the 1930's, its "boomtown" front is elaborately decorated with lions, Roman legionnaires, and bowls of
fruit. When a fire destroyed the roof, the building was used for
a while as a boxing ring beneath the stars. The sherbet-colored
circusy façade was painstakingly restored recently, and inside,
for a time, the interior became a state-of-the-art video, dance,
and music complex with ever-changing shows—rock, reggae,
blues, mud wrestling, male strippers for the ladies, etc. Food
was also served here—most particularly sandwiches named for

Fausto's Food Palace

local politicians. For example, there was the "Bum Farto," in honor of a former Key West fire chief. All this was just too good to last, of course. The money ran out, and The Strand shut down. It has now come back as a **Ripley's Believe It or Not Odditorium**. It's too politically correct in all regards to be truly odd or thrillingly creepy, and somebody keeps stealing the shrunken heads, but going there does seem like a madcap thing to do after dinner or on a rainy day. Pricey at $8.95 for adults, $5.95 for children. Open daily 10 A.M. to 11 P.M. (293-9686).

Somewhere around here there is a shop which has, as part of its window display, a man's bathing suit with an elephant trunk sticking out of it. This has been there *for years*.

The 600 block is the area snatched from the skids in 1976. Merchants and politicians had the year 1910 in mind here, but they wanted the block to appear as it "should" have appeared, not the way it actually did appear. The result was this street of appearances, sticky with fudge and ice-cream nooks, only a pawn shop clinging to the brassy taste of yesterday. The co-op art gallery, **Guild Hall**, is here, near to where the old Picture Show *used* to be. The theater sold beer right along with the popcorn and showed a variety of old, flaky, and message flicks as well as the very funny homage to Key West, *The Key West Picture Show*. You can catch it now only on video.

The Copa

A movie theater built in 1917, it had been showing *Deep Throat* for a decade before it was transformed into this glossy gay cruise bar. Flickering lights and longings and heavy-duty dancing on the big dance floor flanked by bars below. Upstairs is male erotica. Out back is the "Cowboy" bar of pool table and electronic games, then the fresher yet still considerably tumid air of the "Patio" bar, above which, for fern admirers, hangs the largest staghorn in town. The Copa has fascinating entertainment but it varies. You'd better check. You don't want to go down there on Wednesday thinking it's "Doris Day Night" and be disappointed when it turns out to be "Wet Jockey Shorts Night" instead.

The 700 block once had the distinction of having the dustiest and most forlorn collection of seashells in town at the Key West Conch Shell, but someone discovered Windex, then found they didn't want to sell seashells at all. There's something for everyone on this street. The shops and restaurants of upper Duval have all been wrested from what was once a Cuban enclave, but the gentrifiers continue to meet resistance in **Bahama Village**, although inroads have been made. This is the area that Hemingway, with his way with words, called "Jungle Town."

In the 1980's a colorful wrought-iron archway was erected at the intersection of Duval and Petronia and adorned with a flamingo, a marlin, a demi-sun, and conch shells. *Forward,* the swirling iron spelled out—*Forward Together Upward Onward*—but through the splendid passageway moved—nothing. In fact, the adornments were periodically found missing from the gateway. On most tourist maps, Bahama Village does not exist, the town seemingly ending at Whitehead, but it is very much a distinct, special part of Key West, with its simple houses with their neat raked yards, the weedy lots, the crowing roosters, the tiny groceries, and many churches. **Blue Heaven**, a restaurant and seeming time-and-space warp at the corner of

Thomas and Petronia, introduced many people to the special-
ness of Bahama Village, and although not patronized by exactly
the real neighborhood, it has thrived here. Chickens, dogs, a
sweet hippie air, and wonderful food has made it very popular,
particularly on Sunday, when it's almost impossible to get a
table. For some reason *The Tempest* was performed here at one
point. The entire play! Sensational. Aristophanes' ancient
Greek comedy *The Frogs* is going to be next. Across the street is
cool, blue **Johnson's Grocery**. Coldest beer and freshest Miss
Debbie snack cakes in town. More and more people are sallying
forth on their bicycles through these streets, and you can
almost hear them saying, *Why this is delightful, it's so ungen-
trified, look at those gentlemen playing cards.* . . . On the weekends, many of the churches sell fantastically tasty barbeque.
With the flocks of wild parrots flying overhead, you feel you've
discovered something. Something that, blissfully, the Conch
Train has not.

   The Community Swimming Pool at the intersection of
Catherine and Thomas is a terrific place for doing Olympic-
length laps. The pool is clean and alfresco and has a great view
of the ocean.

   Back on Duval, just up from Truman, you will find yourself at
the newly concocted **Duval Square** with its fashionable gym,
its fashionable hair salon, and its fashionable restaurant,
Square One. Beyond is the irresponsibly delicious ice cream at
Flamingo Crossing (do the fresh coconut) and the kayak out-
fitters of **Mosquito Coast**. They have two dockages, one at MM
#9.5 and one farther up on Sugarloaf. You're taken there by van
and have about four hours of water time among the mangroves.
Cost is $45. Call 294-7178. More peculiar land tours are spring-
ing up in Key West's rocky soil. "Catch Donald," someone will
say. "He's very sweet, knows a lot, and probably will split when
his probation is up. . . ." You don't really need all that much help
here with guides—Key West is not, after all, Morocco—but it's
interesting to be instructed by someone other than the Conch
Train. Lloyd, for example, hosts a bike tour. He takes you
through the quieter parts of town. He chats with Conchs on
their porches and invites you to eat peculiar flora as though you
were lost in the desert. Sometimes you can meet a fellow whose
skill is pulling his bottom lip over his nose. It's ninety minutes

of relaxing fun, but Lloyd (294-1882) might not be offering this service forever.

In an old fortune-telling parlor at 1111 Duval is **Baby's Place**, a nifty coffee bar where you can get a rushing jump start on your day. Try "Death by Coffee" or "Baby's Buzz" and have one of their corn muffins while you read a paper from the long-running Valladares newsstand. The automobile graveyard that used to nestle against the old La-Te-Da is gone, as are the beyond-seedy Casa Blanca Apartments (now the **William House**, a red-and-white, proper-enough guest house). New visions are the Miami-style furniture at **Fletcher** (lots of fossil accessories).

Duval is a street one should see through from start to finish, unlike Whitehead, which is hot and tedious. A street that runs straight to the sea is a fine street, and **South Beach**, the little beach that fits so easily on a postcard, is the seaweedy termination to Duval. The pink-and-green Queen Anne mansion beside it at 1400 is the J. Viking Harris House, built before the turn of the century by a judge. For a time it was a nightclub, Casa Cayo Hueso, and is now a private home again. This is **The Southernmost House**.

Key West transportation

The Southernmost Point

This is not at the end of Duval at all but over on Whitehead, at its intersection with South Street. You would logically think the low pink house, lushly compounded and sticking out into the Atlantic beside it would be the Southernmost House instead of the turreted, tottering creation on Duval. And it is! But it's not really because it's not the *original* Southernmost House. The same kind of spirited controversy that swirls around the problem of the Great White and the Great Blue Heron (is the White just a color phase of the Blue? Or is the White a distinct species? If the White *is* just a color phase of the Blue, why do they hate one another so much, unlike other herons which get along quite amicably?) muddies the waters around the *real* Southernmost House.

However, we do have, without question, in the continental United States, which allows us to exclude Hawaii, the Southernmost Point, and this is marked with a black, red, and yellow object of many tons constructed to resemble a nun buoy. The Director of Monuments in Key West, Billy Pinder, designed this. People kept stealing the sign that said Southernmost Point in the USA, so the town decided to install something souvenir-mad tourists couldn't carry off. It is painted in ribbons of bright colors so that it will show up well in photographs. Billy Pinder invited President Reagan to the dedication ceremonies

The southernmost point in the continental United States

for the buoy in 1983, suggesting that if the president came, the town would rename South Street President Ronald Reagan Street. The president did not grace the proceedings, however, and South Street remains South Street. The lady who lives in the house diagonally across from this peculiar and very permanent object that marks the Southernmost Point was so upset by its shape, color, and enormity that she hung her American flag upside down during the ceremony.

Tables are set up here each morning laden with shells. There are, too, lamps made of shells—complete with plastic flamingo and palm tree, ready to brighten your life with a tiny red Christmas tree light—and an assortment of dried and pickled things from the deep—"Honey! Look at this little shark or something in the formaldehyde!" Sponges and shell necklaces hang from the chain-link fence separating the street from Navy property. The conch shells are very rosy, very pretty, but it's supposed to be bad luck to put them in your home, or so the Conchs say. It would be the only revenge the conch could have, in any case. On stormy days, waves crash against the sea wall and surge into the street, soaking the Conch Trains as they make their turns past. Harley guys love to take their hogs and their chicks down here and have their picture taken. Sometimes the rumble of their machines is so loud that it sets off all the car alarms in the neighborhood.

BEACHES AND SALT PONDS

Key West's beaches are not her crowning glory. They are mostly man-made, marly, bumpy, and covered with seaweed, and the waters offshore are shallow. The longest, skinniest beach on the island is **Smathers**, which begins just west of the airport on A1A (South Roosevelt Boulevard). It's lined with cars, taco trucks, and raft and Windsurfer rentals, and parasailors (no age limit, no dress code, and no skill required!) take off from a float on the southern end. All this considerable activity is bleakly gazed down upon by the nervous inhabitants of condominiums.

On the other side of the beach and the highway are the remnants of salt ponds which were once scattered over 340 acres. Evaporation of seawater to make salt, an important preservative before the advent of ice, was an intermittent business here until 1868. Airport construction and condo development have reduced the ponds and the flow of water, but there are still a number of feeding birds to be found back here, particularly early in the morning. The ponds themselves contain extensive grass beds and are filled with blue crabs, shrimp, minnows, and killifish all being lunched upon by herons, egrets, and migratory ducks. A portion of the land is the **Riggs Wildlife Refuge**, and behind a green gate is a small observation deck. You'll be surprised at the serenity to be found here so close to the commerce of traffic and planes.

Just beyond Smathers on Atlantic Boulevard is an area now rudely jammed with condos but once known as Rest or Picnic Trees Beach. Despite its placid names, it has long been a troubled and disturbed area. Early on it was a dump, then the butchering pens for cattle were located here (livestock was also kept in the abandoned West Martello Tower). The pens were torn down in the cleanup of the 1930's and for years it was a spot, not for sunbathing but for digging. People would hunt for old bottles here, the aficionados of that art fashioning bomb-sized craters with their shovels and picks. Intersecting with Atlantic is White Street, which terminates in the **White Street Pier**, a popular crumbling slab of a thing where people fish and hang out. It unquestionably has charm, which is baffling considering the amount of litter wedded to the seaweed on its flank. The "pier" is more like a road to nowhere and the tides simply can't do their jobs removing the junk from the strollers' sight. The second largest beach in town is **Higgs Memorial** right alongside. Families with small children come here because of the playground, and there are picnic tables and a beachside restaurant. Large flocks of skimmers and sea gulls (Were you aware that sea gulls have a high divorce rate? Twenty-five percent of couples split after the first year!) stake out one part of the beach near the West Martello Tower during windy winter months, while gays have reclaimed the rebuilt and oft-described "well extended" Reynolds Street pier nearby.

There are also two tiny patches of landfill where the

undaunted seeker of waterfront can go. At the end of Vernon Street, just beside the restaurant **Louie's Back Yard**, there's a bit of public land—which usually goes topless—with a nice coconut palm and forty feet or so of rocky shoreline. At the end of the sternly unimaginative **Casa Marina** complex on Seminole Street, there's a slice of concrete and a slice of sand where dogs with jaunty bandanas around their necks like to congregate. Snorkeling around the remnants of an old pier is fun here, and a little farther out, just to the east and west of markers that mark a channel through some scattered coral heads, are some nice patch reefs.

The better bodies hang out at Smathers but the best beach in town and really the best place to see the sunset is at **Fort Taylor** (pages 184–87). The entrance to the Fort is through the Southard Street entrance to Truman Annex. The beach is open from 8 A.M. to sunset and has picnic tables and grills. The fee is $1.50 per person, or $3.25 a car and 50¢ a person. Bring sneakers or amphibious sandals because the beach is rough coral. It's difficult getting into the water gracefully at Fort Taylor. People teeter, hobble, crawl. . . . Once in, the tendency is to stay in for a considerable time, putting off the teetering, hobbling, and crawling out as long as possible.

GALLERIES AND ANTIQUES

Lucky Street at 919 and **Gingerbread Square** at 1207 are both on Duval. Lucky Street is the more exuberant. Pottery, jewelry, paintings, books, Arcosanti wind chimes, great receptions. Local sculptor John Martini, whose big studio is an old movie theater in Bahama Village, shows here. A world-class talent, his metal friezes and tall naïf figures are fresh and vigorous. Gingerbread Square is the longest-running gallery in Key West. It frequently shows the soft, otherworldly acrylics of the artist John Kiraly, whose work has been described as "idealized realism" and even "attainable fantasy."

The Haitian Art Company (corner of Francis and Southard). Several rooms jammed with Haitian primitives. Voodoo bottles, spirit flags, gloriously painted boxes. Very reasonable, but you don't get a history lesson with it. Open 10 A.M.–6 P.M.

Perkins and Son is a salty store at 901 Fleming. Great shorts and shirts as well as brasswork, ships' clocks, models, charts, and a nice selection of books about the sea.

The Sea Store (614 Greene). A nice little store. Bottles and old coins. A variety of Keys hardwoods which could possibly be made into something handsomely custom-made for you. The owners, Bill and Fran Ford, are gregarious and knowledgeable about poking around the Keys. They are great birders. If Fran can't get you excited about the Birdathon, the Keys' bird-count day that happens each May 1—"We start in the Dry Tortugas at dawn, spend and hour there, then fly back to Key West for breakfast in the Indigenous Park, and then work our way up the Keys, and by nightfall when we hear the screech owl in Key Largo, we could have one hundred thirty species!"—then nothing ever will. Be sure to call first as they're erratically open (294-3438).

Whitehead Street Pottery at 1011 Whitehead has an elegant offering of original works. **Kalypso** at 609 Whitehead Street has wonderfully winsome hand-painted furniture, and the **Rogue Rooster**, on Thomas Street by Blue Heaven, has colorful primitives, some done on pieces of old tin roofing.

Antiques 'n' Things, on Fleming next to the Key West Island Bookstore, has jewelry, old wicker, and postcards; all matter of things moving in and out. **Sam's Treasure Chest** across the street is junky and jammed, some of the treasures having resided there for years. Many is the old foot from claw-footed bathtubs that has found its way here. **Just Good Stuff** at 1100 White Street has dolls, toys, and a good selection of Deco and old Florida furniture. Get enthused by a *bucce* at the M&M Laundry next door and buy that painting of polar bears you've always wanted.

NEWSPAPERS

The *Key West Citizen* is Monroe County's only daily newspaper, although it does not appear on Saturday. It is a thin paper, sometimes astonishingly thin, and poker-faced in its accountings. It is known as the mullet-wrapper and depicted itself thusly in papier-mâché during one Fantasy Fest parade. A now-departed editor investigated, with two reporters, rumors of occult disturbances at the Little White House. They spent the night in the house where Harry once slept, equipped with high-speed film, a tape recorder, a German shepherd, and notepads. The trio experienced two ghosts. One was a lady named Rose. The other was a slight man with blue eyes named Tom. Tom wore a brimmed felt hat, a cardigan sweater, had thin bony fingers, an eye for the ladies, and owned a green parrot. It is not known what the German shepherd thought, but the reporters' observances were duly reported in the *Citizen*. The pictures of babies, newlyweds, and high school sports are nice, and, of course, the drug trials of prominent local citizens, including police officers and real estate ladies, are followed with great interest, but the most fascinating section of the *Citizen* is by far the police blotter on Page Two. It is here where Key West sings her strange song. It is here where much is exposed, but little explained—the complaints to the police of break-ins where pots of black beans vanish and wet clothes are rearranged. The thefts of car bras and meatball subs. The reports of voodoo roosters and murdered palm trees, the arrests of individuals opening coconuts in a dangerous fashion. The headline of choice on Page Two is *Thieves, Wackos Keep Police Busy*. Or, *Minor Burglaries Galore*.

Solares Hill began in the 1970's as a monthly free paper. It was named in those heady days for the "highest" point on the island, a bit of land sixteen feet above sea level at the intersection of Elizabeth Street and Windsor Lane. (The lowest point in Key West, at least for the undercarriages of cars, is at South and Simonton.) *Solares Hill* is a paper with style and conviction, a community paper of the very best sort with articles on local concerns, politics, and personalities. As well there are helpful supplements for the visitor, such as a walking and biking guide to Old Town. The paper is now published weekly and can be picked up at almost any store or guest house, although some establishments banned it after it printed a picture of fun-loving Spring Breakers on the cover, one of whom, under closer perusal, was starkers.

There are now several good free papers available. People get the *Citizen* for Page Two. They pick up the others—*Key West: The Newspaper* and *Bone Island Sun*—for reviews, disclosures, the style of the Rock, and in-depth eristical attitude.

WRITERS

It is known that writers hang out in Key West, and after the brisk, rather flamboyant tour of the Hemingway House, one is probably curious to catch a glimpse of the other homes where novelists, playwrights, and poets ply their grisly, solitary trade. The Hemingway House is, of course, big business. The other houses can only be reflected upon from outside. Why people are fascinated with the shells these souls inhabit is curious. Perhaps they're actually not that fascinated but have been encouraged to believe they are.

Key West writers have done well. Nine of them have won the Pulitzer Prize—Ernest Hemingway, Elizabeth Bishop, John Hersey, Joseph Lash, James Merrill, Richard Wilbur, Tennessee Williams, Allison Lurie, and Annie Dillard. It almost seems as though with the Pulitzer comes an irresistible urge to move here. Writers like Key West—there may now be more writers in town than bars—but many of them are faithless creatures and they come and they go. One of them, Hart Crane, often mentioned as a Key West writer, was in fact never here at all. The nearest he came was the Isle of Pines in Cuba, although a grouping of his poems was entitled *Key West Sheaf.* Tom McGuane, Philip Caputo, Thomas Sanchez—all are intimately associated with this strange rock, Mile Zero. Their houses of Pepto-Bismol pink and lime green and proper white could be duly noted and located, but this guide, believing that all living

writers have enough problems, most of which are still with
them, prefers to address only those who have passed on in a
permanent sense. More specifically, the former homes of two of
Key West's fixed and illustrious dead—Elizabeth Bishop and
Tennessee Williams.

Elizabeth Bishop and Tennessee Williams

The **Bishop House** is at 624 White Street, not far from the
pale yellow, twin-towered National Guard Armory, now a
Senior Citizens' Center, at 600 White. It is a fine, simple,
weathered structure, almost hidden behind palms and plantings but sporting a new bronze tablet on the gate that quotes a
line from one of her poems—"Should we have stayed at home,
wherever that might be?" Bishop lived here between 1938 and
1942, and many of the poems in her first collection, *Poems:
North and South,* winner of the Pulitzer in 1946, were written
here and are about Florida, the state which she considered to
have "the prettiest name," a "careless, corrupt state, the poorest
postcard of itself." She would be less than inspired, no doubt, by
the view across the street, at the wasteland the Navy has made
of Peary Court, a large green space where there were once softball diamonds, hundreds of trees, and a great many visiting
birds and dogs.

Elizabeth Bishop was a poet of stunning gifts who had a
painterlike fascination with appearances in themselves. Key
West and New England were the early compass points of her
work, although after leaving here, she lived for eighteen years
in Brazil. Two of her wonderful prose pieces concern Key West:
Mercedes Hospital and *Gregorio Valdes.*

Gregorio Valdes was a Cuban sign-painter whom she met
after purchasing one of his paintings out of a barber shop on
Duval. The painting was of a neat row of royal palm trees and
was in the window of the shop, covered with dust and termite
wings.

Bishop wanted him to paint a picture of her green-and-white
White Street house, but she wanted him to add more flowers
and a parrot. She also wanted him to include a monkey that
lived next door and a traveler's-tree. She liked the appearance

Bahama anole lizard under a periwinkle

of the traveler's-tree, which she described as looking like the "fan-filamented antennae of a certain gigantic moth." There being only one such palmlike tree in town at the time, Valdes sketched it separately, then worked from an enlarged photograph of the house Bishop gave him. She was delighted with the final result. "He put in flowers in profusion and the parrot on a perch on the verandah and painted the monkey, larger than life-size, climbing the trunk of the palm tree." But Gregorio Valdes was apologetic because the living tree he had copied had seven branches on one side and six on the other, but in the painting he had given both sides seven to make it more symmetrical.

The **Tennessee Williams House** at 1431 Duncan Street on the corner of Leon is noted for the large, highly *a*symmetrical traveler's-tree in the front yard. A writer of genius in his early years and considered by many to be the greatest living playwright since O'Neill, Williams continued to write prolifically even though his later plays were poorly received, one critic referring to them as "mere mystic mazes of lyrical mumbo-jumbo concerning human despair." This little house with its

tomato-colored shutters is almost a miniature house, reminis-
cent perhaps of one of the small torrid symbols of *The Glass
Menagerie.* On the lot he added a white gazebo, in honor, he
said, of his friend, Jane Bowles; a pool; and a studio where he
produced some of his best-known work, including *The Night of
the Iguana* and *The Rose Tattoo. The Rose Tattoo,* with Burt
Lancaster and Anna Magnani, was filmed in Key West, at this
house and on the Casa Marina grounds, in 1955. Williams loved
his studio, pointing out its "complete bath-shower and female
sockets for electric grills."

Williams was happy in Key West. In the pictures taken of
him here, he is always smiling, happy with his pet bulldogs, his
writing (in which the town never figures), and his friends. He
entertained his beloved, mad sister Rose here. She occupied her
time by watering the trees in his garden with glassfuls of water
from the kitchen sink The master of duality took up painting
here, as did Elizabeth Bishop. He said it was relaxing and
didn't wear him out like writing did.

There was an incident in the late 1970's where Williams and
a friend, Dotson Rader, were roughed up late one night as they
walked drunk and singing up Duval Street. They were singing
the old gospel hymn "In the Garden":

> *Ohhhh He walks with me
> And He talks with me
> And He tells me I am his own
> And the joy we share as we tarry there
> No other has ever known*

. . . the lyrics achieving certain implications never dreamed of
by their creator. Some young toughs pushed the men down and
kicked them, and although the incident was highly publicized
and caused considerable concern among Key West gays, Tennessee dismissed the misadventure. "Well, I suffered no
injury," he said. "Fortunately, an ice-cream shop was being
shut right behind us and a man picked up the phone, called the
police, and said, 'Some men are attacking Mr. Williams on the
street.' "

Three weeks prior to the incident, the caretaker of his house
on Duncan Street had been shot and killed. While going

through his effects, the police found that he had pilfered many of the original copies of Williams' manuscripts. "Well," Tennessee said dryly, "I guess he thought he was going to die after I did."

Tennessee Williams, whose own wish was to be buried at sea between Key West and Cuba, "dropped overboard in a clean white sack," died in 1983 in New York City and is buried in the city he loathed, St. Louis.

Locals like to celebrate his birthday, which is March 25.

The Key West Literary Seminar takes place each January with panels, readings, and, of course, parties. This has become quite a sophisticated event, with well-known and articulate participants and interesting themes. Past topics have included Literature and Film, Travel Writing, and Biography. Call 293-9291 for information. The seminar should not be confused with **Hemingway Days** which take place in the doldrums of July and consist of drinking mostly, plus a costume party where people dress up like Hemingway characters, the winner one year being a fluttering Portuguese Man-of-War from *The Old Man and the Sea*. There is as well a short-story contest where you don't have to write exactly like Hemingway to win.

There are two good bookstores in town. Foremost is **Key**

TRUMAN CAPOTE IN KEY WEST

Truman Capote was in a bar in Key West with Tennessee Williams when a woman came over to the table where they were sitting and asked Capote to autograph her navel with an eyebrow pencil. She handed him the pencil and pulled up her T-shirt. "Just write it like you would the numerals around a clock," she said. So Capote wrote his name around her navel. T-R-U-M-A-N-C-A-P-O-T-E. She returned to her table, but her husband got up, seemingly quite enraged. He came over to Capote, eyebrow pencil in hand and, as Capote relates, hauled out his "equipment" and howled, "Since you're autographing everything, how'd you like to autograph *this*?" Truman paused and said, "Well, I don't know if I can autograph it, but perhaps I could initial it."

West Island Books at 513 Fleming, just off Duval. On the walls is a rogue's gallery of local authors' photographs, and there is an excellent selection of their work and books of local interest. There's also a rare-book room and carefully chosen used books. **Caroline Street Books** at 800 Caroline Street, corner of William, is cozy and airy at once, with a coffee and juice bar. Good contemporary choices and selective used ones. Both stores have lively signing parties in the winter. The pink **Monroe County Library** was built in 1959 and has been recently spruced up. In 1994 a benefactor gave several hundred thousand dollars, not for books but specifically for a palm garden to the side. Overnight, and to considerable amazement, an oasis appeared. Ask the librarians about it and they'll say, "Oh, *that* . . ." A visitor's library card costs $15 and is good for a year. On the first Saturday of each month there's a book sale behind the library. All hardcovers cost 25¢. During the winter there are weekly coffees and talks, some of them *most* intriguing. How could one resist, for example, early on a Monday morning the desire to hear one Poochie Myers discuss "The Serpent Handling Religions of West Virginia."

Hemingway and His House

In 1851, Asa Tift, a "brainy, cultured, suave gentleman" from Groton, Connecticut, a merchant and builder of Confederate ships, built a limestone mansion from native coral rock at 907 Whitehead. With its mansard roof and iron-flanged pillars, of vaguely Second-Empire or Spanish Colonial design, the **Hemingway House** is unlike any other house in town.

Ernest Hemingway and his wife Pauline bought the house in 1931 for $8,000, a monetary gift from Pauline's wealthy Uncle Gus. The house was in a gross state of ill repair, with a grassless yard dotted with a few scraggly trees. It was a "miserable wreck," according to Pauline, who also referred to it as a "damned haunted house" after a piece of plaster fell from the ceiling and lodged in her eye. Nonetheless, just before Christmas, the Hemingways, with their two small sons, nurses, and cooks, moved into rooms still jammed with carpenters, plumbers, plasterers, and crates of furniture shipped from

France. Hemingway worked here winters in a small room over what had once been a carriage house until his divorce from Pauline in 1940. At that time he crated all his belongings—papers, books, guns, and hunting trophies—and stored them in a back room at Sloppy Joe's. (When Mary Hemingway, his last wife, went into the room in 1962 and opened the boxes untouched for decades, she found original manuscripts blackened with mildew and eaten by rats, uncashed royalty checks, and rotted animal skins.) He then went off to Cuba for a new, if brief, marriage with Martha Gellhorn, and a new house, the Finca Vigía or "Lookout Farm," nine miles outside of Havana. It was at the Finca where the ghastly collection of inbred cats roamed and not in Key West, where the pet population, which numbered several peacocks, included only two cats, one of which the children once dyed a dark green, producing unknown consequences. Hemingway, however, did have over fifty cats in Cuba and once boasted of shooting a peasant's dog who had molested one of them. He had intentionally gut-shot the animal so that it would take three days to die.

Ernest Hemingway, as every schoolchild knows, fished, drank, and wrote in Key West. He wrote *Death in the Afternoon, The Green Hills of Africa,* and *To Have and Have Not,* as well as a play, *The Fifth Column,* and a considerable number of short stories, including "The Short Happy Life of Francis Macomber" and "The Snows of Kilimanjaro."

A Farewell to Arms was completed in 1929 in a house he and Pauline had rented at 1100 South Street, the same house where his mother had sent a chocolate cake and the Smith and Wesson revolver his father had used to commit suicide.

"Christ, this is a fine country!" Hemingway wrote a friend, enthusiastic about Key West. Between trips to Arkansas, to shoot grouse, pheasant, ducks, and geese; Wyoming, to shoot bear, elk, mountain rams, and eagles; and Africa, to shoot elephant, lion, rhino, buffalo, and kudu, Hemingway fished the Gulf Stream. As the biographer Carlos Baker remarks, in somewhat of an understatement, he "enjoyed life immensely without being sensitive to it." Once, when the poet Archibald MacLeish visited him and they went kingfishing, they found the fish weren't running so Hemingway "took to shooting terns, taking one with one barrel and the grieving mate with the other."

Besides shotguns, he also carried on board a harpoon and a machine gun for sharks and the stray pod of whales.

Hemingway liked marlin fishing best, for marlin were "fast as light, strong as bucks, with mouths like iron." Tuna, perhaps, were not so exciting, even though they could take just as long to catch. It took him seven hours to land one $11\frac{1}{2}$ foot, 540-pound tuna, and after getting drunk, he strung it up and used it as a punching bag. (Hemingway had also once used the poet Wallace Stevens as a punching bag in Key West. He blackened his eyes and fractured his jaw after the older man had apparently remarked that Hemingway's writing was not his "cup of tea.")

During his first years in Key West, Hemingway had chartered the boats of Bra Saunders, Charles Thompson, and Sloppy Joe Russell. In 1934, at the height of the Depression, and in the same year that the town had declared bankruptcy, Hemingway bought his own boat—a 42-foot black cruiser with mahogany trim built to his specifications in a New York shipyard. "A really sturdy boat," he described her, "sweet in any kind of sea, and she has a very low-cut stern with a large wooden roller to bring big fish over." He called her the *Pilar*, one of his early names for Pauline, as well as the name of a Catholic bullfight shrine in Zaragoza, Spain. He docked her at the Navy station,

The oldest house in Key West, on Duval Street

THE TOUR

You will enter the grounds. The plantings are nice. It is lush. Figs, elephant ears, a magnificent date palm. Then you will see the excessive inauthentic collection of cats, clumping around on their malformed toes—cats eating, cats brawling, cats having more cats in little cages. You will take the tour. It will cost you $6 (children $1.50) and it will take thirty minutes. Four people give tours ten times a day. The most eccentric tour is given by a tiny man with a tiny belly in tiny, tight, shiny black pants. You will be in a mob and he will call you "beanies," he will call you "little sparklers," he will tell you to keep it "flowing and glowing" as you follow him tripping through the rooms. He is a movie buff and you will hear about Loretta Young and Rock Hudson and Lauren Bacall. There's a chair in the bedroom which he will point out because Franchot Tone sat in it in the production of *The Fifth Column*. Franchot Tone was married to Joan Crawford at the time. The bedroom abounds in strange little chairs, uncomfortable chairs, key-hole chairs, even a midwife's chair. Later, of course, you are shown *The* chair, the cigar-maker's chair Hemingway wrote in. The books of the house are all enclosed behind wire mesh, although there is a good selection of his works in paper for sale in the drawing room. "I had no idea he wrote so much," you'll hear. Glance inside the pages. Other than this, his life's work, Hemingway is dead as a doornail in this place.

---

in the submarine pen where he and his friends, the "Mob," liked to swim. She rode out the 1935 hurricane there.

Hemingway did a lot of fishing on the *Pilar*. In 1942, he employed her in a daffy manner as a submarine hunter in the Caribbean, having convinced the Navy to equip her as a Q-boat with a supply of bazookas, grenades, and short-fuse bombs. The *Pilar* was seized by the Castro government in 1960, a year before Hemingway's death, and is now rotting on the lawn in front of the Finca in Cuba.

Hemingway thought his house on Whitehead Street resembled "Joan Miro's 'The Farm' as it might have been painted by Utrillo." If that does not exactly crystallize the vision for you, imagine it being, in the 1930's, the finest house in town, a mansion with tall French windows, staffed with servants on an acre of land and possessing the only basement, bathroom, and swimming pool on the island. The pool is sixty feet long and was dug by pick and shovel for $20,000, an amount which, the guides like to point out, would be equivalent to spending around $225,000 today. Hemingway lived very well here. In 1936, he was putting the finishing touches on his Key West book, *To Have and Have Not,* a novel that showed the poverty-stricken plight of islanders during the Depression, as well as showing Hemingway's considerable disdain for fellow writers, literary hangers-on, Gulf Stream yachtsmen, and tourists. *To Have and Have Not* is actually an unsuccessful attempt to fashion a novel by taking three previously published stories about a fisherman and smuggler named Henry Morgan (based on Sloppy Joe Russell) and attaching them to subplots of love triangles and capitalistic boorishness. But it's Hemingway's Key West book and it captures the jarring rhythms of a town on the skids.

Hemingway became Key West's most famous citizen. In 1937, Toby Bruce, a driver, friend, and general handyman for the Hemingways, built a privacy wall around the property from bricks salvaged from Duval Street, dug up when the town laid down its first sewer system. By 1940, Hemingway was gone. "Those who live by the sword, die by the sword," he said rather uninspiredly, explaining Pauline's replacement by Martha. After all, Pauline had replaced Hadley. And Mary was to supplant Martha. Pauline, who had provided him with the wealth he so enjoyed and despised, died suddenly in Los Angeles in 1951. When asked by Tennessee Williams, who had met her in Key West, how she had died, Hemingway replied, "She died like everybody else and after that she was dead."

FORTS, TOWERS, AND MUSEUMS

The Lighthouse Military Museum

Close across from the Hemingway House, this museum is housed in the lighthouse keeper's cottage. It used to be more interesting, but unfortunately in 1988 a great deal of well-intentioned housekeeping took place and the rooms lost their messy, intriguingly atticy quality. The grounds were once cluttered with various torpedoes, depth charges, and gun mounts, even a Blue Angel stunt jet, all innocently moldering. All of this has been carted off now, even the oddest object of all—a miniature Japanese submarine from World War II. This captured sub (small windows cut in the hull and two mannequins in Japanese uniforms placed inside) toured the country during those war years collecting money to raise the ships sunk at Pearl Harbor. It will be returned there to be part of the *Arizona* Memorial. The museum still includes many artifacts from the *Maine,* including life preservers and a capstan to which the nuns of the Convent of Mary Immaculate added a spire. The new emphasis is on lighthouse history and memorabilia. The impressive original Fresnel lens from the Sombrero Key light is on display, and more interpretative exhibits are planned.

You can climb eighty-eight steps to the top of the lighthouse and get a good gull's-eye view of Key West. When it was built in 1847, it was fifty-eight feet tall, but it had to be raised over the years so that the light could be seen over growing trees and the new buildings of an expanding town. The tower stopped growing at seventy-eight feet and the light was extinguished in 1969. Open 9:30–5. Admission is $5. Children, $1. Telephone: 294-0012.

Fort Taylor

The Fort is scarcely visible from the exterior, either from the land or from water. It is not imposing until one is inside.

Begun in 1845 as part of an ambitious coastal fortifications system and named five years later for President Zachary Taylor, it was originally built 1,200 feet from shore (sand and fill eventually connected it to Key West) and had two tiers plus a top platform for cannon just behind the parapet. The fort is built in the shape of a trapezoid and rests on a foundation of Keys' limestone and New England granite. Millions of bricks, shipped down from Pensacola, were used in the twenty-one-year project, set by slaves and German and Irish masons. (Iron-

ically, the slave population of Key West increased fivefold when
Union authorities imported them to work on military fortifications during the Civil War.) Construction was plagued by
strikes, shortages of material, the antipathy of European
craftsmen toward Negro laborers, and hurricanes. Most impor-
tantly, there were the vicious periodic attacks of yellow fever,
blamed on "miasma" in the air. Indeed, the only time the fort's
cannons were fired was in an attempt to dispel this "miasma."
A swamp close to the workmen's quarters and teeming with
mosquitoes was not suspected.

On the night that Florida seceded from the Union, January
13, 1861, a small group of Union soldiers marched to the fort
and, with the assistance of a Lieutenant Edward Hunt, in
charge of the fort's construction, secured it for the Union, delivering an immediate blow to the Confederacy. Less than fifty
Union men held a crucial fortification in what was the largest
town in Florida. Sentiment in town was mostly Southern, but
there was no attempt to take the fort by rebel sympathizers,
although many of the young men of Key West sailed away

The lighthouse at Key West

immediately to join the Confederate Army. Several months later, with the arrival of additional troops, the Union blockade of the Confederacy began, and captured blockade runners, their ships, and cargoes, were brought into the harbor and anchored beneath the massive guns of Fort Taylor, guns which now numbered almost two hundred. An average of thirty-two ships were stationed here during the war years, and at one time there were three hundred vessels of various description held captive.

Key West was the only city south of the Mason-Dixon line to remain in the hands of the Union during the Civil War, but Washington officials did not consider it that important militarily. Frantic requests for supplies and reinforcements were largely ignored. Many Union commanders considered it a fetid place of disease and desired neither their ships nor their men to come near Key West. In 1862, of the 448 men garrisoned at Fort Taylor, 331 contracted yellow fever and 71 died.

The fort was still in the process of being constructed in 1866 when it was declared obsolete. The innovation of rifled cannon, which projected a spinning cannonball that dug into masonry rather than bounced off it, made huge brick fortresses useless. Only a few soldiers remained stationed here, and it became a favorite spot for the townspeople to picnic. A local druggist, J. Otto, made a written request to the authorities for picnicking privileges using his letterhead:

Apothecaries' Hall
Pharmaceutists and Embalmers
Bodies Disinterred
Hermetically Sealed
and Forwarded to Friends.

In 1867, the president of the defeated Confederacy, Jefferson Davis, visited Key West for a day on his way to Cuba, where he hoped to regain his health. He did not picnic at the fort, but while here he was given a sapodilla to sample. He broke it neatly in half, took a small bite, and put the halves back together again. When asked if he liked the fruit, he said politely, "I cannot say that I care for it particularly, but I fancy some people are very fond of it."

In 1898, for the Spanish-American War, the fort was reacti vated. It was also modernized by cutting it back a level and equipping it with newer weapons. This new emplacement of guns was called Osceola Battery. The refuse from the demolition was packed into the casemates with all the obsolete Columbiad and Rodman cannons, cannonballs, and gun carriages, and the whole thing was covered with cement and sand. Over the years, through World Wars I and II and the Cuban crisis, other weapons, radar, missiles, and antiaircraft guns were mounted and removed, but the treasury of Civil War artifacts, including the Parrott rifle, the type of cannon that had reduced Savannah's Fort Pulaski to rubble, remained untouched. (The Parrott can be identified by the wrought-iron jacket shrunk around the breech and the grooves inside the muzzle.)

By the mid 1960's, Fort Taylor was abandoned, forgotten and buried beneath dredge material and weeds. Then in 1968, the Navy (the Army had turned the fort over to the Navy in 1947) directed their base architect and historian, Howard England, to investigate the site, although they did not want to spend any money for excavation. It is to Howard England that the "discovery" of Fort Taylor should be attributed. With borrowed equipment and volunteer help from townspeople and Navy personnel, including, perhaps most enthusiastically, men from the brig, Fort Taylor emerged. After months and years of hand shoveling, the beautiful vaulted brickwork of the gun rooms was exposed and cannon unearthed. Also discovered was America's first water desalinization plant—Dr. Normandy's Patent Marine Aerated Fresh Water Apparatus—which had once produced 7,000 gallons of fresh water daily from the sea. The military artifacts you will see have been recovered from only two of the fort's twenty-four casemates and represent only a fraction of the buried arsenal which is the largest collection of Civil War cannons in the United States.

The fort and fifty acres of surrounding land is now under the management of the Florida Park Service. It has an interesting little museum and the best swimming in Key West. Don't miss Fort Taylor. Truman Annex at Southard Street. Telephone: 292-6713.

PEARY COURT

Key West is an emotional, obstreperous town, its citizens continually in a lather about something. Everything becomes an issue—sidewalks, the Bubba system, Houseboat Row, the San Carlos, the airport—but nothing has divided the city more than Peary Court, Key West's last green space, thirty acres of sloppy but cherished parkland on the edge of Old Town near Garrison Bight. It had been an Army parade ground, cavalry barracks, and military cemetery for 106 years when the Navy took it over after World War II and used it pretty much as a dump site before "giving" it to the city in 1974. The city cleaned it up, made a couple of softball fields, mowed the grass, and let the trees grow, some sapodilla, fig, and frangipani reaching considerable size. By 1988, when the Navy decided they wanted to build 160 units of military housing there, citing a desperate housing shortage, the town had pretty much forgotten that the park wasn't really theirs. ("This is what happens when you give something to the people. They don't want to give it back," a counsel for the Navy recently said.) Since the military had been downsizing in Key West for the last decade, the "desperate need" rhetoric seemed a little inflated, but the town, which has long loved the Navy here, supported them—though possibly they could build someplace else? On one of their many unused or underutilized sites? In a less socially and ecologically sensitive location? Keep Peary Court Green signs appeared all over town, ratified not only by environmentalists but by a lot of carpenters who liked to play softball. Military cutbacks continued. But it seemed the more the Navy families left Key West, the more determined Naval base commander Michael Currie became. Peary Court was going to be built out, and since it was a federal project, exempt from municipal control, building codes, taxes, and all but the most perfunctory environmental survey, it was going to be built out to the max. Fences went up and most of the trees came down. Bases all across the country continued to close, and in Key West the hydrofoil fleet left, as did two fighter wings from Boca Chica. In 1992 the General Accounting Office concluded that Peary Court was unnecessary. It was still somewhat green, though inaccessible, and could, in theory, be excessed to the city for a dollar, but slabs were poured, the first frames of the eventual 160 houses appeared, and the remaining trees didn't look so good. Captain Currie, in his role as juggernaut (and a successful role it was), maintained that there was a housing shortage until his retirement in 1993, a few months after which an internal Navy report was released saying that the military had a huge surplus of rental units in Key West, but planned to demolish or excess them and continue to construct Peary Court. They wanted higher-quality housing for their personnel. Building began in earnest, the locals marveling at the use of something called oriented strand board instead of plywood in the construction. It looks somewhat like head cheese and was banned in Dade County after Hurricane Andrew because it absorbs moisture and disintegrates when wet. The spring rains came, and with them the growing rumor that the Naval Air Station/Key West would be on the base closure list in 1995.

This was all too much for Harry Powell, a City Commissioner from 1987 to 1991 and leader of the dogged but dispirited Keep Peary Court Green crowd. At eight in the morning on January 14, 1994, he walked into an empty construction trailer just opposite the old armory on White Street with a stick of dynamite and a gallon of gasoline, threatening to blow it and himself up unless he was promised a federal investigation into Peary Court—another GAO audit. The standoff, immediately dubbed Key Waco, ended ten hours later when Powell surrendered. He remains in jail, possibly for a very long time, and further debate and inquiries into the necessity of the housing is moot since all the houses have been built. They're just waiting for someone to move into them.

East Martello Museum and Art Gallery

A charming museum and a great place to acquaint yourself with Key West history.

The Martello Tower was an ancient Corsican means of defense, a cylindrical structure often described as an "upside down flowerpot." Key West's two nontraditional towers were constructed during the Civil War to assist Fort Taylor in repelling a coastal landing force. Begun in 1862, work on them ceased two years later. The towers, like the rest of the Keys' huge brick fortifications, were never completed. Cannon were never installed here. Before the Art and Historical Society took over the East Tower in 1950, there was not even a roof.

The museum has exhibits depicting sponging, turtling, pirating, and whatnot, as well as a Cuban life raft, found floating empty ten miles south of Key West in 1969, made of bamboo, wire, and tractor inner tubes and bearing a feed-sack sail. In the great exodus of 1994, more rafts appeared in the Straits of Florida, some consisting of little more than a wedge of Styrofoam powered by a grass-trimmer engine. U.S. immigration policy changed toward Cuba that August, when automatic asylum was no longer granted and thousands of rafters were returned to Guantánamo Bay by the Coast Guard.

The gallery has rotating shows of contemporary and local art as well as an interesting permanent collection where "the welded found materials" of Stanley Papio of Key Largo and the wood carvings of Old Key West by Mario Sanchez can be found.

Papio was a junk dealer and welder, despised for years by his neighbors on Route 1. After being arrested six times for violating local ordinances concerning orderliness and neatness, a friend suggested he claim the junkyard as an "art museum" and charge 25¢ to see the peculiar and parodic conjunctions made between bedsprings, toilet fixtures, and Buick chrome. Papio is the Keys' John Chamberlain, and his works are witty, crude, and very charming. When he died suddenly in 1982, Key Largo, home of the movie lie and Port Bougainvillea, still had no interest in the collection, and Martello was eventually able to purchase the pieces.

The Cuban primitive Mario Sanchez was born in Key West in 1908 in what was known as "Gato's Village," an area bounded by Truman Avenue and Whitehead, South, and Simonton Streets. This is where the flourishing cigar industry was located—one of the larger rebuilt factories still exists today as the Navy Commissary—and the heart of the Cuban community. It is this lively and departed village that Sanchez recreates in his meticulous, colorful carvings. What is nice about his work is that he, like a kind angel, restores lost things. The Convent of Mary Immaculate was demolished, but Sanchez recreates it, complete with its stupendous plantings. To the sightseer at the corner of Amelia and Duval, the Cuban Club is nothing but a simulation (more shops!)—just a bit of hygienic faux, but

Sanchez paints it as it was when it was the soul of the neighborhood, beside the long-gone El Anón Ice Cream Parlor.

Sanchez first draws his scenes on grocery bags, then transfers them to wood with carbon paper. His tools are chisels, a mallet, a piece of broken glass, and a razor blade. Sometimes he uses coffee grounds, coral rock, or kitty-litter to make streets. He likes horses, parades, funerals, pregnant ladies, chickens, and clouds. In the amazing clouds of Key West, he carves things too—doves, blossoms, trumpets, and even the themes of Mr. Hemingway. In one of the explanatory notes to his carvings in this carefully presented exhibit, Sanchez says, "I have featured two of his best-known works in the clouds: *For Whom the Bell Tolls* and *Death in the Afternoon.*" And there they are.

There is also a "Key West Writers" room, the books of the venerated fixed behind glass. **East Martello Tower**, its museum, gallery, and garden, is right in front of the airport on South Roosevelt Boulevard. Open daily 9:30 to 5:30. Adults, $2.50; ages 7–15, 50¢.

West Martello Tower

The West Tower, on Higgs Beach, between the picnic grounds and the White Street Fishing Pier, is the home of the Key West Garden Club. It is far more low-slung and battered than the East Tower because bored soldiers stationed at Fort Taylor used it for target practice, and since it was closer to town, people pilfered many of the bricks for their walls and gardens.

Within the garden center at West Martello are plant-identification books, seed-pod exhibits, and a tattered arrangement of stuffed birds. There is also a checklist of plants, ninety-two of which are marked in the rambling, ruined confines of the tower's grounds. Below the mounded fortification on the beachward side are topless sunbathers, and above you, according to the season, is flowering or fruiting this and that.

The West Tower is free and erratically open. Each year, in March, there is an orchid show, and on the last Sunday of April there is a large, lush, and frantic plant sale. Open Tuesday through Thursday and Saturday and Sunday, 10 A.M.–noon and 2–4 P.M.

OLD TOWN

Conch Houses

Most of the beautiful old homes and intriguing lanes and alleys of the town can be found in the blocks between Caroline and Angela (which borders the graveyard) and Duval and Francis, and many of these buildings are well documented. *The Pelican Path,* a free descriptive folder published by the Old Island Restoration Foundation, is available from the Hospitality House in Mallory Square. The route is marked with directional yellow signs and the buildings sport neatly numbered plaques. (So much of the Keys seems recently numbered. Even the birds of the air are sometimes seen bearing pancake-size discs on their wings, numbered, by those great numberers, the field researchers, who roam armed with nets and tranquilizing darts.) The Historic Key West Preservation Board has published a striking collection of black-and-white photographs by Sharon Wells and Lawson Little entitled *Portraits: Wooden Houses of Key West.* The oversized paperback costs $10.

"Conch" architecture is the indigenous look of Key West. It is what's here. One of the prettiest houses in town, passionately regarded as "Conch," is the violet-hued **Artist House** (a guest house) at 534 Eaton Street, which can only be described as Key West–West Indian–Colonial-Victorian in design. Conch too is the dignified rawboned **Albury House** at 730 Southard, as is the modest **Eyebrow House** at 1025 Fleming, its attic windows tucked beneath the shelter of the roof; a most efficient breeze-capturing and air-circulating architectural eccentricity and one not found elsewhere in Florida. With this exception, however, the Conch style is not one unique to the country—it is a coalescence of styles, a high density of nineteenth- and turn-of-the-century classically built wooden houses that gives the town such an appealing and distinctive appearance.

The practicalities made necessary by a remote, hot, and wet location were combined with mainland fashion and local wealth. Many of the houses have thermally efficient roofs of galvanized steel, embossed with a pattern, and virtually all have porches. In the case of the larger houses, the porches often curve around three sides of the house with the pattern being repeated on the second story. Top-hung shutters are prevalent as a blind to the sun, and ventilating scuttles (simply a hole on the roof, with a lid) are outlets for hot air. Frequently, houses large and small are built not on foundations but on piers, which may explain why Key Westers so enthusiastically undertake the task of moving them around. Piers are slabs of coral rock which elevate the house, protecting it against rot, flooding, and even hurricane winds.

Paint was not employed until the cleanup of the 1930's. Houses were left to weather and silver in the sun. Plaster was never used. Inside, the wood of preference, pitch-rich pine from Pensacola and Dade County, was used on floors, ceilings, and walls, often hand-planed and fitted without nails. Dade County pine has become extinct, Dade County being Miami now, but the wood lives on in Key West houses, beautiful wood, personalized by each home's resident termite population. Chimneys are rare, except on those Queen Anne mansions whose all-embracing style insisted upon them, but there are a number of cupolas to be seen, resembling the widow walks of New England coastal towns. Here, however, they should be referred to as wrecker's walks, for they were not employed so much by desperate ladies awaiting the return of their men from the sea, but by anyone with an eye out for ships which would hopefully run aground on the reef, providing the household with a variety of new possessions. Another vessel eagerly awaited by all in the 1800's was the ice boat, delivering its precious and disappearing cargo all the way from Maine ponds. Ice was also often used as ballast in ships traveling from the North. Good examples of wreckers' walks can be seen on two houses built before the 1886 fire, the Albury house at 730 Southard and the John Lowe house at 620 Southard. The **Lowe House** is built of heart of pine and Honduran mahogany with all mortise-and-tenon joints secured with wooden pegs so that the house would give in strong winds. An early historian noted that Lowe was rich because he never embarked on a "bubble enterprise." He owned a sponging fleet and enlarged his home as he grew more prosperous. Sponges were responsible for much of the wealth and many of the fine

A GONE GARDEN AND TWO GROWING ONES

People used to love to drop by **Peggy Mills Garden**, once open to the public at 700 Simonton Street, and confer with the awesome plantings. There were real treasures here—huge earthenware jars called *tinajones* from Cuba, orchids and lilies, rare old palms . . . The plants grew so vigorously inside Miss Peggy's that it was said if you parked your car outside on the bougainvillea cuttings, you'd get a flat tire. Over the past years the most intensely planted acreage in Key West has had a series of owners, each adding extensive renovations, which were usually of a non-organic nature. For example, a tennis court. The tennis court has since been felled, and Miss Peggy's place now exists as the very pricey **Gardens Hotel** (see page 208).

The **Botanical Gardens on Stock Island** was the pride and joy of horticultural ladies of the '30's. An intriguing spot with a varied number of trees in a natural hammock setting, it was allowed to decline, its rare and indigenous species pushed out by brazilian pepper and neglect. Difficult to find—it is behind the golf course, sandwiched between the Easter Seal Society, the dog pound, and the jail annex—it has been cleared and replanted, now the pride and joy of the horticultural ladies of the '90's. It boasts three Florida "Champion" trees (which means they're *big*), the Arjan almond, the Cuban lignum vitae, and the Barringtonia; and, once again, the oddities of monkey's dinner bell, egg fruit, horseradish, and soapberry trees grow here.

The **Indigenous Park** at the end of White Street opposite the pier and next to the bocce courts is only a little over three acres but it seems much larger as you wander and linger among these palms and trees—the real natives here. Everything is identified but, relaxingly, not explained. There are over 125 different species of trees and shrubs, which the songbirds like to visit.

homes of Key West, as were foundered ships, turtles, and cigars.

An ice palace, indeed, having been built in 1885 by George Curry, the president of the ice company, is the large classical home at 620 Eaton Street—a temple of columns, porticos, and entablatures, all tropically garnished with louvered porches and Canary Island date palms.

Eaton Street presents many beauties, the lovely triplets at 401-405-409, and the equally impressive clutch at 511-517 and 523. The "tropical Greek Revival" **Donkey Milk House** at 613 is open to the public. Built in 1868, it's been meticulously restored, and its hand-painted ceilings (the Italian artist gave Key West four seasons), century-old Barcelona tile, and distinctive antiques make this a very pretty respite from the street. Open 10 A.M.–5 P.M. Admission is $3. The octagonal tin-towered **Richard Peacon House** at 712 Eaton is somewhat notoriously known for the price it once commanded. It was originally built by a banker and grocer in the 1890's and bought by the late designer Angelo Donghia in the 1970's. Key West realtors went into deliriums when it was later bought by Calvin Klein for close to a million dollars, approximately $700,000 more than everyone admitted the house was worth. Klein said it was "probably crazy" but he "wanted it badly." The house at 724 is a handsome example of a Bahamian house with Victorian influences. Adorned with flourishing columnar trim and cranberry glass, it is owned by the county sheriff.

Two of the most remarked upon homes in Key West were brought here from somewhere else. The **Bahama Houses**, one at 730 Eaton, the other directly behind it at 408 William, were made in the Bahamas, dismantled, brought over by ship, and reconstructed in 1847, after the hurricane of 1846 had destroyed much of Key West. Wood was scarce, so two brothers-in-law, Joseph Bartlum and Richard Roberts, returned to their home in Green Turtle Cay and sailed these structures, made simply of random-width, hand-beveled pine boards, back. The twin-gabled roof, with the valley in between to collect rainwater for the cistern, and the large shuttered windows are of typical Bahamian design. The low ceilings inside indicate the age of the houses, for the cooling benefits of high-ceilinged rooms were only recognized by later Key West builders. Bartlum was a shipbuilder who built the only clipper ship ever made in Key West, the *Stephen Mallory*. The ship was launched in 1856 and bore a life-size figurehead of the cherubic Mallory upon her prow. The Roberts House on William has been very little altered over the years. Crowded at right angles to the street, its

NOT ON THE PELICAN PATH

Just past The Palm Grill at 1017 Southard is a shambly but dignified Conch house where on April 30, 1992, police found a man who had been dead for two months lying on the floor. His roommate, a seventy-eight-year-old gentleman named Thomas Warren, thought he was just being "stubborn" and ignored him, though occasionaly he asked him if he wanted something to eat or drink or wanted to go to the hospital. Annoyingly, the body didn't reply. As his roomie mouldered and melted into the linoleum, Mr. Warren went about his business, stepping over the body, which lay facedown between the kitchen and a bathroom. He told detectives that he thought the fellow, an unlucky man named Delaney, was alive because he appeared to change positions and, even, stretch his legs.

double porches run the length of the house on two sides and are built under the roof. Both houses are rather unassuming, intriguing primarily because of the journey they once took.

Gingerbread, Courtyards, and Shotguns

Key Westers love their gingerbread. The town embraced this fanciful fashion of the mid-1800's and people today are still gleefully remodeling by slapping up baluster patterns of pineapples, fleurs-de-lis, and urns. Most of the elaborately turned railings of Old Town were not made locally but were brought here as stock items for the building trade, although there were several local craftsmen who did scroll-cut work from flat boards. One of these was John Carroll, who set up his turning lathe near the lighthouse in the 1880's and produced brackets, cornices, and trim according to the customer's whim. Another was Francisco Camellon, a black Cuban, whose lathe was turned by a blindfolded horse. His shop was on Simonton Street under a big Spanish lime tree.

There are more than sixty different baluster patterns to be found in Key West, the most popular being Grecian urns, dia-

monds, hearts, ship wheels and—after the railroad reached
Key West in 1912—viaduct arches. Lovely examples of scroll-
cut ship wheels can be found at the **Cuban Consul House** on
the corner of Eaton and Grinnel. The same gingerbread string-
course adorns the house at 615 Fleming.

One of the most intriguing examples of personalized gingerbread and a design that was used for professional advertising is
found on the old Conch house at 1117 Duval. The saloon keeper
who once lived here had this pattern of whiskey and wine bottles and the hearts and diamonds of playing cards sent from
Cuba and installed as balusters.

Two of the most elaborate gingerbread dwellings in town are
the gray Victorian **George Roberts House** at 313 William
Street (its beauty assisted in the late spring and summer by the
blooming of a towering poinciana tree) and the **Benjamin
Baker House** at 615 Elizabeth Street. Baker was the owner of
a lumberyard, a contractor, and an undertaker, and he built
this house for his daughter in 1885 as a wedding present. His
workmen, freed from the rigors of nailing together coffins,
spared no flourish here—the trim is all scroll-cut. The house
was so well built that when a tornado moved it seven feet off its
foundation in 1972, not a single wall or window cracked.

The **William Kerr House** at 410 Simonton Street has gingerbread embellishments of a more Gothic sort. The style of
this little house is unclassifiable, put together by a carpenter-

Examples of gingerbread trimming

architect who had designed many of the striking buildings of
Key West in the last twenty years of the nineteenth century.
Born in Massachusetts Kerr became one of the town's most ver-
satile and original builders, responsible for the design of the
convent, as well as the Customs House and the Old Stone
Church at 600 Eaton Street. The house is heavily ornamented
inside with hand-painted landscapes over the doors and in
indented panels in the ceilings.

A building of erratic history, so common in Key West, is the
structure at 314 Simonton, the old **Trev-Mor** apartments.
Built with bricks taken from the ruins of Fort Taylor, the first
Ford dealership in Key West was located here in 1919. There
were apartments upstairs, and it was here where Hemingway
and his wife Pauline, fresh from Paris, stayed for several weeks
as they awaited the delivery of a new car. It remained a room-
ing house and hotel until the 1970's when it was completely
gutted by fire. The new owners kept the core empty and it is
now a one-bedroom private home with a vast inner atrium. The
old cistern is in the middle of things and is used as a swimming
pool. A number of water craft continue their lives most peculiarly behind these walls. An Ecuadorian canoe is used as a
planter, a glass-topped Haitian dory serves as a coffeetable,
and a wet bar and dumbwaiter have been created from a
lifeboat off the yacht of one no less than Adolf Hitler. It's now
called Casa Antigua and you can see the gardens for $2.

The old **Mercedes Hospital** or **Casa Gato** at 1209 Virginia
Street, just around the corner from the Gulfstream Market on
White, is out of the way but noteworthy. It too has a courtyard,
of an initially more intended sort, and a history even more
eccentric and variable.

Eduard Gato was a wealthy Cuban cigar manufacturer who
had come to Key West in 1868 at the start of Cuba's Ten Years'
War with Spain. The town was jammed with wealthy Cuban
cigar manufacturers building factories, banks, and mansions
and hiring and housing thousands of their fellow emigrés to
work as strippers, trimmers, rollers, pickers, and packers. Gato
built his mansion, embellished with balconies and cupolas, and
enclosed a patio, in the Spanish style, but it appears a little odd
because it was built out of wood, covered with clapboard, and
decorated with a bit of gingerbread. It is a high, square building

with long Gothic windows and large, dark, tall-ceilinged rooms
(eight to a floor) that look out onto the somewhat stern court-
yard. It was said that after Gato got his Spanish courtyard he
was puzzled as to what to do with it, so he stabled his horses
there for several years.

Gato and his family did not live here long. He returned to
Cuba after the Spanish-American War of 1898 (the war in
which Teddy Roosevelt disappointed Key Westers by having his
Rough Riders sally forth from Tampa) and gave the house to
the town to be used as a hospital. The hospital was named for
his wife, Mercedes, but it was locally called *Casa del Pobre*—the
house of the poor. It remained a poorhouse until the 1940's.
Elizabeth Bishop, once paying a call, described a patient as possessing an "apocryphal appearance," her bright, milky blue
eyes seeming "like the flames of a gas burner when they have
just been turned off and are about to sink back into the black
pipes." The Mercedes Hospital had a reputation of harboring
gloomy ghosts, and there are still some old Cubans in town who
refuse to walk on the Casa Gato side of the street.

When its days as a poorhouse had passed, it became an arena
for cockfights and a storage area for newspapers collected during World War II paper-drives. It was "a monster nobody

Sand Key Light

wanted" until the 1970's when it was restored as apartments. Musical events take place here now during Old Island Days. String quartets play, and champagne is served in the court-yard.

Many cigar barons like Gato built houses for their workers, creating instant neighborhoods around their factories. Most of the factories are gone, but many of the little company houses remain. These narrow houses were simplicity itself, consisting of three rooms, one behind the other, the front and rear doors in alignment with the door connecting the rooms, and were called *shotgun* houses, perhaps because of the narrow and uninter-rupted passage the space allowed. Most were no more than twelve by thirty feet in floor area, had galvanized steel roofs and little porches. Tired of termites, many shotgun owners later replaced the wooden pillars and porches with concrete ones. Tidy, cherished examples of shotguns can be found between 822 and 834 Olivia, where the street parallels the graveyard.

THE GRAVEYARD

"I'd rather eat monkey manure than die in Key West," Ernest Hemingway said. He said this one summer day, sweating in the sulfurous, warm, and brownish waters of his swimming pool, years before he chose to die in Idaho. But people not as fortu-nate, one would assume, have died in Key West, and it is here where they remain, smack in the middle of things on the lip of Old Town. This is referred to euphemistically as "The Ceme-tery" in yet another attempt to gingerbread Key West. But what it is is the graveyard. It was established here in 1847, although some of the graves date before that. The original bury-ing ground was closer to the lighthouse but was moved here when many of the graves were disinterred in a hurricane. There are still funeral marching bands in town that will play the dead home.

The graveyard is hot, white, and built up, the graves all in above-ground vaults, both because of the water table and the toughness of coral rock, and it is virtually treeless, although

The graveyard

some citizens are hard at work planting frangipani cuttings
and mock oranges in available scraps of ground. "Palm
Avenue," which intersects the graveyard, is now neatly lined
with tiny Christmas palms. Other citizens, however, are just as
determinedly cutting down large, bearded, Washingtonian
palms, fearing that a high wind will bring them crashing down
on what James Merrill describes as "whitewashed hope chests."
Neither Conchs nor Cubans care for trees as a rule, and in fact
the graveyard is a fine, impressive place without them. There
are flowering shrubs planted here and there and something is
always in bloom. White egrets drift among the markers, giving
an Egyptian effect.

This is a wonderful place to see birds, particularly at the end
of the day. This is the nighthawk's territory, for instance. The
large, mottled bird is known in Key West as the mosquito hawk,
although it is not a hawk at all but belongs to the voracious
insect eaters known as goatsuckers. A flying mouth, it darts
and scoops at twilight here, saying *piskkk*.

A sausage tree, notorious for its preference to be pollinated by
bats, stands at one of the entrances on Angela Street opposite
the remains of the "bottle wall," a Key West landmark demolished by its creator one dark afternoon to the horror of its fans.

Look upon it and be grateful that once again it appears to be fruitless. If R. C. Perky had been successful in raising bats on Sugarloaf, Key West would have been up to its rooftops in sausage trees with their weird seed pods swinging on long stems.

The graveyard is crisscrossed with paths that bear concrete road markers. For example, the brick Otto plot which contains the graves of three Yorkshire terriers—Sunny, Little Boy, and Little Derry Otto—as well as the one of a pet deer, Elfina, is located at the intersection of Second and Laurel. (Sunny might have been something of a pest—his inscription reads *His Beautiful Little Spirit Was a Challenge to Love.*) A varnished marker on the crypt of B. P. Roberts which complains *I Told You I Was Sick* is at the end of Seventh Street just before the fenced Jewish plot. There are angels small and large, including the beautiful Gladys, swans and lambs, open books, and amputated tree trunks. There is a full-sized cement sculpture of a man, done by his friend, utilizing the boots of the deceased. His name is Earle Saunders Johnson and he is smiling. *The Buck Stops Here* one gravestone says. *Here Lies Our Heart* says another. *A Devoted Fan of Singer Julio Iglesias* says a third. People *think* there's a plaque that says *At Least I Know Where He's Sleeping Tonight* but there isn't, though there is the famous "bound woman" near the fence at the intersection of Angela and Grinnel. She's no angel certainly, and her posture seems to suggest something other than grief, but Archibald John Sheldon Yates really really wanted her on his grave and there she is. Wander and read epitaphs of loss—*We Miss You at Home*—longing and regret—*Yesterday Is Gone and Tomorrow Shall Never Be Mine.* Even gratitude—*God Was Good to Me.* There are pictures of some of the dead in small plastic frames. There are benches beside some of the graves and wrought-iron fences around others. There is a pretty plot which contains the graves of the victims of the *Maine* with a handsome statue of a sailor holding an oar. And there is a monument to *Los Martires,* Cubans who died during the Spanish-American War.

An infamous grave that is not marked is the one of Elena Hoyos Mesa, a Cuban girl who died of tuberculosis in the 1930's but who even more unfortunately was the object of affection of an elderly and lunatic X-ray technician named Karl von Cosel.

Before he met Elena, von Cosel's obsession was with air-planes. He was building an experimental craft that would land on either water or land. The plane had huge wheels made of wooden slats and covered with paper. After Elena died, von Cosel was seen visiting her tomb just off Francis more than fre-quently. He played records and sometimes cooked breakfast there. Eventually he carted the body off in the plane to his house where he loved, lived with, and experimented on Elena for seven years until the grisly affair was discovered. Held together with wire and waxy compounds and wearing a wed-ding gown, the corpse had glass eyes, fabricated breasts, and, according to a doctor who testified at the trial, "a tube in the vaginal area wide enough to permit intercourse." Poor Elena was viewed by thousands of Key West citizens at the Lopez Funeral Home before she was interred again.

The dead are always with us, some more than others.

The graveyard's gates are open from sunrise to sunset. Tours are available on the weekends for $5. These leave from the Mar-garet Street entrance at 10 A.M. and 4 P.M. They even have a breakfast tour on Memorial Day. Have a pastry and contem-plate the ever-approaching nothing.

WHERE TO STAY

There are many quaint, elegant, and/or decadent places to stay in Key West. There are guest houses and motels (chain and unchain) and condominiums as well as suites in time-share resorts that can be rented by the day and week. The Key West Visitor's Bureau puts out an accommodation directory with rates and a helpful visitor "type" category. You can get one by writing to Box 1147, Key West, FL 33041 or calling (305) 294-2587.

If you're planning a longer stay you may be interested in renting a home by the month or for the season. Most of the real estate agencies have furnished houses for rent. Knight Realty, in the oldest school house, 336 Duval (294-5155), is one of the larger ones. Or try Prudential, 507 Whitehead (296-8516). Spe-cializing in vacation rentals is Property Management of Key

West, 517 Eaton Street (296-7744). They have about forty houses in and out of Old Town that they'll rent daily, weekly, or monthly. They provide maid service and have their own maintenance department and will try to match your vacation needs, even your desires, with present availability—just like a dating service.

Remember, prices here are probably already history. Undoubtedly, they have risen. And will rise. In season, nonrefundable deposits and two- or three-day minimum stays are often required.

Chains

The chains are on North Roosevelt Boulevard as you come into town. The prospect—a jumble of the familiar, plus a highly harrowing four-lane highway teeming with illogical and neurotic traffic—is not pleasing. It's awful. There is the water, but it looks so *sad*. Beware of ads promising Gulf views in this area. It's not that they're exactly lying, it's merely that you might be disappointed. Here are **Holiday Inn**, **Howard Johnson**, **Quality Inn**, **TraveLodge**, and **Day's Inn**. Prices are usual for chains in resort areas—$140–$200 a night, $75–$125 off season.

On South Roosevelt Boulevard (A1A) the expected appears much nicer. Set back from the ocean by the airport in pleasantly landscaped grounds are the **Best Western** (296-3500), $150–$185 a night, and the **Key Wester** (296-5671). The Key Wester has tennis courts and a good resident pro. Prices are $150–$300 in season, down to $60–$150 off.

South Street–Simonton Street Beach Area

There are a number of reasonable motels here, all within walking distance of town, including the classic, old-timer **The Santa Maria** (296-5678), now cramped and dwarfed by the pink four-story **Reach**. The Santa Maria has nice rooms overlooking a huge pool. Rates are around $145, out of season $75.

There are the swimming-pool-in-the-middle-of-the-parking-lot variety like **The Blue Marlin** (294-2585), and the swimming-pool-on-the-street variety such as **Southernmost** (296-6577) and **The Spanish Gardens** (294-1051). Rooms here run $110–$150 a night for a double in season, slightly more for an efficiency, and drop $20 in price from June until December. **Atlantic Shores** (296-2491) is a big place, no beauty on the street side but with a handsome swimming pool decked out on the ocean and a 150-foot pier. Rooms around $125, $50 in summer. Sunday night there's a rambunctious "tea dance" at their bar, **Papillon**. (A tea dance in Key West is bare-chested bump-and-grind boogie. **La-Te-Da** began tea. The 801 Bar has "pre-tea," the **Copa** "after-tea." The **One Saloon** at 524 Duval gets right down to it and just has Sleazy Sundays, in their desire to make Sunday night the naughtiest night of the week.) The more subdued and better designed **South Beach Motel** (296-5611) is next door with pool, pier, and balconied rooms. Rates are $160–$190, Christmas through April; in summer, $100–$135. Upstairs rooms with a balcony overlooking the ocean are $135. **La Mer** (296-5611) is a turn-of-the-century home renovated as a small hotel with eleven rooms. Once somewhat dreary, it has been recently redone and it sparkles—the only bed-and-breakfast on the ocean. It has a swell little beach and some of the rooms have efficiencies. It's gotten a reputation as a honeymoon destination, and children under twelve are not permitted. $110–$150 in summer; $175–$245 in season.

Posher and pricier is the **Coconut Beach Resort** run as a time-share at 1500 Alberta Street near the Casa Marina (294-0057). Very pretty, sophisticated rooms on a hidden beach. All the suites are on the ocean and have complete kitchens. They cost about $300 a night in season. A studio not on the beach costs $170–$195. Minimum stays apply, and prices go up $40 for holidays—Christmas, Easter, and **Fantasy Fest**, which takes place the last week in October and has developed a quite indescribable life of its own. Invented fifteen years ago to break up the summer doldrums, there are several events, including a "Pretenders-in-Paradise" costume party—tons of feathers, foil, and Mylar, much smoke, and many mirrors. It all culminates in a big parade up Duval Street which doesn't necessarily get better as the years go by. Sometimes its outrageous, sometimes corny, sometimes just raunchy.

Deluxe

Henry Flagler planned a chain of luxury resort hotels, which he referred to as "Halls of Joy," along his Florida train route. **The Casa Marina**, with its Spanish Renaissance design, tiled roof, arched windows, colonnades, and loggias, in a beautiful garden setting at the end of the road on the Atlantic, was to be the ultimate. The Casa opened New Year's Eve 1922, eight years after Flagler's death. It was a popular spot for the rich and famous until 1943, when the government leased it for Navy housing during the war. It returned to hotel status in 1945 but was taken over by the Army in 1962 during the Cuban missile crisis. Sentries replaced doormen, missile battalion troops were quartered in the rooms, and the beach was strung with barbed wire. After the Army left, it was declared out of commission as a hotel. Indeed, it was described as a "termite-ridden firetrap." For the next ten years, only the dance patio and the Birdcage lounge remained open, and it was messy and popular until 1978, when the Marriott chain took it over, renovating it completely, tearing down the Birdcage and adding a new, ugly four-story wing. The elegance is all beach-side. They don't do pretty for the street. The old building is grand, its walls "battered in" for hurricane proofing, receding in thickness from 22 inches at the foundation to 12 inches at the roof. The black cypress lobby is impressive, the grounds immaculate. The Casa has a 1,100-foot beach, tennis courts, and several bars and restaurants, including **Flagler's**. Thirty-dollar lamb chops here in a reserved, even solemn, setting. It seems very far from town. And it is. In fact, going downtown from the Casa feels like a foray into exotic, uncontrolled, and unsecured territory. The Casa is great-looking but can't quite shake—despite her pig roasts and steel drum music—her reputation as being a bit . . . boring. Suites range from $320 to $695 in season. Ocean-view rooms are $345. The least expensive room is $240, $155 in summer. Reynolds Street on the Atlantic. Toll-free: 800-228-9290, or direct: (305) 296-3535.

The Pier House (1 Duval Street, 294-9541. Toll-free: 800-327-8340.) The Pier House is well known and very popular. Reservations should be made in advance even during the off-season, when the rooms may all be filled with powerboat racers or rafters or fantastic participants in the Fantasy Fest revels of Halloween. The hotel is subtly and handsomely laid out, the rooms tasteful, the grounds palmy. Low-key, efficient, and friendly. At the Caribbean Spa annex next door, there's an awesome health club. The standard room here in season is $265. A nicer room in the courtyard by the pool is $325, and one overlooking the harbor is $385. From April 15 to December 20, these are $150, $195, and $235 respectively. Suites run from $450 to $750 in season, but if elaborate suites are your desire, you might be more content across the street at

Ocean Key House (Zero Duval Street, 296-7701. Toll-free: 800-328-9815.) The Ocean Key House, when built, was notorious for counting bay-bottom acreage in their density computations. Out of scale with an enormous parking garage at its base which one must pass through to attain either one's room or the pool, the exterior is heavy-handed. But the rooms are perhaps the most luxuriously furnished on the island, all decorated in soft, tropical shades, with large balconies and kitchens. The showers are motel basic; you're supposed to luxuriate in the immoderate Jacuzzi in the bedroom. Suites overlook the street, the Gulf, and Mallory Square parking lot. You may come back from breakfast, open the door, and have the sensation of a cruise ship having entered your living room. Very comfortable one-bedroom suites run from $310 to $450 in season, $60 to $100 less April to December. Two-bedroom suites, $385–$450.

The Reach (Simonton Street on the ocean, 296-5000. Toll-free: 800-822-4200.) The Reach is somewhat brutish in design, even though it's pink. One hoped that this would be the south end of town's answer to The Pier House, but it has little of The Pier House's gracious ease. Beautifully situated on the water with a great beach, pool, and pier, it has developed a somewhat crabbed and suspicious attitude toward its guests. Taken over in 1994 by Marriott, the new management fired the pastry chef (a genius!), banalized the restaurants, and hired tall men in

black pants, white shirts, and walkie-talkies to patrol the
beach. Ask for their desired guest profile. They must have
someone in mind. A one-bedroom suite on the ocean is $375 in
season, $285 summer and fall. There are 149 rooms here, half of
which have a glimpse of the water, which makes a big difference.

Hyatt Key West (601 Front Street. Toll-free: 800-228-9000.)
Part of the new chic-ing-up of Key West. They call it a boutique
resort as it has only 120 rooms. The beach could be the world's
smallest, but the rooms with balconies are sited well for sunset-
watching. The lowest rate in season is $200 a night. A suite is
$450. If Fate brings you to the Rock in August, say, a suite is
yours for $250.

The Marquessa Hotel (600 Fleming Street, 292-1919). This
old boardinghouse was refurbished in 1988 and it's charming.
Fifteen lovely big high-ceilinged rooms with generous baths.
One suite has a private balcony overlooking the street, and
many of the rooms have pretty window seats that are right out
of a Jesse Wilcox Smith painting. Charming, but costly. Rooms
and suites $185–$260. $115–$165 in summer.

The Gardens Hotel (526 Angela Street, corner of Simonton,
294-2661). The newest deluxe re-do. Pretty, gleaming, and
serene but a far cry from the jumble of a jungle it was. Big white
marble bathrooms very much in the European fancy mode (one
of the suites even has a sauna). Very prettily lit at night. $625
for the master suite in the old main house. The humbler, new
rooms in the tasteful buildings out by the pool run from $225 to
$315.

Moderates

Near the Casa and not far from the beach is the secluded **El
Patio Motel** (800 Washington Street, 296-6531). This is a discovery—quiet, clean, and pleasant with a garden patio and a
terrific rooftop sun deck where you can sail your gaze over the
tops of palms to the ocean. The rooms are large with little view

of their own but with classic Cuban-tile floors. This is the best of the little motels in the area. Rooms are $89 in season, $52 otherwise. Rooms with two double beds are $98 down to $58. **The Sea Shell Motel** at 718 South Street is a lighthearted, unexacting youth hostel which takes no credit cards and is $38 a night. It has a dormitory where one can sleep for $18. During spring break, however, the rooms are $100 a night because ". . . the kids trash the rooms" (296-5719). With a pool and accepting credit cards and even pets are **The Key Lodge Motel** at 1004 Duval (296-9915) and the **El Rancho** at 830 Truman (294-8700). The Key Lodge is $75 a night in season, $45 in summer and fall. El Rancho, away from the action but on busy Truman, is $99 a night in season, $89 at other times. Recently, a guest here called police to report that he couldn't find the cocaine he had hidden in his room and feared that it had been stolen. (At your basic little bar on Applerouth Lane, **The Bamboo Room**, people often call the police too, many times to turn themselves in . . . "I'm a fugitive from Texas and I just can't take it anymore. . . ." Maybe they just couldn't find a cheap room.)

Downtown

La Concha (430 Duval, 296-2991). You can't be closer to the heart of things than this. Pleasant rooms done in a '20's tropo style, a great bar at The Top from which you can see Key West in all its improbable selfness, even a pool on one level. A room with a queen-size bed is $160–$300 December through April. Drops $50 summer and fall. A suite is $200–$500. In March, the dreaded "Breaker" month, you might want a room *away* from the street.

The Curry Mansion (511 Caroline Street, 294-5349). Stay in the Mansion with its Tiffany glass and lovely paneling and verandas. The kitchen is the revered site of the creation of the first Key lime pie. (An Aunt Sally did it.) The new rooms built around a small pool are pleasant but plain. There's free breakfast and a complimentary cocktail party daily as well as beach-club privileges at both The Pier House and the Casa Marina.

Rates in season $150–$200. Nonseason from $110 to $160. The Mansion is often rented for "events," so you'll frequently find yourself part of a party, even a wedding party.

Guest Houses

Guest houses abound in Key West, and most of them are very pretty, private, and friendly places with lovely gardens and dramatic pools. (The 1990's brought an explosion of them on Truman Avenue. Every old manse on the block became one. They almost ran out of names.) Many do not accept children sixteen and under either, because of the cozily affectionate milieu or because patrons want to enjoy their complimentary quiche breakfasts and Jacuzzis in peace. A pleasant place that will take families is **The Island City House**.

The Island City House (411 William Street, 294-5702). Smack in the middle of the historic district with all its regal houses, Island City was built in the 1880's and served as a guest house as early as 1912. Another building in this small compound is **The Arch House**, which faces Eaton. Restored and renovated down to its last nail, each unit is an apartment with full kitchen. The rooms are rather dark but high-ceilinged and beautifully furnished. Bromeliads bloom profusely over an old cistern. Pleasant pool, rampant garden, breakfast bar. One-bedroom suites are $165–$200. Two-bedroom $100 more. **The Island City House** should not be confused with **Island House**, a men-only cruise complex on the corner of Fleming and White (294-6284) that has rooms, a pool, and a complete gym.

Two small classic guest houses are The Artist House and The Pilot House. Neither has a pool.

The Artist House (534 Eaton Street, 296-3977). Built in 1890, each room in this sweet old house is uniquely decorated. The large room in front has a pretty winding staircase which leads to a sleeping loft in the tower. The side rooms have claw-foot bathtubs on an enclosed porch. In one of the suites you can even bubble bathe under a chandelier. The garden is tiny and unmysterious, although it does have a lion's head sluicing water into a Jacuzzi and an obscure stone saint by the fish pond. The Artist House is formal, filled with seventeenth-century antiques, and can be noisy, particularly the rooms on the street. **The Pilot House**, behind it at 414 Simonton Street (294-8719), is more casual, with a number of larger, often connecting, rooms with kitchens. A bedroom in The Artist House is $125; $165–$190 for a suite. Suites in The Pilot House are about the same, but the double suites are $275.

Two attractive, voguish, more freewheeling guest houses are Heron House and Merlinn.

Heron House (512 Simonton, 294-9227). One of the prettiest and best-located guest houses in Key West. Seventeen high-ceilinged, beautifully furnished rooms are available. Great attention to detail and design. Handsome yet lightly tropical. Rooms $125–$175 in winter, $75–$150 June 1–November 30. A lot of style for the money. Pool.

Merlinn (811 Simonton Street, 296-3336). The rooms here are a bit peculiar, narrow and very high, rather monkish in aspect. The garden, sunning decks, and pool, however, are decidedly not. Merlinn is a real charmer, a bosky retreat from the street with a beautiful, high-ceilinged pine kitchen from which delicious breakfasts are served. There's also an aviary and a library with free drinks and hors d'oeuvres served at the important sunset hour. Cocktails, coffee cake, and cockatoos . . . what sort of heart could desire more? Rooms are $90–$100 December through April. Larger rooms with kitchens, $125–$150. The singular "Treehouse" with its private sundeck is $130.

If you'd like to have the illusion of staying with your neat hippie sister when Key West was cool and casual, try **Key West Bed and Breakfast** (The Popular House) at 415 William Street, only a few blocks away from the town's beloved Bight. A 100-year-old house with great porch-top views and lots of fresh fruit for breakfast. Most of the high-ceilinged, individually furnished rooms share a bath. Jacuzzi, no pool. Your cohosts are the golden retrievers Sam and Dave. $80–$175 in season. Otherwise, $40–$125. Call 296-7274.

The Eden House (1015 Fleming Street, 296-6868) has been around since 1924 when it operated as The Gibson Hotel. This is some ways from downtown, but in a great walking and biking neighborhood. A simple, tropical inn with fans and iron beds, it's been recently modernized with phones, air conditioners, and private baths. Just as the sprucing up was completed, Hollywood arrived and wanted to re-funk the place for the movie *Criss Cross*. Many coats of paint were employed to make the place look unpainted, and its engaging, slightly seedy quality was reinstated. After the filming, it was all turned around again. A great old place. It seems to have interesting tenants, feeling rather like the Gramercy Park of Key West guest houses. A conch house next door has been converted into fancier suites ($135–$250) but you can still get the old rooms with the big porches overlooking Fleming Street for $75 ($20 less out of season), and other rooms with a bath down the hall are about the same. Rockers on the porch; pool; little restaurant (**Martin's**) to the rear. **Martin's** serves serious German food. Veal, veal, veal—enough to make a cow never want to have her calf. It may seem odd to chow down potato soup and Wiener

Night-blooming cirrus at 413 William Street

schnitzel in the tropics, but the chef here enjoys preparing it for you. He wants to, and he does.

Of the gay guest houses—**Big Ruby's** on Applerouth Lane has the distinction of being the oldest in the country—**The Brass Key** at 412 Francis (296-4719) is newly elegant, mature you might say, while the all-male **Lighthouse Court** at 902 Whitehead is edgier and younger—New York–style, so described. **Colours**, **Coconut Grove**, and the all-male **Oasis** are all on Fleming. **Colours** (410 Fleming, 294-6977) is in a lustrously restored Victorian mansion, and **Coconut Grove** at 817 Fleming (296-5107) is a sprawling, breezy white gingerbread inn with lots of balconies and porches. Rates here run between $75 and $180, $55–$100 in summer. "Socializing is a requisite," and around the pools and sun-traps "clothing optional."

Simonton Court (320 Simonton, 294-6386) is in an 1880 building which was originally a cigar factory. Down a little alley are a number of well-designed wooden cottages with kitchens, porches, and private bedrooms as well as sleeping lofts. There are two dramatic pools here, one black, and one set within the crumbling brick foundations of an old house. The cottages, which accommodate four people, are $260 in season, $180 in summer and fall. No kids here though. This is an adults-only compound which caters, as the owners say, to visitors who appreciate a "varied" life-style . . . showing, once again, that euphemisms make strange bedfellows.

WHERE TO EAT
Breakfast

Breakfast is extremely important to some people who firmly believe that a magical amount of day-long energy and luck is inherent in an eggy morning plate. These are the same people who need to be apprised practically at sunup of world news— the bombings and threats, the kidnappings and disasters, the shocking and the pathetic—and read the newspaper while they eat. An odd marriage, but one indulged in by many. There are others who desire coffee only, perhaps a bun. Still others who prefer brunch: eggs Benedict, corned beef hash, steak . . . practically anything, really, as long as it can be accompanied by a Bloody Mary.

Hemingway, before going fishing, would ingest simply of a piece of Cuban bread, a glass of Vichy, and a glass of milk. But alas, Mrs. Rhoda's electric kitchen, where he indulged, is gone, as is, more recently, **shorty's** on Duval, famous for their biscuits and strange French toast since 1942. Shorty's had the thinnest, palest waitresses in the Keys, and the day the joint closed was the day Truman Annex developer Pritam Singh announced that Ritz-Carlton would build a hotel on "Sunset Island." Everyone felt this said it all—the Rock vas ruined. But the Ritz hasn't materialized. And probably never will.

For those who believe in breakfast, here are some possibilities:

Dennis Pharmacy (Simonton and South streets). Everyone who stays in the beach motels ends up here. Plainclothesmen can be overheard discussing cases. (They were nevertheless caught flat-footed when in 1994 the owner-pharmacist was accused of dealing drugs.) The intriguing thing about the Pharmacy is that although the waitress never acknowledges your order, you end up being served anyway. Don't even dream about trying to jolly these ladies up.

South Beach (1405 Duval, 294-2727). A shambly place directly on the ocean. It's fun to start your day right on the beach, although the beach patrons at certain times can be pretty low-crust. The fruit plate's healthy but pricey. They make up for this by giving you three times more than you could possibly eat. Open until 10 P.M. with an extensive seafood and raw bar menu. Full bar.

Camille's (703 Duval). Going strong. Classical music, homemade muffins, powerful espresso and con leche. Built breakfasts (some so complicated you feel you need directions to eat them), fresh and imaginative specials. Locals love this cozy, crowded spot. Popular Sunday brunch 8–3. Open for dinner too, Tuesday through Saturday.

Chit-Chat (821 Duval). A simple enough breakfast for 99¢ (not including coffee) served by rather flamboyant middle-aged males with astonishingly flat midriffs, which they expose.

Croissants de France (813 Duval). The Breton owner has expanded this tiny pastry shop where you once had to sit on the curb to eat your croissant into a pocket-sized café where you can now wait in line for a table. Somewhat elevated from the street with a European clientele. People exclaim over the extensive menu here in many languages. Transcendental crêpes and croissants.

Blue Heaven (corner of Thomas and Petronia). Best pancakes in Key West, perhaps anywhere. Or you can get two eggs, grits, coffee, and banana bread for $2. This place is charming, though not for those with a fear of chickens. Apparently fowl phobia does exist. But most people love it here. Maybe you'll even have a favorite hen.

Lunch

Lunch can be an occasion, a necessity, or just a habit. You can munch on Conch fritters, Philippine food, or a dolphin sandwich with fries from street vendors, or be healthy and buy a fruit smoothie. If you want to watch the street you can sit more or less *in* the street at **Mango's** (700 Duval). Good food, but occasional large parked delivery trucks with their motors running can make conversation difficult. Where are the drivers? Perhaps at the next table, enjoying their shrimp caesar. Good Cuban sandwiches can be had at **5 Brothers Grocery** (corner Southard and Grinnel) or at **Sandy's** in the **M&M Laundry** walk-up at 1026 White. Best place to eat in the Mallory Square area is the gardeny **Rooftop Cafe** at 310 Front Street. Opens at 9 in the morning and moves right past midnight. Good burgers and wonderful Apalachicola oysters can be had at **Pepe's Cafe** (806 Caroline), a place of varnished walls, booths, and tiller-topped tables. An awesome ceiling fan rotates slowly, slowly overhead. There's a nice patio here with bougainvillea vines thick as trees. It's popular for dinner too, though the wait is often endless, the rule appearing to be that *just* as you get seated, the place clears out. And the bill always comes to more than you had guessed. The **Half-Shell Raw Bar** across the way in Land's End Village rides rather overconfidently on its popularity. You are one of many, many served here. On windy days there is no outside seating as the Bight would be quickly paved in flying plastic. Buy a T-shirt and enjoy the conch, which is good in all its guises. For a trip into less terra cognita, drive out to Stock Island to the **Rusty Anchor** (294-5369), a fine old favorite. The **Margaritaville Cafe** at 500 Duval is where to go for a cheeseburger and a bracing brace of margaritas to get your afternoon going. Jimmy Buffett himself is wont to drop into his place some nights for the music—which always gives the tourist a tingle. **The Indigo Island Bistro** at 730 Duval serves great pizzas, soups, sandwiches, and salads. It becomes a little deep purple and self-conscious at dinner, but lunch is a great deal. Long wine list. **Bagatelle** is a pretty old house at 115 Duval, and eating on the cool verandas gives you a real sense of being on holiday. Very nice for lunch, but dinner finds the Bag in more disarray. They will possibly be careless with your meal, perhaps be annoyed by your very presence. Once, when a patron protested some fish he felt was "funny," the kitchen said, "The kitchen does not agree with you." And that was that. The long pier at the **Ocean Key House** has both a grill and a raw bar. You can linger here, watching the boats right into the sunset hour. Remember, don't bolt as soon as the sun disappears. The real effect takes place twenty minutes later. **The Pier House** is always fun. Good raw bar, conch fritters, conch salad, fruit plates, and the best margaritas around. They have two Key lime pies available, frozen or chilled. Choose neither, for they are not very good. However, you should feel easy here, as though eating lunch is *exactly* what you should be doing. Strangely, there are often pigeons about, not on the grass, of which there is none, but on the deck, on the railings, on empty tables, eying you with their pigeon eyes, as though all the world were their monument. The management has had string wire around to interrupt their flight patterns.

Dinner

Dinner is a far more serious engagement. It costs so much more and one is usually expectant, or at the very least, hopeful. One might even be dressed up.

Key West restaurants are notoriously unreliable. *The* place to be one season will be empty as a weekday church the next. Proprietors have nervous breakdowns. Chefs are shot. People get bored. The kitchen help's minds wander to thoughts of affairs, windsurfing, or cocaine. Restaurants are as capricious as the weather, as quickly changeable as the tides. And yet the number of pretty and ambitious restaurants here is very impressive and should be investigated with enthusiasm. All the restaurants serve Key lime pie, but they have all become somewhat wary of recommending it. Really good Key lime pie is elusive. The bars have begun serving Key lime shooters with enthusiasm. They taste exactly like what you've been looking for but they're more fun.

Some very grand cuisine and prices have struck Key West. **Cafe des Artistes** (1007 Simonton) and **Flagler's** at the Casa Marina both offer meals and wines not to be undertaken with a skinny wallet. These are enclosed, dark, well-mannered establishments, indicating the seriousness of their rich fare—buttery steaks, creamed chickens, stuffed shrimp, fish in pastry puffs. To leave the streets of Key West and enter them is to feel like Captain Kirk might on opening the door to an alternate world— like Sarasota.

The pretty restaurant in the corner of the Marquessa (600 Fleming) was called Mira when it began, and was so awesomely expensive that it unnerved even the rich. You could charter a boat for weeks for the cost of dinner. But then they simplified themselves somewhat, painted over most of the trompe l'oeil, changed their name to **Cafe Marquessa**, and became one of the smartest restaurants in town. Delicious food with particularly inventive soups and desserts. Everything's chic here.

od-looking people. In a way it could be called Resemblances,
everyone looks vaguely "known." Open 6–11 (292-1244).

ouie's Backyard (corner Vernon and Waddell off South
Street, 294-1061). In a lovely old house of the palest pink on the
Atlantic is the best-known restaurant in town, and the one with
the best views. Deck dining offers spectacular arboreal
prospects, particularly in summer, when silent lightning leaps
across the sky. Porches, stars, excellent service and food.
Sophisticated, pricey, and romantic, though there's a feeling in
town that people are becoming a little weary of Louie's "reputation." Even so, it remains every traveler's culinary destination.
In the winter at the shuttle terminal in Miami, everybody on
the telephone is calling here, desperate for a reservation. Plead-
ing and begging. Lying! ("We'll be out by eight, we promise . . .")
Lunch can be less tense, even more fun.

La-Te-Da the institution is gone. And its progenitor, Larry
Formica, and his pink Cadillac, gone too. All the effects auc-
tioned off one afternoon, one by one, from the chaises which
once supported the sassiest bodies in town to the Art Deco sofas
to the mirrors, which must have seen a great deal, to the champagne flutes to the black-mirrored tables to the rose-colored
linens. Brunches lasted for hours here, diners toppled into the
pool, dogs had their very own fashion show with prizes ("The
Look-Alike trophy went to Frank Cicalese and his Chihuahua
Sam. They appeared as identical, perfectly pink Easter bunnies
in identical bunny suits, slippers and hats carrying matching
Easter baskets. Both wore sunglasses . . ."). Proper middle-aged
ladies with their purses firmly in hand could ascend the steps to
the Crystal Cafe and be misplaced for the season. And the
shrieks from the Sunday afternoon tea dance could be heard for
miles. Oh, it's all still *there,* white now instead of pink, more
open to the street, more obvious if not exactly more straightfor-
ward. But upstairs there's a disco now, and the restaurant,
which is called Charms, is currently a misnomer.

Palm Grill (1029 Southard, corner of Francis, 296-1744). A
rickety apricot-and-blue building which is mostly delightful

Mexican flame vine

patio, this place is friendly, intimate, and has a fresh, sophisticated menu. Lots of restaurants try to garden up their places
with the ubiquitous high-white lattice, but here it works—the
uneven brick, the old shutters, the big breadfruit tree, the quiet
night, the great bluesy vocals from the record machine. It's a
shanty with style. Try the gumbo or the pork chops with pecan
stuffing or the snapper with Key lime *crème fraîche*. There are
lighter offerings as well, salads and pizza and exceptional
desserts such as a Mandarin creamsickle or Bananas Foster.
Smooth wines but no bar. Dinner 6–10:30. Closed Sundays.

La Trattoria Venezia (524 Duval, 296-1075). A stylish
restaurant in the heart of town with a sleek bar, excellent service, and delicious food. The charming owners, two brothers
from Sicily, keep everything running smoothly. Opens at 6. Try
to get one of the two pretty tables in the window.

The Lighthouse Cafe (917 Duval, 296-7837) looks destitute
by day but from 6–11 pleasantly lit and engaging. Try to be
seated outside in the very back where the effect is tropical.
Good squid and conch dishes as well as seafood brochette. Wine,
no bar. Good pasta which is not administered by the bucket as
is the case at **Mangia Mangia** (corner Southard and Margaret,
294-3466), a place whose popularity eludes some. Always a
wait, no place to wait, mundane sauces, enormous portions.

"You just don't know how to order there," a fan says. "You avoid the pasta, you avoid the red sauce, you order the grilled chicken sandwich and tell them to leave off the bread."

An inexpensive restaurant fancied by the locals is **PT's** (920 Caroline Street). Pool tables, a couple of big TV's, smokey, and dim. The fare is ribs, pot roast, meat loaf, mashed potatoes and gravy. Nothing nouvelle about this cuisine. It's pretty good actually, although it all gets to taste like meat loaf. Open till 4 A.M.

Chico's Cantina, on the way out of town at the turn to Stock Island, is a pretty good Mexican restaurant, even though they do have fake cacti. Everything's homemade; the tamales go fast. Open 11:30 A.M. to 9:30 P.M. Beer and wine. Closed Mondays (296-4714).

Dim Sum (613 $\frac{1}{2}$ Duval, to the rear, 294-6230). This seems to be the place you go to on your fourth night in town. Thai, Chinese, and Indian food, though none of it is truly spicy or intriguing. Eating with chopsticks helps. Tiny and pretty. Maybe you'll love it and want to top off your experience with a dessert of bananas steamed in coconut milk. Opens at 6 P.M. Wine and beer.

There are several Cuban restaurants in town. **La Lechonera** (3100 Flagler, 296-7881) has what might be, perhaps, the best collection of pig photographs in the state on the wall, but the food tends to be fatty. **El Siboney** (900 Catherine Street, 296-4184) boasts less decor but is reliable. ("Well, that wasn't so bad, was it?" an out-of-towner said to her husband upon emerging one evening. "No, no," the man said. He looked a little startled. ". . . But it wasn't very good either." But people are increasingly "discovering" this place, even sweeping up to it by pedicab. **José's Cantina** (800 White Street, 296-4366) may be the best. The fluorescent-light decor has been toned down some and there are even paintings on the walls. Who *is* that lady with the rhinestone glasses? Have the shredded pork, the *plantanos* (lovely soft green bananas), the *casava* (tastes a little like delicious cold cream). You can get great *ropa vieja* and palomilla steak. Fresh sangria too. If you have a pretty place you can take takeout *to,* you're in great luck. All Cuban restaurants close early, usually at 9, and none have decent wine. But the servings are abundant, and the prices low.

For late-night suppers, **PT's** is available, and the upstairs **Café at Louie's. Sloppy's** serves up their Sloppy food window-service style until 4 A.M., and the **Hungry Sailors' Garden Cafe and Bar** at the back of 618 Duval is open twenty-four hours.

BARS

Ah, the bars of Key West, some more famous than the finest homes! It's said that the three hurricanes that hit town in the early 1900's blew down all the churches but left the bars standing. They change hands, clientele, and whole personalities, and some, like so many of the structures in Key West, are even moved from one block to the next, or are burned or razed. But few are ever forgotten.

The oldest bar is **Captain Tony's** on Greene Street. Names of the famous are paint-printed on the bar stools. Martha Gellhorn's name should be on one of the stools, for she was sitting in this joint when Hemingway first saw her in December of 1936. She would become the reason for his breakup with his second wife, Pauline; his third wife (people said that together they looked like Beauty and the Beast); and the reason for his move from Key West to Cuba in 1939. The bar is quaint as the dickens (a plastic shark mouths a lady mannequin and there is junk and bric-a-brac and signs hanging everywhere), and grizzled Captain Tony himself is a cutie. He doesn't own the bar anymore. He sold it after owning it for thirty-one years. He was once elected mayor and is now the honorary mayor of Key West. You can buy a poster of the Captain with the adage, *All you need in life is a tremendous sex drive and a great ego—brains don't mean a shit.* The bar began as The Blind Pig. The Blind Pig begat Sloppy Joe's which begat The Duval Club which begat The Oldest Bar which begat the bar that bears Tony's name today. Captain Tony's, when it was Sloppy Joe's between 1933 and 1937, was Hemingway's favorite bar. It was named for a popular hangout in Cuba and was owned by Joe Russell, who Hemingway liked to call Josie Grunts. Their friendship began when Russell cashed a Scribner's royalty check for Hemingway, something the fine old bank down the block refused to do. Russell was a rumrunner and charterboat captain, and before he bought the *Pilar,* Hemingway did all his fishing aboard Russell's *Anita.*

But *before* Sloppy Joe's was legitimately at the Greene Street location after the repeal of Prohibition, it was a speakeasy by the Naval base. It was not one of the better bars in town. Prohibition meant absolutely nothing to Key West. There were great drinking establishments everywhere—Pena's Garden of Roses, The Tropical Club, Baby's Place, Raul's, and Delmonico's. And there was the infamous Havana-Madrid Club located on Front and Duval across from the bank, only a short distance away from Big Annie's whorehouse. It had a huge dance floor of white Cuban tile and a rambling combination of indoor and outdoor rooms where "music, dancing, gambling, and fistfights went on twenty-four hours a day."

In 1937 the rent was raised a dollar a week at Sloppy Joe's on Greene Street, so Russell bought the building across the street on Duval—it had once been a restaurant—and in the middle of one night he and "every drunk in town" moved the bar. And here it remains, almost fifty-five years later, still Hemingway's "favorite" bar, still pushing the *Papa Dobles* ($2\frac{1}{2}$ jiggers of white rum, juice of two limes and a grapefruit half) and now offering a taco stand, a rock and roll band, and a T-shirt kiosk. You can't miss Sloppy's—it would be like going to Freeport, Maine, and not being able to locate L. L. Bean.

In the 1940's, the highway down the Keys was remembered as a mangrove tunnel with birds screeching and nesting within overhanging branches that completely covered the road in shade. But in Key West there were forty-eight bars on and near Duval Street, plus strip joints and tattoo parlors. Where a score of gentle shops exist now, selling suntan lotions, fabrics, and postcards, were the hard-core dives—the Midget Bar, The Conch Gardens, the Wagon Wheel, and four or five saloons known commonly as the Bucket of Blood. "The town was filled with beautiful men," an old girl remembers. "No one took any-

Captain Tony's Saloon

thing seriously. Life was sweet, lighthearted, and fun." There was the Mardi Gras, where a stripper named Dixie Lee performed with a little white muff held demurely before her. Inside the muff was a snarling chihuahua that would bite any sailor's hand that ventured near. Delmonico's boasted the only trapeze stripper in show business. Her name was Alma and she swung just above the heads of the drinkers. The very popular Tradewinds Restaurant and Night Club at the corner of Duval and Caroline occupied the historical Caroline Lowe House. Caroline Lowe was the young wife of a Confederate blockade runner during the Civil War. Martial law was in effect, yet every time Union troops went marching down Duval, Caroline would wave a Confederate flag from the cupola on the roof. The soldiers could never find the flag, which she would hide in a newel-post. The Tradewinds was torched by an arsonist in the mid-1950's and later demolished.

Gone, gone but not forgotten! Gone are the Cave Inn and the 25¢ double martinis at the Garden of Roses. Gone are The Monster, the hot gay disco on Front Street, and The Big Fleet on Caroline, where strippers danced for the shrimpers day and night, and the Boca-Chica Lounge, the grisly, hard-core Navy institution on Stock Island. Most recently down (it seems but a weird dream) is The Full Moon, the legendary bar of the 1980's.

But there remains a plentitude of bars in Key West. Drinking here is almost an obligation, and close to being an art. As in Ireland, it's not the thing to drink at home.

The Bull and Whistle (224 Duval). Super-loud and rowdy. Open to Duval's parade with another bar and balcony upstairs. Cover charge for live rock and roll, which can be heard for ten blocks.

The Green Parrot (400 Southard). A well-known old-time funky bar. "See the lower keys on your hands and knees" is a popular adage here, and the philosophy of the place is that of the famous bumper sticker, *Shit happens*. Pool tables, darts, pinball. Great murals on the walls, professional drinks. A Key West classic. They even have poetry readings, the most famous being their Valentine's Day Poetry Slam. Reading to this mob is not for the overly sensitive, to say nothing of the overly accomplished. Parrotheads go for the more arcane kind of metaphor—"That woman was so beautiful, she was the clean-your-snorkel kind of gorgeous . . ." Have another margarita.

Hog's Breath Saloon (400 Front Street). On the site of the legendary Monster. A nice breeze blows through the Hog's Breath (better than no breath at all, as Granny would say). Sometimes they sell more T-shirts than drinks here, and they sell a great many drinks.

Schooner Wharf (at the Key West Bight Marina down William Street). This looks seedy but it's theatrically seedy. You expected Key West to be sort of like this, and here it is. All types of hip here. Dark, dark dance floor. It's always fun to watch the *Sebago* hustle away from its mooring as the *Wolf* returns to its berth after its sunset cruise. Chaos, cool heads, zippy comments.

Casa Marina (Reynolds Street on the Atlantic). There is the Calabash Lounge off the lobby and the Sun-Sun outside bar. Pricey, but incomparable views. As you wander about with your Poinciana (champagne, cranberry, cassis) across the greensward to the dimpled shore, note the sign that earnestly

alerts guests to the great untoward—Marine Life Exists
Beyond This Point . . .

Rumrunners (200 block Duval). Has a garden bar, a piano
bar, a rooftop bar, and two other bars they haven't even both-
ered to name. Live music goes until midnight, after which
canned disco plays until 4 A.M. Pizza and burgers are served
until 3 A.M. Somewhere here too is a strip joint. Lap-dancing,
other vile goings-on.

VooDoo (700 Duval). A lively dance club with lots of "alternative dance" music. Odd 16-millimeter films are always running
on a large screen. The deal is now a $2 cover, which entitles you
to both a free drink *and* a free condom. Drag persons with great
legs and a talent for lip-synching are the entertainment some
late evenings.

Pier House (1 Duval). **The Chart Room** is dark and small
and can be very crowded late at night. The word is that important people hang out here so the drinks are expensive. **Havana
Docks** is up a story and over the water. Dancing and live music
inside. Generous decks outside. Very popular, of course, for
sunset watching, though the deafening "island" music can be
overwhelming. The **Ocean Key House** next door has a 200-
foot dock running across the Gulf and gets you real close to the
water. People like to come down here too and see the fish swimming under the lights at night.

Louie's. On the other side of the island at the corner of Vernon
and Waddell, this is the quieter, classier place to be when the
sun goes down. The outdoor bar on the Atlantic is called **The
Afterdeck** and is simply splendid. Open until 2 A.M.

The Conch Flyer (at the airport). Used to be open 24 hours,
encouraging some of the most sinister types in Key West to drop
by for a 5 A.M. nightcap. Now it's only open 21 hours a day. It's a
shame. The bar is barely separated from the airstrip and it has
a tropical Casablanca air. Have a beer and a chilli dog for
breakfast and watch the little planes drop in and out of paradise. The airport is being "improved," much to everyone's dis-

may, partially in anticipation of the opening of Cuba, a twenty-
minute flight away.

FISHING, DIVING, AND THE
WATERS BEYOND

The personality of a fishing guide, in terms of *your* personality,
is almost as important as his expertise in leading you to fish. To
find your guide you have to inquire, observe, be willing to ask
questions, and know what you want. In Key West, the charter
boats are at Garrison Bight on Charter Boat Row. There are
now, in the area of Key West, 40 full-time light-tackle boats, 40
trolling boats, 20 flats boats, and a half dozen head boats (for
those who want a gnarly, plebian experience). Do you really
want to go out on a boat called *No Mercy*? Well, you can. You
can even go out on *Fishbuster,* ignominious for running
aground on Western Sambo Reef in 1994, chewing a path 15
feet wide and 120 feet long through the corals. Or you can damn
everything and go out on the 21-foot *Tailhooker* (never apolo-
gize and never explain), captained by the same Navy commander, Michael Currie (now retired), who led the battle of
Peary Court and without question won it. (See Peary Court,
page 188.) Gulf Stream prices are $150 per person a day, and
the boats take four to six fishermen. Light-tackle guides who go
into the back country charge around $250 a day for two fisher-
men. If you cruise in your car past the Bight in the slow summer months, unhired captains or their mates often beckon to
you like true hookers—making an imaginary cast, reeling an
imaginary reel. Go to the Bight around four when the boats are
returning and make your arrangements there, firsthand. This
is also a good place to buy your fresh fish or be given it. The Key
West Fishing Tournament runs from April 15 to November 30
with lots of prizes for dead fish and even some awards for tag-
ging and releasing live ones. Some sportsmen enjoy using
extra-light tackle—6- to 15-pound test line for the big ones, sailfish and marlin. Those billfish have a tournament all their own
in October. *Tight lines and screaming reels to you!* the fishing
interests like to say.

Captain Vicki Impallomeni on her 22-foot boat *Imp II* puts together wonderful day trips into the back country of the Great White Heron National Wildlife Refuge. These are private, personalized trips. You can fish for grouper and snapper, snorkel, beach picnic, and bird-watch. She's an animated and knowledgeable guide and the trips are a good deal of fun. Charters are $250 for four hours, $350 for a full 9–5 day. Telephone: 294-9731.

Captain Lynda Schuh also offers smart and sensitive trips on her 16½-foot boat *Eco Charters*. $125 for two for a half day. $200 for four. Very nice. Call 294-4213.

In the **Key West Bight Marina** at the end of William Street is the *Wolf*, a great-looking topsail schooner which offers afternoon and sunset sails ($35 and $28) and can be chartered for parties (296-9653). Free Bubbly. They also do a starlight cruise for an hour and a half on Saturday nights. Here too is *Stars and Stripes*, a replica of Dennis Conner's champ catamaran. Masterfully skippered by Don Kincaid, *Stars and Stripes* glides out among the islands, and you can have a memorable day exploring reefs and beaches from 10–4 for $65 (call 294-7877). They provide snorkeling equipment and refreshments, you bring your own lunch. Go to the **Waterfront**, everyone's favorite market, close by at 201 William Street and create a picnic from their deli.

There are three sight-seeing boats that depart from downtown. The *Fireball* and *Coral Princess* are glass-bottom boats while the *Miss Key West* is more of an aquatic Conch Train. Hers is the shortest cruise at little over an hour. The *Fireball*'s trip to the reef is two hours long. Cost is $12, $6 for children. You'll often see nothing through the glass but undifferentiated turbulence. Just as often you'll get to pitch and yaw a lot.

To dive the reef contact **Reef Raiders** on Duval and Front (294-3635); **Lost Reef Adventures** at Land's End (296-9737); or the **Key West Pro Dive Shop** at 1605 N. Roosevelt Boulevard (296-3823). They all regularly dive the Sand Key Light, Eastern and Western Dry Rocks, and Cottrell Reef, which is on the Gulf side. Remember, coral is protected. Enjoy looking at it and leave it where it lives. **Sand Key** is heavily dived—it can even be crowded. **Eastern Dry Rocks** and **Rock Key**, about a mile east, are noted for their wrecks and pretty stones. **West-**

ern Dry Rocks is about three miles from the light and has the clearest waters and the most caves. It also has lobsters and sharks. **Cottrell Reef** is best for beginning snorkelers.

For scuba divers, the dive shops make trips to various deepwater wrecks as well as **The Outside Reef** or **Ten Fathom Ledge**, or they can be chartered for longer trips to **The Lakes** (a series of shallow lagoons protected by islands and reefs), the **Marquesas** (the only atoll in the Atlantic, formed not by a volcano but possibly by a prehistoric meteor), or the Tortugas, where you are getting into deep, wild water with large coral formations and big turtles and fish.

A real treat is to sail to the Marquesas, then explore the beaches and mangrove rivers there by kayak. **Cayo Caribe Kayaks** has a weekend trip for $250 per person on a 40-foot sloop. You'll realize you've forgotten there are so many stars in the sky. Call 296-4115 or 296-3009.

FORT JEFFERSON AND THE DRY TORTUGAS

Nothing will really prepare you for seeing this gigantic fort in the middle of vast waters, seventy miles from Key West. Most people fly here by seaplane. Boats can take anywhere from hours to days.

Fort Jefferson is doomed and has always been luckless. Planned by Thomas Jefferson to dominate the Gulf of Mexico with walls fifty feet high and eight feet thick and with facilities for 1,500 men and 450 cannon, construction on the largest of America's coastal forts was begun in 1846 on Garden Key, enclosing a lighthouse that had been built there in 1825. Ten years later, with fantastic supply and construction problems to overcome, its hexagonal walls had risen only a few feet above the surrounding waters. Ten years after that, with almost 16 million bricks having gone into its construction, it was found to be sinking, the weight of the walls squeezing the sand out from beneath the foundation. The 16-acre key on which it was built did not consist of solid coral, as was believed, but of sand, shell, and loose coral rock. True coral lay 80 feet below the surface.

Fort Jefferson, like its smaller, trapezoidal sister, Fort Taylor, never fired a shot at an enemy and was obsolete before it was finished. Like many monuments of far more ancient times, the fort was built by slaves and prisoners, overseen by craftsmen and guards. When the slaves were freed by the Emancipation Proclamation of 1863, the Army employed prison labor —the death sentences of Union deserters were often commuted to work on Fort Jefferson, the very name of which was supposed to cause hardened criminals to shudder. Prisoners were frequently forced to carry cannonballs around all day or were hung by their thumbs.

The fort's most famous prisoner was the phlegmatic Dr. Samuel Mudd, the doctor who set the broken leg of assassin John Wilkes Booth after the murder of President Lincoln. Convicted of conspiracy and sentenced to life, Dr. Mudd spent most of his time in the scorching heat making little chests and boxes of mahogany and crabwood and writing to his wife. He missed his children and the Maryland winters, writing, "I sometimes fancy I can see the dear little creatures coming in with chattering teeth and little snotty noses, shivering with cold."

Shortly after his arrival in 1865, Mudd attempted to escape in a departing ship, was discovered, and was confined for a time to a desolate gun room, a dungeon which can be seen today. One of his duties was to clean old bricks. "I worked hard all day," he wrote, "and came very near finishing one brick."

In 1867 a yellow fever epidemic swept through the fort; 270 people suffered from it and 38 died, among whom were small children of the officers and the fort's physician. Although Mudd made no discoveries in treatment or prevention, he assiduously nursed the ill, and when cooler weather came and dispelled the disease, Army officers sent a petition to President Andrew Johnson requesting the doctor's release. However, Mudd was not pardoned until the last day of Johnson's presidency, February 8, 1869, and was not released from the fort until March 11. He had been imprisoned for three years, seven months, and twelve days. A reporter from the *New York Herald* saw him at his Maryland farm and wrote, "In his sunken, lusterless eyes, pallid lips and cold, ashy, complexion, one can read the word 'Dry Tortugas' with a terrible significance."

Victims of disease and mishap were buried on a nearby key, a mortuary island bitterly called Hospital Key. The officers had fine quarters, perhaps the most comfortable and luxurious barracks in the United States, with roofs of Vermont slate, stairways of New England granite, stately verandas, and beautifully furnished rooms, but none of this splendid display protected the men from boredom, yellow fever, brackish water (the cisterns cracked and seawater fouled the fresh), crushing heat, drought, and hurricanes. The fort was abandoned in 1874, although it was briefly reactivated by the Navy in 1898 as a coaling station. The fort's bad luck was as virulent as ever. It was here where the battleship *Maine* coaled up on her way to Cuba. It is now believed that the explosion of the ship was caused not by a Spanish mine but by the spontaneous ignition of the gunpowder stored in the magazine, gunpowder which could be carried safely enough in wooden-hulled ships but exploded in the heat of steel ships powered by coal.

Hurricanes and fires have destroyed the coaling docks, the officers' quarters, and the soldiers' barracks. The vast parade ground is empty now except for the palms and trees introduced by the National Park Service, and the hot-shot ovens which once heated cannonballs so they could more effectively destroy their wooden targets. A Rodman cannon was capable of throwing a 300-pound shell three miles. But there were never any targets to destroy. And nothing attacked Fort Jefferson but Nature herself, in the inexorable guise of wind, water, and time.

Many people in Key West speak of going to the Tortugas, but few ever make the trip. Good weather is necessary, and money. **Key West Seaplane Service** on Stock Island (294-6978) flies year round and charges $120 a person for a half day. A full day costs $195. Flights leave at 8 A.M. and noon. The trip takes about a half hour, which allows you $2\frac{1}{2}$ hours at the fort. Most people think this is all the time they need on this desolate spot, but a full day is much more enjoyable, giving you time to snorkel, swim, picnic, and explore.

Bart's at the Key West Airport (294-0999) also flies to the Tortugas. The cost is $120 for a half day (only $30 more for a full day), with discounts for college students and the military.

Bart's at this time operates only during the season, December through April.

Bring a picnic lunch, cold drinks, snorkeling equipment (although the ranger will provide it free if you're without), and binoculars.

The flight to the Tortugas is astonishing. The planes fly low over the clear and multihued water, and you will see wrecked ships gleaming in the depths of reefs. You'll see living sharks and rays and the bleached bones of whales. You'll also see the macabre scrawl of hundreds of motorboat prop scars crisscrossing the seagrass beds. And then, there are miles of glittering ocean wastes, dotted by the whites of waves cresting the shoals and by the gliding shadows of birds, and then the fort rises into view in all its dark improbability. A short distance away is the lighthouse of Loggerhead Key, and close to the fort is Bush Key, where thousands of noddy and sooty terns arrive to nest each spring. The terns mate in the air at night, as angels must, and when they land on the key, egg laying begins immediately, each couple staking out a two-foot homestead in the sand. The Tortugas are a major rest stop for migratory birds, and in the spring, anything—warblers, hummingbirds, thrushes, tanagers, buntings, orchids, swallows—might show up and linger for a while, but it is the sheer number of the nesting terns that is so thrilling. Bush Key is off limits to people from March through September, and all the nearby keys, with the exception (ironically enough) of Loggerhead are closed May through September during the time the sea turtles lay their eggs. The moat around the fort is filled with young turtles ten inches long, part of a National Park Service project which collects hatchlings from the Atlantic coast and protects them for a year before release.

You have to really want to get to Fort Jefferson, for it is far beyond Mile #0. People who have lived in Key West for some time and still haven't gone to the Tortugas blame it on "Tropical Creep" of the suddenly "Seven Years Came and Went" variety. Others, here for a short time, are rushed to do many things and opt for easier (and cheaper) memories—a party fishing boat or a group dive. You can sign up as a standby passenger on board the National Park Service supply boat that goes to the Tortugas biweekly. If they have room, they'll take you. Or you can stay out there several weeks as a volunteer, an experience many rave about. Contact the National Park Service.

The fort is civilized enough these days. It has a pier and a helicopter pad. It has a fifteen-minute slide program and, like all national monuments, informative signs on a self-guided walk. There are picnic tables and grills and even rest rooms. You are not going into the heart of darkness after all. There is a sandy beach and snorkeling is excellent, both around the moat walls and on the reefs of Loggerhead Key. Camping is available here for up to twenty days, but as the ranger says, you "must provide for your own existence." There is nothing here but the beach, the bricks, the constant wind, the water, and the sky, in which the magnificent frigate-birds soar. Their bones are hollow, their color black, their elegant hooked wings span seven and a half feet. They are thieves and dandies, stealing fish from other birds, never getting themselves wet. They ride the currents of the air and there you are below them, far from home, almost nowhere.

INDEX

About the Author

JOY WILLIAMS is a novelist and short story writer.

About the Artist

ROBERT CARAWAN is a native-born Key West Conch. His etchings and serigraphs may be seen at the Gingerbread Square Gallery on Duval Street.

About the Type

This book was set in Century Schoolbook, a member of the Century family of typefaces. It was designed in the 1890's by Theodore Low DeVinne of the American Type Founders Company, in collaboration with Linn Boyd Benton. It was one of the earliest types designed for a specific purpose, the *Century* magazine, because it was able to maintain the economies of a narrower typeface while using stronger serifs and thickened verticals.